Renaissance and Baroque Poetry of Spain

with English prose translations

Renaissance and Baroque Poetry of Spain

with English prose translations

INTRODUCED AND EDITED BY ELIAS L. RIVERS

WAVELAND PRESS, INC.
Prospect Heights, Illinois

For information about this book, write or call:
Waveland Press, Inc.
P.O. Box 400
Prospect Heights, Illinois 60070
(312) 634-0081

1988 reissued by Waveland Press, Inc.

ISBN 0-88133-363-8

Printed in the United States of America

9 8 7 6 5 4 3 2 1

Contents

Preface 9
Introduction 11

POETS OF THE RENAISSANCE

Juan Boscán (ca. 1490–1542) 31
Sonetos I, LXI, LXXXI

Cristóbal de Castillejo (ca. 1490–ca. 1550) 33
Soneto; "Da mi basia mille" (Catulo)

Garcilaso de la Vega (1503–1536) 34
Sonetos I, IV, X, XI, XIV, XXIII,
XXIX, XXXII; Canciones III, V; Elegía II; Églogas I, III

Gutierre de Cetina (ca. 1516–ca. 1555) 82
Madrigales I, II; Sonetos I, III, V, VI

Francisco de la Torre 86
Sonetos V, XX, XXIII; Endecha II

Hernando de Acuña (ca. 1520–1580) 90
Soneto al rey nuestro señor

Fray Luis de León (1527–1591) 91

Odas I, III, VII, VIII, X, XVIII,
XIX, XXII; Décima

Baltasar del Alcázar (1530–1606) *111*
Canción I; Soneto

Fernando de Herrera (ca. 1534–1597) *113*
Canción en Alabanza de la divin majestad . . . ;
Sonetos I, XIV, XVIII, XXI, XXVI, XXXVIII, XL, LXV

Francisco de Aldana (1537–1578) *126*
Sonetos XIII, XVII, XXX, XXXIV, XXXVII

Anónimo *129*
Soneto a Cristo crucificado

San Juan de la Cruz (1542–1591) *130*
Canciones I, II, III; Coplas I, II, III;
Canción IV; Cantar

BAROQUE POETS *151*

Lupercio (1559–1613) & Bartolomé (1562–1631) L. de Argensola *153*
Sonetos I, II, III, IV, V, VI

Luis de Góngora (1561–1627) *157*
Sonetos LIII, LIV, LXIX, LXXXII, LXXXVI, CIII, CIX
CLXV, CLXVI; *Fábula de Polifemo y Galatea;*
Letrillas XIX, XXIII, XLVIII; Romances XVII, XXXII, XLIX

Lope de Vega (1562–1635) *198*
Romances primeros; Canciones populares; Sonetos;
Canción III, from *La Arcadia*; Romances from *Los Pastores de Belén* and *La Dorotea*

Juan de Arguijo (1567–1623) *240*
Sonetos XII, XVI, XXIII; XLIII, XLIV, XLV, XLIX

Francisco de Medrano (1570–1607) *244*
Sonetos XI, XXIX, XXX, XXXIX

Rodrigo Caro (1573–1647) *247*
Canción a las ruinas de Itálica

Andrés Fernández de Andrada (fl. ca. 1610) *251*
Epístola moral a Fabio

Pedro Espinosa (1578–1650) *259*
Sonetos

Francisco de Quevedo (1580–1645) *260*
Poemas metafísicos; Poemas morales; Poema religioso; Epitafios; Poemas amorosos; Poemas satíricos

Francisco de Rioja (ca. 1583–1659) *305*
Sonetos VIII, XII; *Silvas* X, XI

Esteban Manuel de Villegas (ca. 1589–1669) *310*
Cantilenas VII, XXXIV; Sáficos

Sor Juana Inés de la Cruz (1651–1695) *314*
Romances; Redondillas; Sonetos;
Primero Sueño (fragmento)

Biobibliographical Notes *337*

General Bibliography *350*

Preface

The history of Spanish poetry has yet to be written. Among foreigners the Romantic movement aroused interest in Spain's older literary traditions, in particular the folk-ballads *(romances)*, but the Renaissance tradition has generally received little attention abroad. This volume, while including many of the usual anthology pieces, provides a sampling of the major genres of poetry associated with that tradition, omitting only, for reasons of space, the classical epic. Familiarity with this selection should give the interested reader a foundation for further, independent exploration in a vast area of curious and often exciting poetry. The introduction to this volume is an attempt to define the genres included herein and to indicate briefly the lines along which they developed; it is hoped that such an essay, albeit premature, may be helpful in sketching a perspective within which a formal history of the Renaissance tradition in Spanish poetry may some day be written.

As for the English prose translations, one can only be apologetic; at best, they may be of use to the reader whose Spanish is weak. They are mere approximations, sometimes oversimplifying the sense of the Spanish text. Even in those cases where the translations themselves seem poetic, the poetry of the original may be quite different; and where the English translations are most crudely prosaic, the Spanish may often be at its highest level of pure poetry.

I acknowledge with appreciation the permission of Dell Publishing Co., Inc., and of Charles Scribner's Sons to reprint this anthology, first published in 1966 and reprinted in 1972; in both of these editions it has been used extensively at the undergraduate and graduate levels. A few textual corrections and bibliographical additions have been made in this second reprinting.

May, 1988 —ELIAS L. RIVERS

Introduction

In the year 1543 the cultural revolution known as the Renaissance yielded more than one epoch-making book. In Latin, the international language of European science, a radical reorientation was imposed upon the macrocosmos of astronomy by Copernicus's *De revolutionibus orbium coelestium,* and upon the microcosmos of physiology by Vesalius's *De fabrica humani corporis.* In the new national language of Spain's rapidly emerging empire, it was not a new science, but a new poetry whose birth was being facilitated by the printing press. Precisely on the 20th of March, 1543, a Catalan printer in Barcelona finished work on *Las obras de Boscán y algunas de Garcilaso de la Vega.*

We can understand revolutions only in terms of the conditions that lead up to them. What were in fact the conditions, or, better, the traditions, that Boscán and Garcilaso deliberately turned away from? What traces of continuity do we nevertheless find in their works? And what traditions do they turn toward in their search for new forms and sources of inspiration?

The oldest fragments of Hispanic lyric poetry, preserved in the refrains (*kharjas*) of eleventh-century poems written in Arabic and Hebrew, are predominantly love songs, snatches of lamentations in which a girl bewails the absence of her lover. Quite similar are the *cantigas de amigo* found in the thirteenth-century Portuguese song collections (*cancioneiros*), and so are the *villancicos,* often, of Castile. The doubtless prehistoric oral tradition to which such *Frauenlieder* belong certainly antedates the courtly love poetry of the Provençal troubadours, in which we hear the man's voice submitting, with adoring reluctance, to the cruel discipline of his lady. Another folk tradition in Spanish poetry, that of the ballads *(romances),* seems to stem primarily from the feudal epic tradition of Castile, which had itself died out by the fifteenth century. There had also been a monastic or clerical tradition, transferring from Latin or French into Spanish verse the numerous miracles of the Blessed Virgin and knightly legends of Alexander the Great; and clerical poetry had sometimes been rather Goliardically bawdy, reminding us more of Chaucer's Wife of Bath than of pious monks or gentle knights.

But the literary lyric, as independent written poetry, became established much later in the central Spanish dialect (Castilian) than it did in Portuguese or Catalan, the northwestern and northeastern dialects of the peninsula. Early Catalan poetry itself belongs, in fact, to the closely related linguistic and cultural domain of the Provençal troubadours; in the fifteenth century, Ausias March brings this Catalan tradition of courtly lyrics to its highest level of anguished perfection. The poetic sophistications of courtly love first reached Castile by way of Portuguese. It was between 1350 and 1450 that Spanish lyric poetry finally shifted from Portuguese to Castilian; the *Cancionero de Baena* (1445) was the first great collection reflecting the shift. In it we may already note the allegorical and philosophical influence of Italian poetry, particularly that of Dante, but it is the troubadour tradition that predominates. The most typical genre is the *canción de amor,* a love song written presumably to be set to music. Short lines (usually of eight syllables each) forming a few short stanzas that repeat the same rhyme scheme are its most obvious external characteristics. Its theme is typically that of a man's suffering for his lady's love, an erotic martyrdom; its abstractly intellectual style is based on lexical repetition (polyptoton), antitheses, paradoxes, and wordplay. Let us consider, for example, this fifteenth-century poem by Jorge Manrique:

No tardes, Muerte, que muero;
ven porque viva contigo;
quiéreme, pues que te quiero,
que con tu venida espero
no tener guerra conmigo.

Remedio de alegre vida
no lo hay por ningún medio,
porque mi grave herida
es de tal parte venida
que eres tú sola remedio.

Ven aquí, pues, ya que muero;
búscame, pues que te sigo;
quiéreme, pues que te quiero,
y con tu venida espero
no tener vida conmigo.

("Don't delay, Death, for I'm dying; come that I may live with you; love me, since I love [=want] you, for with your coming I hope not to be at war with myself. A gaiety cure by no means exists, because my serious wound has come from such a source that you alone are the cure. Come here, then, since I'm dying; seek me, for I follow you; love me, since I love you, and with your coming I hope not to be at life with myself.") We can see at once that this is poetry of a very special sort; its formal limitations are a real challenge to emotional and technical virtuosity on the part of the poet.

The more ambitious poets of the fifteenth century, such as the Marquis of Santillana and Juan de Mena, cultivated, in addition to the *canción de amor,* long allegorical narratives and philosophical poems. An interesting pre-Renaissance product of Santillana's final twenty years, in the middle of the fifteenth century, is over forty sonnets, the first to be written in any language other than Italian; they reveal the influence of the *"dolce stil nuovo"* and of Petrarch. And Mena's rhetorical grandiloquence, Latinized vocabulary, aesthetic use of classical allusion, and emphatic nationalism make of him, too, a very significant herald of the Renaissance in fifteenth-century poetry.

Toward the end of that century religious poetry had taken on a more personal, sentimental coloration in the semi-popular works of certain Franciscans. And there had sprung up a new interest, on the part of literate poets, in the folk tradition; *villancicos* and *romances* were being collected, elaborated upon, and published. All of the above elements are to be found in the great folio *Cancionero general,* a late medieval corpus of poetry, first published in 1511 and republished, with modifications, several times during the sixteenth century.

BOSCÁN AND GARCILASO

Returning now to the spring of 1543, as we pick up the newly printed volume of *Las obras de Boscán y algunas de Garcilaso . . .*, we notice little that is strange in the first few pages; in fact, these troubadour-style *canciones* could easily belong to the *Cancionero general.* But on page 38 of the text begins the manifesto of a poetic revolution that had been brewing since 1526, when, at the court of Charles V in Granada, the Venetian ambassador Andrea Navagero had suggested to Boscán that he try his hand at writing sonnets and other Italian forms in Spanish. Defending these innovations, Boscán declares that, compared to traditional Spanish courtly poetry, the Italian manner is "más grave y de más artificio y mucho mejor" ("more serious and more artistic and much better"). He recounts the consequences of his conversation with Navagero: on his way home to Barcelona from Granada, as he rode along, he had tried composing the difficult new lines in his head, and later, with his friend Garcilaso's encouragement and help, he began to feel that he was achieving some measure of success. He has found in the new style a greater flexibility, more appropriate for the imitation of classical authors: "una disposición muy capaz para recebir cualquier materia: o grave o sotil o dificultosa o fácil, y asimismo para ayuntarse con cualquier estilo de los que hallamos entre los autores antiguos aprobados." And, in fact, the poetry that follows this manifesto is quite different from any published before in Spanish.

The basic new Italianate meter, instead of the octosyllabic line, is a hendecasyllabic, or eleven-syllable, one, with a fixed accent on the tenth syllable and hovering accents tending to gravitate toward the fourth, sixth, and/or eighth. This is, in fact, the Spanish equivalent of the iambic pentameter of Renaissance poetry in England. The new, longer line makes for a less emphatic rhythm and rhyme; it could even be used with no rhyme at all, as blank verse, approximating the unrhymed hexameters of classical antiquity. But not only is the basic meter different: the new Italian genres bear little resemblance to anything in the Spanish medieval tradition. Perhaps the closest to the troubadour style are the sonnets and *canzoni* (*canciones* or *odas,* made up of stanzas combining seven- and eleven-syllable lines) with which both Boscán and Garcilaso introduce their collections of new poetry. This particular combination, of sonnets and odes, is typically Petrarchan; Boscán's *canzoniere,* consisting of 90 love sonnets interspersed with ten *canzoni,* is a coherent sequence, telling the psychological story of a tortured sensual love, in the sinful courtly tradition, which finally gives way to a quite different, chaste matrimonial affection. We may here recognize many familiar troubadour elements, but the brief rationally constructed sonnets and the long subjective, introspective odes encourage a more classical treatment of the themes than did the rapid rhymes and wordplay of the old-style *canciones de amor*. And two of Garcilaso's poems are more radically different: his Canción III introduces a new evocation of classical landscape, and his Canción V, written in an unusually short five-line stanza subsequently called the *"lira,"* imitates closely the linear development of an Horatian ode. Also quite different is Boscán's *Leandro,* a long narrative poem in blank verse (*versos sueltos*), retelling after Musaeus the tragic love story of Hero and Leander; here descriptions of legendary scenes, including a visit to the submarine court of Neptune, bring to Spanish poetry a new level of realistic fantasy.

In a somewhat shorter narrative poem, Boscán uses the *ottava rima* stanza (eight hendecasyllabic lines, rhyming ABABABCC). This form, of course, breaks up the flow of his narrative into neat, compact units; if his *Leandro* may be criticized as occasionally prosaic, his *ottava rima* allegory of love, influenced by Bembo and Poliziano, is more ornately beautiful, but also, I think, more medieval in tone, less humanistic.

Terza rima, consisting of an indefinite series of three-line units with interlocking rhymes (ABA, BCB, CDC, . . . XYXY), is the form preferred by Boscán and Garcilaso for epistolary poems. This essentially discursive genre may be divided into several sub-genres. Boscán has two *capitoli d'amore,* or plaintive love letters, in the style of Serafino dell' Aquila; somewhat similar in tone is Garcilaso's Elegía II, a poetic epistle addressed to Boscán. His Elegía I, based on Latin and Italian models, is elegiac in the more usual sense: it was written to the Duke of Alva to console him for the death of his brother and expresses an elevated half-Platonic, half-Stoic moral attitude toward life on earth and hereafter. Somewhat less elevated is the philosophical epistle in the style of Horace; urbane Epicureanism blends with Stoicism and Aristotle's golden mean in Boscán's *Respuesta a don Diego de Mendoza,* which is probably his poetic masterpiece. Garcilaso's brief blank-verse epistle to Boscán is much less ambitious, but perhaps for this very reason more genuinely Horatian in its modest simplicity of tone.

To Garcilaso alone belongs the final innovation, his Virgilian eclogues. More than half of the space in his section of the 1543 volume is devoted to three pastoral poems. The one he wrote first (Egloga II) is long and quite heterogeneous; it seems, in fact, to be an attempt to fuse into a single poem several of the Italian verse forms (including *rima al mezzo*) and of the classical genres of poetry. The whole work is put into the mouths of four characters (two shepherds, a hunter and a huntress). The first part of the poem is devoted to the love story of hunter and huntress; he tells one of the shepherds how their innocent childhood companionship has changed on his part into a passionate sensual desire that is driving him mad. The climax of this section is a violent scene in which the two shepherds restrain their friend the hunter by force. The second part of the poem is made up of a long narrative in which one of the shepherds tells the other of the family background, education, marriage, and military career of the Duke of Alva. The frustrated eroticism of *"loco amor,"* in a half-medieval, half-Renaissance pastoral mode, is balanced by sane matrimony and crusading campaigns against the infidel. In his other two, much shorter eclogues Garcilaso explicitly disavows, in his introductory lines, any epic ambitions, and the results are considerably more coherent. Egloga I is composed of two neatly balanced shepherds' plaints, in *canzone* form; the first shepherd accuses his former mistress of having broken her vows in abandoning him for another, and the second laments the untimely death of his lady, ending in a vision of reunion in the pastoral meadows of Venus's heaven. The third and final eclogue is less directly sentimental, more elaborately artificial, in the tradition of Sannazaro's *Arcadia:* four lovely nymphs rise from the depths of the Tagus River near Toledo and weave into tapestries of silk and gold the tragic love stories of Orpheus and Eurydice, Daphne and Apollo, Venus and Adonis, and finally of our bereaved Spanish shepherd of the Egloga I and his dead nymph Elisa. The raw immediacies of grief are given the aesthetic distance of classical antiquity and of pictorial art. An epilogue of shepherds' songs in the background, extolling their ladies, further softens any direct emotional impact caused by the death which occupies the central scene; art and nature are merged to convert grief into beauty.

These new genres, incarnating the Renaissance, or rebirth, in Spanish of the Greek and Latin literary traditions, gradually took root in Spain, marking a distinct shift of poetic sensibility. The success of this revolution was due largely to the superior aesthetic gifts of Garcilaso, who not only assimilated the Italian metric forms, but also captured an essential part of the Renaissance spirit in his poetry: a sensuous, metaphoric flow of bucolic, erotic, and mythological images, motifs, and themes expressing a new sense of subdued, half-melancholy joy in idealized classical attitudes and landscapes. The poetry of Boscán and Garcilaso was republished together many times during the sixteenth century. Garcilaso's poetry was published separately for the first time in 1570; it was treated as a humanistic classic by being annotated by Francisco Sánchez de las Brozas, or El Brocense, professor of rhetoric at the University of Salamanca, in 1574 and 1577, and by the scholar-poet Fernando de Herrera, of Seville, in 1580. Thus Garcilaso's approximately 35 sonnets, his five odes, two elegies, one epistle, and three eclogues became the foundation of a Renaissance tradition of poetry in Spain; actually one may say that since the sixteenth century very little poetry has been written in the Spanish language that has not been influenced to some extent by that of Garcilaso de la Vega. There was a half-serious movement of conservative, nationalistic resistance against the new Italian poetry, headed by Cristóbal de Castillejo; his own poetry, however, while avoiding the new meters, frequently reflects the Renaissance spirit much more than it does the spirit of the Spanish fifteenth century.

SALAMANCA AND SEVILLE

One of El Brocense's colleagues at Salamanca was the Augustinian friar, Luis de León, a Biblical scholar and professor of the Hebrew Scriptures. He tried to keep secret his interest in poetry, but in manuscripts there began to circulate his verse translations of the Psalms, of Virgil's eclogues, of Horace's odes. He had recognized in Garcilaso's Canción V the obvious formal model for Horatian odes in Spanish; his own original poems, also circulated surreptiously in manuscript, consist almost entirely of odes written in this *"lira"* stanza, combining the intellectual traditions of Christian idealism with the classical urbanity of the Renaissance. With sober vigor and moral seriousness, Fray Luis de León managed to fuse the satirical rusticity of Horace with a soaring Neoplatonic Catholicism which at times approaches true mysticism; the linear development of his odes rises and falls in climax and anticlimax as he seeks heaven and then returns to earth. Because of its explicit moralistic content, his poetry often attracts a more philosophical attention than does that of Garcilaso; it seems to reconcile once more the Greco-Roman and the Hebraic-Christian traditions, and it frequently achieves a restrained formal perfection. Fray Luis's poetry sets the tone for the so-called Salamanca school of Castilian poets.

Also written predominantly in the *"lira"* stanza are the most important of a very small body of lyrics by the reformed Carmelite monk, Fray Juan de la Cruz (later canonized by Rome as St. John of the Cross); but it is significant that he also writes in the popular traditional genres of *villancico* and *romance*. His poetry, at its highest, is much more ethereally mystical than that of Fray Luis. His major poem, the *Cántico espiritual,* draws directly upon the Song of Solomon and indirectly upon Garcilaso's eclogues; the resultant pastoral imagery, tremulously sensual, lends itself to an extended allegory of the soul's passionate longing for God. Nowhere else in Western poetry is erotic intensity so essential to the expression of an overwhelming religious experience. Not published until about 1620, San Juan's poetry does not really belong to the central tradition of Renaissance poetry in Spain, but rather brings to its climax a special tradition of Carmelite religious verse.

At the same time, on a lower plane, other poets continue to use the traditional Spanish meters, especially the octosyllabic line. Scholastic wit of a fifteenth-century sort is revived for religious purposes in the *Conceptos espirituales* (1600), for example, of Alonso de Ledesma (1562–1633).

The most deliberate attempt to continue Garcilaso's tradition was that of his Andalusian annotator, Fernando de Herrera, the central figure in a school of more humanistic poets developing in southern Spain, principally in Seville. His voluminous notes to Garcilaso's works are, in fact, a poetic manifesto of an erudite, Neoplatonic sort. Herrera declares that classical learning is necessary for great poetry, that the Spanish language is as richly expressive as the Italian, and that the poetic genius perceives divine reality. His own erudition is inexhaustible; in his notes he writes veritable histories of the poetic genres and uses a large Greek vocabulary in making rhetorical analyses. Thus his *Anotaciones* (1580) are a major contribution to Renaissance poetics, second in Spain only to the Aristotelian *Filosofía antigua poética* (1596) of A. López Pinciano.

Having taken minor orders, Herrera devoted his entire life to scholarship and poetry. He wrote several Pindaric odes or heroic hymns on national themes. But the social center of his life was the literary *tertulia,* or salon, of the Count and Countess of Gelves; here Herrera found it natural to focus his poetry, in the manner of Petrarch, upon the lovely young countess. His *canzoniere* is comparable in many ways to that of Boscán. These sonnets, odes, and elegies reflect primarily a literary experience within an aristocratic, scholarly setting; they won for him the title of "the Divine" when, in 1582, a year after the countess's death, he published some of them with the modest title of *Algunas obras de Fernando de Herrera.* This poetry sets the tone for the so-called Sevillian school of Andalusian poets, usually characterized by spectacular erudition, verbal musicality, and an archaeological interest in classical ruins, in pagan mythology, and in Stoicism. (Herrera may also be viewed as a "mannerist," or a transitional figure linking Garcilaso, the great poet of the Renaissance, to Góngora, the great poet of the Baroque period in Spain.) Other poets traditionally associated with this Andalusian school are Pedro de Espinosa, Francisco de Rioja, and Francisco de Medrano.

Mention might here be made of Renaissance epic poetry. Spain has nothing to compare with Portugal's *Lusiadas* (1572), but the epic of the conquest of Chile, *La Araucana* (1569–1590), by Alonso de Ercilla (1533–1596?), can still be read with interest and occasional moments of aesthetic pleasure. Particularly worthy of note in this poem is the literary treatment of the Indian chieftain, Caupolicán, as a "noble savage."

BAROQUE DEVELOPMENTS

Don Luis de Góngora, like Juan de Mena, was born in Cordova and, like Herrera, took minor orders entitling him to an ecclesiastical benefice; in classical erudition and aristocratic intellect he was second to neither of his Andalusian predecessors, and he rivals Garcilaso himself as a major creative figure in Spanish poetry. In a sense he continues and elaborates upon Garcilaso's tradition, carrying each of his stylistic traits out to its ultimate poetic consequences, achieving an aesthetic purity almost devoid of any everyday human emotion deriving directly from such basic themes as love, religion, or war.

Like other major poets of seventeenth-century Spain, Góngora cultivated poetry, not only in the Italianate meters of the Renaissance tradition, but also in the octosyllabic and shorter lines of the older tradition. His *romances, villancicos,* and *letrillas* often reveal a thorough familiarity with the more popular themes and meters; Góngora characteristically polishes and elaborates upon them, however, in such a way that we could seldom mistake his exquisite poems for those of the anonymous tradition. He also uses octosyllabic forms for treating typically Renaissance subject matter in a somewhat burlesque mode, as in his *romances* of "Angélica y Medoro" and "Píramo y Tisbe." (He himself seems to have considered the latter to be his best poem.) And in his sonnets, whether heroic, funereal, erotic, or burlesque, he realizes a final formal perfection. His most ambitious classical poems are quite difficult, both because of their unusual syntax and word order and because of the intellectual complexity of their metaphors, conceits, and mythological allusions. His masterpieces in this style are baroque pastorals: the *Fábula de Polifemo y Galatea,* based on Ovid's Polyphemus episode and written in octavas, like Garcilaso's Egloga III, and the *Soledades,* the "plot" of which is more original, though hardly a line is without classical allusions. This style of his, traditionally labeled *culteranismo,* though widely imitated in Spain, Portugal, and Spanish America, was never surpassed by any of his imitators. The world of Góngora's major poems is a material world juxtaposing colorful solid substances and glitteringly deceptive appearances; the poet, using words, attempts to rival the artificiality of nature, of *natura artifex,* herself. It is no accident that a taste for this poetry has been revived in the twentieth century by Spain's most sophisticated modern poets; it clearly belongs to Yeats's Byzantium.

The more sentimentally human strains in Garcilaso are developed by Lope de Vega, the creator of Spain's lyrical Golden Age theater; he was a very productive poet, his sonnets alone numbering 1,600 or more. He wrote several long narrative poems, of which perhaps his Tassoesque *Jerusalén conquistada* is the most noteworthy. Between 1602 and 1632 he published five important collections of his lyrics; they are not so polished as those of Góngora, but they are full of variety, spontaneity, and flowing grace. His odes, eclogues, elegies, and sonnets belong quite evidently to Garcilaso's classical tradition, with light baroque elaborations of all sorts; he only occasionally attempts to compete with Góngora as a *cultista.* His poems do, obviously, surpass Góngora's in subjective personal emotion, if not in erudition and technical skill. In the other tradition, Lope's popular lyrics are unexcelled; unlike Góngora's, they are often quite indistinguishable from anonymous, oral ones. And his ability to fuse these two traditions, the learned and the popular, is also unexcelled. No other poet could compete with Lope de Vega's facile abundance; he was indeed, as his contemporaries called him, a veritable phenomenon, "el monstruo de la naturaleza."

Finally, to mention only briefly a third great poet of Spain's seventeenth century, Francisco de Quevedo, though his poetry too shows considerable variety, brings chiefly a severe moralistic tension, an awareness of universal human corruption and death, to Spain's baroque poetry. His love poetry ranges from the lowest physical lust to the heights of desperate Neoplatonic hyperbole. An incisive satirical wit characterizes much of Quevedo's poetry, which at times is quite obscene; his colloquial puns and other witticisms are often very funny, in a grim sort of way. His profoundest lyrical note is struck when he faces death with Stoic desperation.

It is traditional, though misleading, to list Spain's other seventeenth-century poets either as showy *cultista* followers of Góngora, or as intellectual *conceptistas* like Quevedo. As a matter of fact, classical erudition and mythological allusions, the trademarks of *culteranismo,* were almost universal in seventeenth-century poetry; and most poets used puns, conceits, and other forms of baroque wit. The question is, with regard to each poet, how he developed an individual style and poetic mode as he made use of the contemporarily popular devices. The modern critic can usefully study the poetics of the period: the *Libro de erudición poética* (1611) by L. Carrillo y Sotomayor; the *Discurso poético* (1623) by J. de Jáuregui; and, above all, the *Agudeza y arte de ingenio* (1642), in which the great Jesuitical *conceptista*, B. Gracián (1601–1658), cites Góngora, significantly, far more than he does any other poet.

CONCLUSION

The poetic movement initiated by the posthumous publication, in 1543, of Boscán's and Garcilaso's experimental Renaissance verse came to an end in 1695, in a convent near the Mexican court of the Spanish viceroy, with the death of Sor Juana Inés de la Cruz. This erudite Jeronymite nun, born in New Spain, is unique in the history of Spanish Golden Age poetry. She is its only noteworthy woman, its only native of the New World. Although in many ways her poetry simply continues the baroque tradition of Spain, in both its *culterano* and its *conceptista* aspects, her major poem, the *Primero sueño,* is philosophically much more ambitious, as a highly personal essay on epistemology, than is any other poem written in Spanish during the sixteenth and seventeenth centuries. The richly materialistic style belongs to Góngora's world of deceptive appearances, but the psychology seems to approach that of a more Faustian modern skepticism. For Sor Juana's *Sueño,* or *Dream,* expresses poetically the failure of the human mind to grasp reality by means of purely intellectual activity, whether intuitive or discursive. In her last years her library was sold; she gave up her studies and subjected herself to the most ascetic disciplines of her religious order. Thus the highest spiritual ambitions of Renaissance humanism are finally seen as wholly vain; disillusion is the only subject matter left for poetry, until disillusion itself collapses, leaving nothing:

> . . . es cadáver, es polvo, es sombra, es nada.

A NOTE ON SPANISH VERSIFICATION

A regular line of Spanish verse consists of a fixed number of syllables. One conventionally counts the syllables of any line by beginning with the first syllable and ending with the last stressed syllable plus one. Thus the following are all considered metrically to be eight-syllable lines (*octosílabos* or *versos octosilábicos*), a basic form in the popular tradition:

1 234 56 7 + 1
el tesoro celestiál (verso agudo)

1 2 3 4 5 6 7 8
sola tú la venturósa (verso llano)

1 2 3 4 5 6 789 – 1
es de veras muy fantástico (verso esdrújulo)

The most common line in the Renaissance tradition is the *endecasílabo* (11 syllables). In the following stanza, called the *"lira," endecasílabos* are combined with *heptasílabos* (seven syllables):

Si de mi baja lira
tanto pudiese el son que en un momento
aplacase la ira
del animoso viento
y la furia del mar y el movimiento ...

When two vowels are not separated by an intervening consonant, they usually merge to form a single syllable; thus the following is an *endecasílabo:*

Huye el monstruo a exhalar su acerba pena.

The rhythm, or pattern of accents, is seldom rigidly fixed in Spanish versification; usually an alternation of stressed and unstressed syllables tends to prevail. The pattern is most flexible toward the beginning of a line; the final stress, on the other hand, is always fixed (syllable 6 in the *heptasílabo,* 7 in the *octosílabo,* 10 in the *endecasílabo).*

Rhyme is of two types: *rima asonante,* or vowel rhyme,

and *rima consonante,* or full rhyme (of vowels and consonants). *Rima asonante* is characteristic of the popular tradition, particularly the *romance* (ballad), written in *octosílabos* with a continuous *rima asonante* at the ends of the even-numbered lines:

Bañando en sudor y llanto
el esparcido cab*e*ll*o*,
el blanco rostro encendido
de dolor, vergüenza y mi*e*d*o*,
deteniendo con sus brazos
los de un loco rey manc*e*b*o*,
una débil mujer sola,
ausente del padre y d*e*ud*o*s,
así le dice a Rodrigo
ya con voces, ya con ru*e*g*o*s ...

Rima consonante is characteristic of both the troubadour and the Renaissance traditions; except in blank verse (*versos sueltos)* and in a few special types of stanza such as the *silva,* each line of classical Spanish poetry normally rhymes with one or more other lines. Of particular importance in this anthology are the following stanzaic forms:

terceto italiano (*terza rima*):

¡Oh natura, cuán pocas obras cojas	A
en el mundo son hechas por tu mano!	B
Creciendo el bien, menguando las congojas,	A
el sueño diste al corazón humano	B
para que al despertar, más se alegrase	C
del estado gozoso, alegre o sano;	B
que como si de nuevo le hallase,	C
hace aquel intervalo que ha pasado	D
que el nuevo gusto nunca al bien se pase ...	C

"lira" (see above; rhyming aBabB, this combination of *heptasílabos* and *endecasílabos* is a special variety of the *canzone* stanza, which is usually longer).

octava real (*ottava rima*):

Cerca del Tajo, en soledad amena, A
de verdes sauces hay una espesura B
toda de hiedra revestida y llena, A
que por el tronco va hasta el altura B
y así la teje arriba y encadena A
que el sol no halla paso a la verdura; B
el agua baña el prado con sonido, C
alegrando la hierba y el oído. C

soneto:

Pedís, reina, un soneto: ya le hago; A
ya el primer verso y el segundo es hecho; B
si el tercero me sale de provecho, B
con otro verso el un cuarteto os pago. A
Ya llego al quinto: ¡España, Santiago! A
Fuera, que entro en el sexto: ¡sús, buen pecho! B
Si del séptimo salgo, gran derecho B
tengo a salir con vida de este trago. A
Ya tenemos a un cabo los cuartetos. C
¿Qué me dices, señora, no ando bravo? D
Mas sabe Dios si temo los tercetos. C
Y si con bien este soneto acabo, D
¡nunca en toda mi vida más sonetos! C
Ya de éste, gloria a Dios, he visto el cabo. D

The rhyme scheme in the quatrains (*cuartetos*) is practically invariable; in the tercets (*tercetos*), instead of two different rhymes, as above, there are often three (CDE, CDE, etc.).

NOTE ON ORTHOGRAPHY

The spelling of the Spanish texts is in most cases the standard modern spelling. In a few cases, however, the older spelling has been kept. This older spelling reflects the existence of a set of six phonemes where modern Spanish has only three: ç [ts] and z [dz] = c,z [θ or s]; ss [s] and s [z] = s [s]; and x [sh] and j [zh] = j [χ]. Thus, certain consonantal rhymes that exist in modern Spanish did not exist in older Spanish: *la caça* did not rhyme with *la raza; impresso* did not rhyme with *queso; dixo* did not rhyme with *hijo*. It should also be noted that, in the older pronunciation, aspirate *h* (derived from Latin *f*) was a consonant and could impede the merging of two vowels (synalepha).

Poets of the Renaissance

Juan Boscán
(ca. 1490–1542)

SONETO I

Nunca de amor estuve tan contento
que en su loor mis versos ocupase,
ni a nadie consejé que se engañase
buscando en el amor contentamiento.

Esto siempre juzgó mi entendimiento:
que de este mal todo hombre se guardase;
y así, porque esta ley se conservase,
holgué de ser a todos escarmiento.

¡Oh! vosotros que andáis tras mis escritos
gustando de leer tormentos tristes,
según que por amar son infinitos,

mis versos son deciros: "¡Oh benditos
los que de Dios tan gran merced hubistes
que del poder de amor fuésedes quitos!"

SONETO LXI

Dulce soñar y dulce congojarme,
cuando estaba soñando que soñaba;
dulce gozar con lo que me engañaba,

SONNET I: I was never so happy with love as to use my poetry in its praise, nor did I ever advise anyone to be so foolish as to look for happiness in love. This has always been my firm belief: that everyone should be on guard against this misfortune; and so, to help this law, I was glad to be exhibited as an example for all to avoid. Oh, you who seek out my writings and enjoy reading of my sad sufferings, which being caused by love are infinite, my poetry is to tell you: "Oh, happy are you who have received so great a favor from God as to be free from the power of love!"

SONNET LXI: A sweet dream and sweet thrill, when I was dreaming that I dreamt; a sweet delight in what would deceive me, if only I could have

si un poco más durara el engañarme;

dulce no estar en mí, que figurarme
podía cuanto bien yo deseaba;
dulce placer, aunque me importunaba
que alguna vez llegaba a despertarme:

¡oh sueño, cuánto más leve y sabroso
me fueras si vinieras tan pesado
que asentaras en mí con más reposo!

Durmiendo, en fin, fui bienaventurado,
y es justo en la mentira ser dichoso
quien siempre en la verdad fue desdichado.

SONETO LXXXI

Un nuevo amor un nuevo bien me ha dado,
ilustrándome el alma y el sentido,
por manera que a Dios ya yo no pido
sino que me conserve en este estado.

A mi bien acrecienta el mal pasado,
tan sin temor estoy de lo que ha sido;
y en las hierbas compuestas que he bebido,
mi fuerza y mi vivir se han mejorado.

Anduvo sobre mí gran pestilencia

deceived myself a little longer; a sweet not being in myself, for I could imagine every good thing I desired; a sweet pleasure, though so pressing that at times it reached the point of awakening me: oh dream-laden sleep, how much lighter and enjoyable you would have been for me if you had settled down more heavily and calmly upon me! While I slept, in sum, I was in bliss, and it is fitting that one should be happy in deception who has always been unhappy in truth.

SONNET LXXXI: A new love has given me a new happiness, enlightening my soul and mind, so that I no longer ask God for anything but that he keep me in this state of grace. My happiness is increased by past sorrow, since I am now so unafraid of what no longer is; and the poisons that I have imbibed have improved my strength and health. I was suffering under a great plague which even killed the birds as they flew and almost every living creature; this deadly influence gradually went away, and so, as a result of this fierce mortal illness, what has survived is healthier than ever.

hasta matar los pájaros volando
y casi cuanto en vida fue crïado;

este influjo crüel se fue pasando,
y así de esta mortal, brava dolencia
con más salud quedó lo que ha quedado.

Cristóbal de Castillejo

(ca. 1490–ca. 1550)

SONETO

Garcilaso y Boscán siendo llegados
al lugar donde están los trovadores
que en esta nuestra lengua y sus primores
fueron en este siglo señalados,

los unos a los otros alterados
se miran, demudadas las colores,
temiéndose que fuesen corredores
o espías o enemigos desmandados;

y juzgando primero por el traje,
pareciéronles ser, como debía,
gentiles españoles caballeros;

y oyéndoles hablar nuevo lenguaje,
mezclado de extranjera poesía,
con ojos los miraban de extranjeros.

SONNET: Garcilaso and Boscán having come to where the troubadours are, who in our language and its beauties were once famous in this world, the two groups look at each other in alarm, their colors paling, fearing that they are scouts or spies or renegade enemies; and judging them first by their clothes, they took them to be, as was right, gentle Spanish knights; and hearing them speak a new language, mixed with foreign poetry, they looked at them with the eyes of foreigners.

"DA MI BASIA MILLE" (*Catulo*)

Dame, amor, besos sin cuento,
asida de mis cabellos,
y mil y ciento tras ellos,
y tras ellos mil y ciento,
y después
de muchos millares, tres;
y porque nadie lo sienta,
desbaratemos la cuenta
y contemos al revés.

Garcilaso de la Vega

(1503–1536)

SONETO I

Cuando me paro a contemplar mi estado,
y a ver los pasos por do me ha traído,
hallo, según por do anduve perdido,
que a mayor mal pudiera haber llegado;
mas cuando del camino estó olvidado,
a tanto mal no sé por dó he venido;
sé que me acabo, y más he yo sentido
ver acabar conmigo mi cuidado.

"GIVE ME A THOUSAND KISSES" (CATULLUS): Give me, love, countless kisses, holding tight to my hair, and eleven hundred after that, and after that eleven hundred, and after many thousands, three more; and, so that no one can resent it, let's mix up the accounts and start counting backwards.

SONNET I: When I pause to consider my state and to look at the road along which I have been brought, I discover, to judge by the nature of the road, that I might well have ended in a greater evil; but when I ignore the road, I don't know how I have reached such evil; I know I've reached my end, and I regret the more to see my sufferings end along with me. I shall end, for I

Yo acabaré, que me entregué sin arte
a quien sabrá perderme y acabarme
si ella quisiere, y aun sabrá querello;
que pues mi voluntad puede matarme,
la suya, que no es tanto de mi parte,
pudiendo, ¿qué hará sino hacello?

SONETO IV

Un rato se levanta mi esperanza.
Tan cansada de haberse levantado
torna a caer, que deja, mal mi grado,
libre el lugar a la desconfianza.
¿Quién sufrirá tan áspera mudanza
del bien al mal? ¡Oh, corazón cansado!,
esfuerza en la miseria de tu estado,
que tras fortuna suele haber bonanza.
Yo mismo emprenderé a fuerza de brazos
romper un monte que otro no rompiera,
de mil inconvenientes muy espeso.
Muerte, prisión no pueden, ni embarazos,
quitarme de ir a veros, como quiera,
desnudo espirtu o hombre en carne y hueso.

SONETO X

¡Oh dulces prendas, por mi mal halladas,
dulces y alegres cuando Dios quería!

have yielded myself unreservedly to one who can end and destroy me if she wishes to, and she can even wish to; for since my own will can kill me, hers, which is not so much on my side, being capable of doing so, what else will it do?

SONNET IV: For a while my hope rises. It falls again so tired at having risen that, despite me, it leaves open the way for despair. Who can bear so abrupt a change from good to bad? Oh, tired heart, endure the misery of your condition, for after a storm there is usually good weather. I myself will undertake by the strength of my hands to break through a forest which no one else would, densely overgrown with a thousand difficulties. Neither death nor prison nor obstacles can keep me from going to see you, one way or another, as a naked spirit or as a man of flesh and blood.

SONNET X: Oh sweet souvenirs, discovered to my sorrow, sweet and happy as long as God so willed! You are all together in my memory, and conspiring

Juntas estáis en la memoria mía,
y con ella en mi muerte conjuradas.
¿Quién me dijera, cuando en las pasadas
horas en tanto bien por vos me vía,
que me habíades de ser en algún día
con tan grave dolor representadas?
Pues en un hora junto me llevastes
todo el bien que por términos me distes,
llevadme junto el mal que me dejastes;
si no, sospecharé que me pusistes
en tantos bienes porque deseastes
verme morir entre memorias tristes.

SONETO XI

Hermosas ninfas que, en el río metidas,
contentas habitáis en las moradas
de relucientes piedras fabricadas
y en colunas de vidro sostenidas:
agora estéis labrando embebecidas,
o tejiendo las telas delicadas;
agora unas con otras apartadas,
contándoos los amores y las vidas;
dejad un rato la labor, alzando
vuestras rubias cabezas a mirarme,
y no os detendréis mucho, según ando;
que o no podréis de lástima escucharme,
o convertido en agua aquí llorando,
podréis allá de espacio consolarme.

with memory against my life. Who could have told me, when in time gone by you caused me so much joy, that you would some day return to me in the company of so great a grief? Since in one moment you have taken from me all the joy that you granted me little by little, take from me now the sorrow that you've left me; if you don't, I'll suspect that you placed me among so many joys because you wanted to see me die among sad memories.

SONNET XI: Lovely nymphs who, deep in the river, live happily in mansions built of shining stones and upheld by crystal columns: whether you are now busily embroidering or weaving fine fabrics, or whether in little groups you are telling one another of your loves and lives, lay aside your work for a moment, raising your golden heads to look at me, and it won't take you long, in my sad state; for either you'll be too sorry to listen, or else, changed into water by weeping here, you'll have plenty of time to console me down there.

SONETO XIV

Como la tierna madre que el doliente
hijo le está con lágrimas pidiendo
alguna cosa, de la cual comiendo,
sabe que ha de doblarse el mal que siente,
y aquel piadoso amor no le consiente
que considere el daño que haciendo
lo que le pide hace, va corriendo,
y dobla el mal, y aplaca el acidente:
así a mi enfermo y loco pensamiento,
que en su daño os me pide, yo querría
quitar este mortal mantenimiento,
mas pídemelo, y llora cada día
tanto que cuanto quiere le consiento,
olvidando su muerte y aun la mía.

SONETO XXIII

En tanto que de rosa y azucena
se muestra la color en vuestro gesto,
y que vuestro mirar ardiente, honesto,
enciende al corazón y lo refrena;
y en tanto que el cabello, que en la vena
del oro se escogió, con vuelo presto,
por el hermoso cuello blanco, enhiesto,
el viento mueve, esparce y desordena:
coged de vuestra alegre primavera
el dulce fruto, antes que el tiempo airado

SONNET XIV: Like the fond mother whose sick child tearfully begs her for something which, if he eats it, she knows will double his suffering, and yet her indulgent love does not let her consider the harm that she does by doing what he asks, and she runs to him and doubles his illness by alleviating a symptom: so, from my madly infirm mind which, to its own hurt, asks me for you, I should like to withdraw this deadly nourishment, but it begs me and weeps each day so much that I allow it everything that it wants, oblivious of its death and even of my own.

SONNET XXIII: While the colors of roses and lilies are still to be seen in your face, and while your ardent, chaste eyes inflame the heart and restrain it; and while your hair, selected from veins of gold, in a flutter about your lovely neck, so long and white, is blown, scattered and disarranged by the wind: gather the sweet fruit of your joyful springtime before sullen time

cubra de nieve la hermosa cumbre.
Marchitará la rosa el viento helado,
todo lo mudará la edad ligera
por no hacer mudanza en su costumbre.

SONETO XXIX

Pasando el mar Leandro el animoso,
en amoroso fuego todo ardiendo,
esforzó el viento, y fuése embraveciendo
el agua con un ímpetu furioso.
Vencido del trabajo presuroso,
contrastar a las ondas no pudiendo,
y más del bien que allí perdía muriendo
que de su propia vida congojoso,
como pudo esforzó su voz cansada
y a las ondas habló desta manera,
mas nunca fué la voz dellas oída:
—Ondas, pues no se escusa que yo muera,
dejadme allá llegar, y a la tornada
vuestro furor esecutá en mi vida.—

SONETO XXXII

Estoy continuo en lágrimas bañado,
rompiendo el aire siempre con sospiros;
y más me duele nunca osar deciros
que he llegado por vos a tal estado
que viéndome do estoy y lo que he andado
por el camino estrecho de seguiros,

covers with snow your lovely head [cf. mountain peak]. The icy wind will shrivel the rose, fleeting time will change everything in order not to change its usual custom.

SONNET XXIX: While the manful Leander was crossing the sea, all burning with the fire of love, the wind picked up, and the water began to get rough, to rage and to pound. Overcome by the strain and effort, no longer able to fight the waves, and rather dying because of happiness lost than concerned for his own life, he raised his tired voice as much as he could and spoke to the waves as follows, but they never heard the voice: "Waves, since it is not permitted that I escape death, let me reach the other side, and when I return, vent your fury upon my life."

si me quiero tornar para huiros,
desmayo viendo atrás lo que he dejado;
  si a subir pruebo en la difícil cumbre,
a cada paso espántanme en la vía
ejemplos tristes de los que han caído.
  Y sobre todo, fáltame la lumbre
de la esperanza, con que andar solía
por la escura región de vuestro olvido.

CANCIÓN III

  Con un manso ruido
de agua corriente y clara,
cerca el Danubio una isla que pudiera
ser lugar escogido
para que descansara
quien, como yo estó agora, no estuviera;
do siempre primavera
parece en la verdura
sembrada de las flores;
hacen los ruiseñores
renovar el placer o la tristura
con sus blandas querellas,
que nunca día ni noche cesan dellas.

  Aquí estuve yo puesto,
o por mejor decillo,
preso y forzado y solo en tierra ajena;

SONNET XXXII: I am continually bathed in tears, always rending the air with sighs; and what makes it even more painful is that I can never dare tell you that it is because of you that I have reached such a state that, seeing where I am and how far I've come along the narrow way of following you, if I try to turn around and flee, I faint to see what I have left behind; if I try to climb up the painful peak, at every step I'm frightened along the way by the sad sight of those who have fallen. And more than anything else I lack the light of hope with which I used to walk through the dark regions of your forgetfulness.

ODE III: With a gentle sound of clear running water, the Danube encircles an island which could be a place chosen for one to rest who wasn't in the state that I'm in now; where always springtime appears in the verdure sown with flowers; the nightingales cause the renewal of joy or of sadness with their gentle plaints, never ceasing from them night or day. Here I was placed, or to express it better, imprisoned by force and alone in an alien land; they

bien pueden hacer esto
en quien puede sufrillo
y en quien él a sí mismo se condena.
Tengo sólo una pena,
si muero desterrado
y en tanta desventura:
que piensen por ventura
que juntos tantos males me han llevado;
y sé yo bien que muero
por sólo aquello que morir espero.

El cuerpo está en poder
y en manos de quien puede
hacer a su placer lo que quisiere;
mas no podrá hacer
que mal librado quede,
mientras de mí otra prenda no tuviere.
Cuando ya el mal viniere,
y la postrera suerte,
aquí me ha de hallar,
en el mismo lugar,
que otra cosa más dura que la muerte
me halla y ha hallado;
y esto sabe muy bien quien lo ha probado.

No es necesario agora
hablar más sin provecho,
que es mi necesidad muy apretada;

can easily do this to one who can stand it and who willingly convicts himself. I have only one regret, if I die in exile and in such misfortune: that they may think perchance that so much suffering all together has destroyed me; and I know quite well that I'm dying for that alone for which I hope to die. My body is in the power and hands of him who can do at his pleasure what he likes; but he can not make me end in misfortune so long as he has no other hold upon me. When at last death comes and my final fate, it will find me here, in the same place, for something more cruel than death finds me and has found me already, and this he knows quite well who has experienced it. It is not necessary now to speak further to no avail, for my necessity is most pressing: one moment has destroyed all that on which my entire life was spent. And after such a campaign, do they think they can frighten me? Let

pues ha sido en un hora
todo aquello deshecho
en que toda mi vida fué gastada.
¿Y al fin de tal jornada
presumen espantarme?
Sepan que ya no puedo
morir sino sin miedo;
que aun nunca qué temer quiso dejarme
la desventura mía,
que el bien y el miedo me quitó en un día.

Danubio, río divino,
que por fieras naciones
vas con tus claras ondas discurriendo,
pues no hay otro camino
por donde mis razones
vayan fuera de aquí, sino corriendo
por tus aguas y siendo
en ellas anegadas:
si en tierra tan ajena
en la desierta arena
fueren de alguno acaso en fin halladas,
entiérrelas, siquiera,
porque su error se acabe en tu ribera.

Aunque en el agua mueras,
canción, no has de quejarte,
que yo he mirado bien lo que te toca;
menos vida tuvieras
si hubieras de igualarte

them know that I can no longer die except fearlessly, for never have I been left anything to fear by my misfortune, which destroyed my joy and my fear on the same day. Oh Danube, divine river which through fierce nations flows along with your bright waves, since there is no other way by which my words can leave this place except by flowing with your waters and being drowned in them: if in so foreign a land, on the desert sand, they should perchance finally be found by someone, let him bury them, at least, so that their wanderings may end upon your banks. Though you die in the water, song, you are not to complain, for I have considered well your deserts; you would have

con otras que se me han muerto en la boca.
Quién tiene culpa desto,
allá lo entenderás de mí muy presto.

CANCIÓN V

Si de mi baja lira
tanto pudiese el son, que un momento
aplacase la ira
del animoso viento,
y la furia del mar y el movimiento,

y en ásperas montañas
con el suave canto enterneciese
las fieras alimañas,
los árboles moviese,
y al son confusamente los trajese:

no pienses que cantado
sería de mí, hermosa flor de Nido,
el fiero Marte airado,
a muerte convertido,
de polvo y sangre y de sudor teñido,

ni aquellos capitanes
en las sublimes ruedas colocados,
por quien los alemanes,
el fiero cuello atados,
y los franceses van domesticados;

mas solamente aquella
fuerza de tu beldad sería cantada,

a shorter life if you had the same fate as others which have died in my mouth. Who is to blame for this, you will soon find out from me down there.

ODE V: If the sound of my lowly lyre were so powerful, that in one moment it could placate the wrath of the vigorous wind, and the fury and movement of the sea, and in the rough mountains with gentle song it could melt the hearts of the fierce beasts, could move the trees and draw them in confusion toward the sound: don't think that I would sing, oh Gnido's lovely flower, of fierce angry Mars, who concentrates upon death, stained with dust and blood and sweat, or of those leaders exalted upon sublime wheels [of triumphal chariots], by whom the Germans, bound by their proud necks, and the

y alguna vez con ella
también sería notada
el aspereza de que estás armada,

y cómo por ti sola,
y por tu gran valor y hermosura,
convertido en vïola,
llora su desventura
el miserable amante en tu figura.

Hablo de aquel cativo
de quien tener se debe más cuidado,
que está muriendo vivo,
al remo condenado,
en la concha de Venus amarrado.

Por ti, como solía,
del áspero caballo no corrige
la furia y gallardía:
ni con freno le rige,
ni con vivas espuelas ya le aflige.

Por ti, con diestra mano
no revuelve la espada presurosa,
y en el dudoso llano
huye la polvorosa
palestra como sierpe ponzoñosa.

Por ti, su blanda musa,
en lugar de la cítara sonante,
tristes querellas usa,

French are led captive; but only that power of your beauty would be sung, and occasionally, along with it, would also be pointed out the cruelty with which you are armed, and how because of you alone, and your great worth and beauty, the wretched lover, transformed into a pale violet, laments his misfortune in this form. I am speaking of that prisoner of whom greater care should be taken, who is dying a living death, sentenced to the oar, tied down in Venus's shell. Because of you he no longer controls, as he used to, the fury and vigor of the untamed horse: he neither guides him with bit, nor punishes him any longer with lively spurs. Because of you, with dextrous hand he does not wield the swift sword, and on the doubtful plain he avoids the dusty list like a poisonous snake. Because of you, his tender

que con llanto abundante
hacen bañar el rostro del amante.

Por ti, el mayor amigo
le es importuno, grave y enojoso;
yo puedo ser testigo,
que ya del peligroso
naufragio fuí su puerto y su reposo;

y agora en tal manera
vence el dolor a la razón perdida,
que ponzoñosa fiera
nunca fué aborrecida
tanto como yo dél, ni tan temida.

No fuiste tú engendrada
ni producida de la dura tierra;
no debe ser notada
que ingratamente yerra
quien todo el otro error de sí destierra.

Hágate temerosa
el caso de Anajérete, y cobarde,
que de ser desdeñosa
se arrepintió muy tarde;
y así, su alma con su mármol arde.

Estábase alegrando
del mal ajeno el pecho empedernido,
cuando abajo mirando,
el cuerpo muerto vido

muse, instead of the sounding cythera, uses sad plaints, which with abundant tears bathe the lover's face. Because of you, his greatest friend is for him annoying, vexatious, and tiresome; I can bear witness, who was once in the hazardous shipwreck his haven and repose; and now grief so overcomes his lost reason that no poisonous beast was ever so abhorred as I by him, nor so feared. You were not engendered or born of the hard earth; she should not be pointed out as erring ungratefully who avoids all other errors. Be warned by the case of Anaxarete and made afraid, who repented too late of being scornful; and so her soul burns along with her marble. Her flinty heart was rejoicing at another's suffering, when looking down, she saw the dead

del miserable amante, allí tendido,

y al cuello el lazo atado,
con que desenlazó de la cadena
el corazón cuitado,
que con su breve pena
compró la eterna punición ajena.

Sintió allí convertirse
en piedad amorosa el aspereza.
¡Oh tarde arrepentirse!
¡Oh última terneza!
¿Cómo te sucedió mayor dureza?

Los ojos se enclavaron
en el tendido cuerpo que allí vieron;
los huesos se tornaron
más duros y crecieron,
y en sí toda la carne convirtieron;

las entrañas heladas
tornaron poco a poco en piedra dura;
por las venas cuitadas
la sangre su figura
iba desconociendo y su natura;

hasta que, finalmente,
en duro mármol vuelta y trasformada,
hizo de sí la gente
no tan maravillada
cuanto de aquella ingratitud vengada.

body of the miserable lover, stretched out there, and tied to his neck the rope with which he released his anguished heart from the chain, who with his brief suffering purchased another's eternal punishment. She then felt transformed into loving pity her harshness. Oh tardy repentance! Oh final tenderness! How were you replaced with greater hardness? Her eyes became fastened upon the stretched out body which they saw there; her bones turned harder. and grew and transformed into themselves all the flesh; the icy entrails gradually turned into hard stone; in the anguished veins the blood was losing its form and nature; until finally, transformed into hard marble, she made people not so much amazed at her as avenged upon her ingratitude.

No quieras tú, señora,
de Némesis airada las saetas
probar, por Dios, agora;
baste que tus perfetas
obras y hermosura a los poetas

den inmortal materia,
sin que también en verso lamentable
celebren la miseria
de algún caso notable
que por ti pase, triste y miserable.

ELEGÍA II

Aquí, Boscán, donde del buen troyano
Anquises con eterno nombre y vida
conserva la ceniza el Mantuano,
debajo de la seña esclarecida
de César Africano nos hallamos
la vencedora gente recogida:
diversos en estudio, que unos vamos
muriendo por coger de la fatiga
el fruto que con el sudor sembramos;
otros, que hacen la virtud amiga
y premio de sus obras, y así quieren
que la gente lo piense y que lo diga,
destotros en lo público difieren,
y en lo secreto sabe Dios en cuánto
se contradicen en lo que profieren.

Don't you, my lady, try to test angry Nemesis's arrows now, for heaven's sake; let it suffice that your perfect deeds and beauty give to poets immortal material, without their also celebrating, in plaintive verse, the wretchedness of some noteworthy accident happening because of you, sad and wretched.

ELEGY II: Here, Boscán, where Anchises the good Trojan's ashes, as well as his eternal life and fame, are preserved by the Mantuan Virgil [i.e., in Sicily], under the bright banner of Caesar Africanus [i.e., Charles V] we victorious forces find ourselves gathered: differing in our purposes, for some of us are eager to gather for our labors the harvest that we sowed with sweat; others, who make of virtue itself the sponsor and reward of virtue's works, and wish it so to be thought and spoken of by men, differ from the former in public, but in secret God knows how much their thoughts do contradict

Yo voy por medio, porque nunca tanto
quise obligarme a procurar hacienda,
que un poco más que aquéllos me levanto;
ni voy tampoco por la estrecha senda
de los que cierto sé que a la otra vía
vuelven de noche, al caminar, la rienda.
Mas, ¿dónde me llevó la pluma mía?
que a sátira me voy mi paso a paso,
y aquesta que os escribo es elegía.
Yo enderezo, señor, en fin, mi paso
por donde vos sabéis que su proceso
siempre ha llevado y lleva Garcilaso;
y así, en mitad de aqueste monte espeso
de las diversidades me sostengo,
no sin dificultad, mas no por eso
dejo las musas, antes torno y vengo
dellas al negociar, y variando,
con ellas dulcemente me entretengo.
Así se van las horas engañando,
así del duro afán y grave pena
estamos algún hora descansando.
De aquí iremos a ver de la Serena
la patria, que bien muestra haber ya sido
de ocio y de amor antiguamente llena.
Allí mi corazón tuvo su nido
un tiempo ya; mas no sé, triste, agora
o si estará ocupado o desparcido.
De aquesto un frío temor así a deshora

their words. I take the middle road, for I have never been quite so eager to acquire wealth, and hence I rise a little higher than the former; nor do I follow the straight and narrow path of those who, I surely know, shift over from one path to another in the dark of night. But where has my pen taken me? For I'm gradually moving into satire, and what I'm writing you is an elegy. I, sir, direct at last my footsteps toward where you know that his fate has always borne, and bears, Garcilaso; and so, in the midst of this dense wood of diversities I sustain myself, not easily, I admit, but nevertheless I do not abandon the Muses, but rather return to them again and again from my work, and by this variety I pleasantly entertain myself with them. Thus the hours slip away, thus from harsh tasks and sad regrets we take a little respite. From here we'll go to see the Mermaid's land [i.e., Naples], which one can easily see in ancient times overflowed with love and leisure. There my heart once had its nest, some time ago; but I don't know, alas, now whether it's occupied or destroyed. Hence a chill fear that this has hap-

por mis huesos discurre en tal manera
que no puedo vivir con él un hora.
Si, triste, de mi bien estado hubiera
un breve tiempo ausente, yo no niego
que con mayor seguridad viviera.
La breve ausencia hace el mismo juego
en la fragua de amor, que en fragua ardiente
el agua moderada hace al fuego,
la cual verás que no tan solamente
no lo suele matar, mas lo refuerza
con ardor más intenso y eminente,
porque un contrario con la poca fuerza
de su contrario, por vencer la lucha,
su brazo aviva y su valor esfuerza;
pero si el agua en abundancia mucha
sobre el fuego se esparce y se derrama,
el humo sube al cielo, el son se escucha,
y el claro resplandor de viva llama,
en polvo y en ceniza convertido,
apenas queda dél sino la fama.
Así el ausencia larga, que ha esparcido
en abundancia su licor, que amata
el fuego que el amor tenía encendido,
de tal suerte lo deja que lo trata
la mano sin peligro en el momento
que en aparencia y son se desbarata.
Yo sólo fuera voy de aqueste cuento,
porque el amor me aflije y me atormenta,

pened, untimely, runs along my bones in such a way that I can not endure it for a moment. If, alas, I had been absent but briefly from my love, I don't deny that I would be living less uneasy. Brief absence has the same effect upon love's flames as in a blazing forge a small amount of water has upon fire, for you'll see that this water not only doesn't put out the fire, but reinforces it with a more intense and flaming heat, because one substance, challenged slightly by its opposite, in order to win the fight, strengthens its own arm and spurs its courage; but if water in great abundance is sprinkled and poured upon the fire, smoke rises skyward, noise is heard, and the bright gleam of the living flame, changed into dust and ashes, almost completely disappears, except for its memory. Thus prolonged absence, having sprinkled abundantly its liquid, which puts out the fire that love has lit, leaves it in such a state that one's hand can touch it without danger when finally in a blaze of noise it destroys itself. Only I am an exception to this rule, for love afflicts and torments me, and in absence the pain grows that I feel; and I

y en el ausencia crece el mal que siento;
  y pienso yo que la razón consienta
y permita la causa deste efeto,
que a mí solo entre todos se presenta,
  porque, como del cielo yo sujeto
estaba eternamente y deputado
al amoroso fuego en que me meto,
  así, para poder ser amatado,
el ausencia sin término, infinita
debe ser, y sin tiempo limitado;
  lo cual no habrá razón que lo permita,
porque, por más y más que ausencia dure,
con la vida se acaba, que es finita.
  Mas a mí ¿quién habrá que me asegure
que mi mala fortuna con mudanza
y olvido contra mí no se conjure?
  Este temor persigue la esperanza
y oprime y enflaquece el gran deseo
con que mis ojos van de su holganza;
  con ellos solamente agora veo
este dolor que el corazón me parte,
y con él y conmigo aquí peleo.
  ¡Oh crudo, oh riguroso, oh fiero Marte,
de túnica cubierto de diamante,
y endurecido siempre en toda parte!,
  ¿qué tiene que hacer el tierno amante
con tu dureza y áspero ejercicio,
llevado siempre del furor delante?
  Ejercitando, por mi mal, tu oficio,

think that reason consents and permits this effect to be caused, as it happens to me alone among all men, because, since by heaven I have been eternally subjected to, and chosen for, the fire of love into which I plunge, hence, for it to be extinguished, absence must be endless, infinite and without any limit of time; and this is contrary to reason, for, no matter how long an absence lasts, it ends with one's life, which is finite. But as for me, who can assure me that my bad fortune will not conspire with change and forgetfulness against me? This fear pursues the hope and oppresses and weakens the great desire which my eyes have to behold their joy; all that I can see with them now is this suffering which rends my heart, and against it and myself I'm struggling now. Oh cruel, oh harsh, oh fierce Mars [i.e., war] covered with a tunic of diamond and hardened forever everywhere!, what does the tender lover have in common with your hardness and rough activity, always swept along by ferocity? As I unfortunately engage in your business, I am

soy reducido a términos que muerte
será mi postrimero beneficio.
  Y ésta no permitió mi dura suerte
que me sobreviniese peleando,
de hierro traspasado agudo y fuerte,
  por que me consumiese contemplando
mi amado y dulce fruto en mano ajena,
y el duro posesor de mí burlando.
  Mas, ¿dónde me trasporta y enajena
de mi proprio sentido el triste miedo?
A parte de vergüenza y dolor llena,
  donde si el mal yo viese, ya no puedo,
según con esperalle estoy perdido,
acrecentar en la miseria un dedo.
  Así lo pienso agora, y si él venido
fuese en su misma forma y su figura,
tendría el presente por menor partido,
  y agradecería siempre a la ventura
mostrarme de mi mal sólo el retrato
que pintan mi temor y mi tristura.
  Yo sé qué cosa es esperar un rato
el bien del proprio engaño, y solamente
tener con él inteligencia y trato.
  Como acontece al mísero doliente,
que del un cabo el cierto amigo y sano
le muestra el grave mal de su acidente,
  y le amonesta que del cuerpo humano

reduced to such straits that only death can be my final reward. And my cruel fate did not allow death to come upon me in battle, pierced through by sharp strong steel, in order that I might destroy myself by seeing my sweet, beloved flower in another's hand, and the cruel possessor making fun of me. But where am I being taken and alienated from my own reason by sad fear? To a place full of shame and grief, where, if I saw the worst, I could not now suffer a bit more than I do, since in anticipating it I'm already devastated. So I think now, but if the worst should come in its true form and figure, I would consider my present suffering as a lesser evil, and I would always be grateful to my luck for showing me only an imaginary picture of my fate, painted by my fear and sadness. I know what it is to put one's brief hopes in the joy of self-deception and to have dealings and communication only with that joy. As it happens with a man who is mortally ill, shown, on the one hand, by his sane and truthful friend the seriousness of his illness and warned that he should begin to raise up, from his human body to a better place, his soul, set free in weightless flight; but, on the other hand, his

comience a levantar a mejor parte
el alma suelta con volar liviano;
  mas la tierna mujer, de la otra parte,
no se puede entregar a desengaño,
y encúbrele del mal la mayor parte;
  él, abrazado con su dulce engaño,
vuelve los ojos a la voz piadosa,
y alégrase muriendo con su daño:
  así los quito yo de toda cosa,
y póngolos en solo el pensamiento
de la esperanza, cierta o mentirosa;
  en este dulce error muero contento,
porque ver claro y conocer mi estado
no puede ya curar el mal que siento,
  y acabo como aquel que en un templado
baño metido, sin sentillo muere,
las venas dulcemente desatado.
  Tú, que en la patria entre quien bien te quiere
la deleitosa playa estás mirando,
y oyendo el son del mar que en ella hiere,
  y sin impedimento contemplando
la misma a quien tú vas eterna fama,
en tus vivos escritos, procurando:
  alégrate, que más hermosa llama
que aquella que el troyano encendimiento
pudo causar, el corazón te inflama;
  no tienes que temer el movimiento
de la fortuna con soplar contrario,
que el puro resplandor serena el viento.

tender wife can not surrender to despair and conceals from him the greater part of his illness; he, in the embrace of his sweet deception, turns his eyes toward her kind voice and rejoices as he dies, to his soul's hurt: so I take my eyes off everything and set them only upon the thought of hope, whether true or false; in this sweet deception I die happy, for to see clearly and recognize my condition can no longer do my illness any good, and I end like him who in a warm bath dies without feeling it, having gently opened his own veins. You, in your native land, with those who love you, are looking at the delightful beach and listening to the sound of the sea that breaks upon it, and with no obstacle are looking at her to whom you, in your immortal writings, are striving to give eternal fame: rejoice, for a more beautiful flame than that which caused the Trojan conflagration inflames your heart; you have no reason to fear the changing of stormy fortune with contrary blast, for that pure gleam calms down the wind. I, like a driven mercenary, go where for-

Yo, como conducido mercenario,
voy do fortuna a mi pesar me envía,
si no a morir, que aquesto es voluntario.
Sólo sostiene la esperanza mía
un tan débil engaño que de nuevo
es menester hacello cada día;
y si no lo fabrico y lo renuevo,
da consigo en el suelo mi esperanza,
tanto que en vano a levantalla pruebo.
Aqueste premio mi servir alcanza,
que en sola la miseria de mi vida
negó fortuna su común mudanza.
¿Dónde podré huir que sacudida
un rato sea de mí la grave carga
que oprime mi cerviz enflaquecida?
Mas ¡ay! que la distancia no descarga
el triste corazón, y el mal, doquiera
que estoy, para alcanzarme el vuelo alarga.
Si donde el sol ardiente reverbera
en la arenosa Libia, engendradora
de toda cosa ponzoñosa y fiera,
o adonde él es vencido a cualquier hora
de la rígida nieve y viento frío,
parte do no se vive ni se mora:
si en ésta o en aquélla el desvarío
o la fortuna me llevase un día,
y allí gastase todo el tiempo mío,
el celoso temor con mano fría
en medio del calor y ardiente arena

tune sends me against my will, except to death, where I go willingly. My hope is sustained only by so fragile a deception that it must be made anew each day; and if I do not build and renew it, my hope falls to the ground so hard that in vain I try to raise it. My service is given this reward, for only in the misery of my life has fortune restrained its usual fickleness. Where can I flee so that for a moment may be shaken from me the heavy weight that oppresses my weakened neck? But, alas, distance does not release the sad heart, and suffering, wherever I am, stretches out its flight to reach me. If where the burning sun reverberates upon sandy Libya, which engenders all things poisonous and fierce, or where the sun is overcome in a moment by the hard snow and cold wind, where no one lives or dwells: if either to the former or the latter place madness or fortune should some day take me, and I should spend there all my life, jealous fear with cold hand in the midst of the heat

el triste corazón me apretaría;
 y en el rigor del hielo, en la serena
noche, soplando el viento agudo y puro
que el veloce correr del agua enfrena,
 de aqueste vivo fuego en que me apuro
y consumirme poco a poco espero,
sé que aun allí no podré estar seguro;
y así, diverso entre contrarios, muero.

ÉGLOGA I

 El dulce lamentar de dos pastores,
Salicio juntamente y Nemoroso,
he de contar, sus quejas imitando;
cuyas ovejas al cantar sabroso
estaban muy atentas, los amores,
de pacer olvidadas, escuchando.
Tú, que ganaste obrando
un nombre en todo el mundo
y un grado sin segundo,
agora estés atento sólo y dado
al ínclito gobierno del Estado
Albano; agora vuelto a la otra parte,
resplandeciente, armado,
representando en tierra el fiero Marte;
agora de cuidados enojosos

and burning sand would seize my sad heart; and in the rigor of the ice, on a calm night when the wind blows sharp and pure which restrains the swift flow of water, against this living fire in which I am refined and hope gradually to be consumed, I know that even there I'll have no protection; and so, torn between extremes, I die.

ECLOGUE I: The sweet lamentations of two shepherds, Salicio together with Nemoroso, I am going to relate, imitating their complaints; their sheep were listening attentively to the pleasant song, forgetting to graze as they heard of love. You, who by your works have won a name throughout the world and a unique title [i.e., Don Pedro de Toledo, Viceroy of Naples], whether you're now devoting yourself exclusively to the distinguished direction of the Alban State, or whether now turned in another direction, clad in resplendent armor, representing fierce Mars on earth; whether, free of annoying cares and business, perchance you are now at hunt, belaboring the forest upon an eager horse, who presses on running after the timid deer,

y de negocios libre, por ventura
andes a caza, el monte fatigando
en ardiente jinete, que apresura
el curso tras los ciervos temerosos,
que en vano su morir van dilatando:
espera, que en tornando
a ser restitüido
al ocio ya perdido,
luego verás ejercitar mi pluma
por la infinita innumerable suma
de tus virtudes y famosas obras,
antes que me consuma,
faltando a ti, que a todo el mundo sobras.
En tanto que este tiempo que adivino
viene a sacarme de la deuda, un día,
que se debe a tu fama y a tu gloria
(que es deuda general, no sólo mía,
mas de cualquier ingenio peregrino
que celebra lo dino de memoria),
el árbol de vitoria
que ciñe estrechamente
tu gloriösa frente
dé lugar a la hiedra que se planta
debajo de tu sombra, y se levanta
poco a poco, arrimada a tus loores;
y en cuanto esto se canta,
escucha tú el cantar de mis pastores.
Saliendo de las ondas encendido,
rayaba de los montes el altura
el sol, cuando Salicio, recostado

who in vain delay their deaths: wait, for when again I have been restored to my lost leisure, you will see my pen devoted at once to recounting the infinite sum of your virtues and famous deeds, before I die, neglecting you, who exceed everyone. While this time which I foresee is approaching, to discharge me some day of the debt which is owed to your fame and glory (which is a general debt, not mine alone, but incumbent upon every distinguished genius who celebrates that which is worthy to be remembered), let the laurel branch of victory which tightly binds your glorious brow give way to the humble ivy that is planted beneath your shade and rises little by little, supported by your praise; and until this is sung, listen to the song of my shepherds. Rising crimson from the waves, the sun's rays were striking the

al pie de un alta haya en la verdura,
por donde un agua clara con sonido
atravesaba el fresco y verde prado,
él, con canto acordado
al rumor que sonaba,
del agua que pasaba,
se quejaba tan dulce y blandamente
como si no estuviera de allí ausente
la que de su dolor culpa tenía;
y así, como presente,
razonando con ella, le decía:

Salicio

¡Oh más dura que mármol a mis quejas,
y al encendido fuego en que me quemo
más helada que nieve, Galatea!,
estoy muriendo, y aún la vida temo;
témola con razón, pues tú me dejas,
que no hay, sin ti, el vivir para qué sea.
Vergüenza he que me vea
ninguno en tal estado,
de ti desamparado,
y de mí mismo yo me corro agora.
¿De un alma te desdeñas ser señora,
donde siempre moraste, no pudiendo
della salir un hora?
Salid sin duelo, lágrimas, corriendo.
El sol tiende los rayos de su lumbre
por montes y por valles, despertando

heights of the mountains when Salicio, reclining at the foot of a lofty beech upon the green, where clear sounding waters trickled across the fresh green grass, Salicio, I say, with song attuned to the sounding echo of the passing water complained as sweetly and softly as if she were not absent who was to blame for his grief; and so, as though present, reasoning with her, he said: *Salicio:* Oh harder than marble against my complaints, and against the blazing fire in which I burn more frozen than snow, Galatea!, I'm dying, and I still fear life; I have reason to fear it, for you're leaving me, and without you there is no purpose in living. I'm ashamed for anyone to see me in such a state, abandoned by you, and I even get angry at myself now. Do you scorn being the mistress of a soul in which once you always dwelt, being unable to leave it for one moment? Flow forth, tears, painlessly. The sun extends its rays of light over mountains and valleys, awakening birds

las aves y animales y la gente:
cuál por el aire claro va volando,
cuál por el verde valle o alta cumbre
paciendo va segura y libremente,
cuál con el sol presente
va de nuevo al oficio,
y al usado ejercicio
do su natura o menester le inclina:
siempre está en llanto esta ánima mezquina,
cuando la sombra el mundo va cubriendo
o la luz se avecina.
Salid sin duelo, lágrimas, corriendo.
¿Y tú, desta mi vida ya olvidada,
sin mostrar un pequeño sentimiento
de que por ti Salicio triste muera,
dejas llevar, desconocida, al viento
el amor y la fe que ser guardada
eternamente sólo a mí debiera?
¡Oh Dios!, ¿por qué siquiera,
pues ves desde tu altura
esta falsa perjura
causar la muerte de un estrecho amigo,
no recibe del cielo algún castigo?
Si en pago del amor yo estoy muriendo,
¿qué hará el enemigo?
Salid sin duelo, lágrimas, corriendo.
Por ti el silencio de la selva umbrosa,
por ti la esquividad y apartamiento

and animals and people: some go flying through the bright air, others over green valley or high peak go grazing safely and freely, the others with the sun's presence go again to their jobs and to the customary occupation to which their nature or necessity inclines them: but my miserable soul is always grieving, when shadows are covering the world or when light approaches. Flow forth, tears, painlessly. And you, forgetful now of this life of mine, without showing the least regret that Salicio is sadly dying for you, are you ungratefully allowing the wind to blow away the love and faith which you should have kept eternally for me alone? Oh, God, why at least, since from your height you see this false perjurer causing the death of a close friend, doesn't she receive some punishment from heaven? If in return for my love I'm dying, what can happen to her enemies? Flow forth, tears, painlessly. Because of you the silence of the shady forest, because of you the unsociable remoteness of the lonely woods used to please me; because of

del solitario monte me agradaba;
por ti la verde hierba, el fresco viento,
el blanco lirio y colorada rosa
y dulce primavera deseaba.
¡Ay, cuánto me engañaba!
¡Ay, cuán diferente era
y cuán de otra manera
lo que en tu falso pecho se escondía!
Bien claro con su voz me lo decía
la siniestra corneja, repitiendo
la desventura mía.
Salid sin duelo, lágrimas, corriendo.
¡Cuántas veces, durmiendo en la floresta,
reputándolo yo por desvarío,
vi mi mal entre sueños, desdichado!
Soñaba que en el tiempo del estío
llevaba, por pasar allí la siesta,
a beber en el Tajo mi ganado;
y después de llegado,
sin saber de cuál arte,
por desusada parte
y por nuevo camino el agua se iba;
ardiendo yo con la calor estiva,
el curso enajenado iba siguiendo
del agua fugitiva.
Salid sin duelo, lágrimas, corriendo.
Tu dulce habla ¿en cúya oreja suena?
Tus claros ojos ¿a quién los volviste?
¿Por quién tan sin respeto me trocaste?

you I longed for the green grass, the cool breeze, the white lily, the red rose and sweet springtime. Oh, how deceived I was! Oh, how different and how completely otherwise was what lay hidden in your false heart! This was told me clearly by the voice of the sinister crow, repeatedly foretelling my misfortune. Flow forth, tears, painlessly. How often, while sleeping in the woods, though I considered it mere nonsense, did I see my misfortune in dreams, poor wretch! I would dream that in the summertime I was taking, to spend there the noonday heat, my sheep down to the Tagus to drink; and after getting there, not knowing how it happened, the water would change its course and flow another way; burning with the summer heat, I would try to follow the diverted course of the fleeing water. Flow forth, tears, painlessly. In whose ear now is your sweet voice murmuring? Upon whom have you turned your fair eyes? For whom so unfaithfully have you exchanged me? Where

Tu quebrantada fe ¿dó la pusiste?
¿Cuál es el cuello que, como en cadena,
de tus hermosos brazos anudaste?
No hay corazón que baste,
aunque fuese de piedra,
viendo mi amada hiedra,
de mí arrancada, en otro muro asida,
y mi parra en otro olmo entretejida,
que no se esté con llanto deshaciendo
hasta acabar la vida.
Salid sin duelo, lágrimas, corriendo.

¿Qué no se esperará de aquí adelante,
por difícil que sea y por incierto?
O ¿qué discordia no será juntada?,
y juntamente ¿qué tendrá por cierto,
o qué de hoy más no temerá el amante,
siendo a todo materia por ti dada?
Cuando tú enajenada
de mi cuidado fuiste,
notable causa diste,
y ejemplo a todos cuantos cubre el cielo,
que el más seguro tema con recelo
perder lo que estuviere poseyendo.
Salid fuera sin duelo,
salid sin duelo, lágrimas, corriendo.

Materia diste al mundo de esperanza
de alcanzar lo imposible y no pensado,
y de hacer juntar lo diferente,

have you put your broken promises? What neck have you entwined, as in a chain, with your lovely arms? No heart is strong enough, even if it were of stone, seeing my beloved ivy torn from me and clinging on another wall, and my grapevine entwined with another elm, not to destroy itself in tears until its life ends. Flow forth, tears, painlessly. What can't be expected from now on, no matter how difficult and dubious? What discordant elements will not be joined, and, at the same time, what can the lover count on with certainty, and what won't he fear from this time on, since you have furnished a precedent for anything at all? When you abandoned my love, you gave ample reason, and an example to everyone under heaven, for the surest man to fear suspiciously the loss of whatever he then possessed. Flow painlessly, flow forth, tears, painlessly. You gave the world cause to have hope of achieving the impossible and unthinkable, and of making different things join, by giving your perverse heart to whom you did, taking it away from me with such

dando a quien diste el corazón malvado,
quitándolo de mí con tal mudanza
que siempre sonará de gente en gente.
La cordera paciente
con el lobo hambriento
hará su ayuntamiento,
y con las simples aves sin ruido
harán las bravas sierpes ya su nido;
que mayor diferencia comprehendo
de ti al que has escogido.
Salid sin duelo, lágrimas, corriendo.
Siempre de nueva leche en el verano
y en el invierno abundo; en mi majada
la manteca y el queso está sobrado;
de mi cantar, pues, yo te vi agradada
tanto que no pudiera el mantuano
Títiro ser de ti más alabado.
No soy, pues, bien mirado,
tan disforme ni feo;
que aun agora me veo
en esta agua que corre clara y pura,
y cierto no trocara mi figura
con ese que de mí se está riendo;
¡trocara mi ventura!
Salid sin duelo, lágrimas, corriendo.
¿Cómo te vine en tanto menosprecio?
¿Cómo te fuí tan presto aborrecible?
¿Cómo te faltó en mí el conocimiento?
Si no tuvieras condición terrible,

an abrupt change that the news of it will always resound from nation to nation. The patient lamb with the hungry wolf will join together, and with simple noiseless birds the fierce serpents will now make their nests; for I consider that there is even greater difference between you and the man you have chosen. Flow forth, tears, painlessly. Always, in summer and in winter, I have plenty of fresh milk; in my sheepfold there is more than enough butter and cheese; and I have seen you so pleased with my singing that not even the Mantuan Tityrus [i.e., Virgil's poetic shepherd] could be more highly praised by you. And, well considered, I am not so misshapen or ugly; for even now I see myself in this water running clear and pure, and I would certainly not exchange my looks with him who is laughing at me now; but I would exchange my luck! Flow forth, tears, painlessly. How did I come to be so despised by you? What made me so quickly become abhorrent to you? How could you cease to understand me? If your disposition were not cruel,

siempre fuera tenido de ti en precio,
y no viera de ti este apartamiento.
¿No sabes que sin cuento
buscan en el estío
mis ovejas el frío
de la sierra de Cuenca, y el gobierno
del abrigado Estremo en el invierno?
Mas ¡qué vale el tener, si derritiendo
me estoy en llanto eterno!
Salid sin duelo, lágrimas, corriendo.
 Con mi llorar las piedras enternecen
su natural dureza y la quebrantan;
los árboles parece que se inclinan:
las aves que me escuchan, cuando cantan,
con diferente voz se condolecen,
y mi morir cantando me adivinan;
las fieras, que reclinan
su cuerpo fatigado,
dejan el sosegado
sueño por escuchar mi llanto triste:
tú sola contra mí te endureciste,
los ojos aun siquiera no volviendo
a lo que tú heciste.
Salid sin duelo, lágrimas, corriendo.
 Mas ya que a socorrer aquí no vienes,
no dejes el lugar que tanto amaste,
que bien podrás venir de mí segura.
Yo dejaré el lugar do me dejaste;

I would always be highly esteemed by you, and I would not witness this separation from you. Don't you know that countless sheep of mine seek in summer the cool of the Cuenca mountains, and the protection of warm Extremadura in the winter? But of what value are possessions if I am melting away in eternal tears! Flow forth, tears, painlessly. When I weep, the stones soften and break their natural hardness; it seems that the trees lean down; the birds that hear me, when they sing, show sympathy by a change in their voices, and in their songs foretell my death; the wild beasts, who recline their tired bodies, abandon restful sleep to hear my sad lament: you alone have hardened your heart against me, not even turning your eyes toward what you yourself created. Flow forth, tears, painlessly. But since you aren't coming here to comfort me, don't abandon this spot that you loved so well, for you may come here in safety from me. I shall abandon the spot where you aban-

ven, si por solo esto te detienes.
Ves aquí un prado lleno de verdura,
ves aquí una espesura,
ves aquí una agua clara,
en otro tiempo cara,
a quien de ti con lágrimas me quejo.
Quizá aquí hallarás, pues yo me alejo,
al que todo mi bien quitarme puede;
que pues el bien le dejo,
no es mucho que el lugar también le quede.—
Aquí dió fin a su cantar Salicio,
y sospirando en el postrero acento,
soltó de llanto una profunda vena.
Queriendo el monte al grave sentimiento
de aquel dolor en algo ser propicio,
con la pesada voz retumba y suena.
La blanca Filomena,
casi como dolida
y a compasión movida,
dulcemente responde al són lloroso.
Lo que cantó tras esto Nemoroso
decildo vos Piérides, que tanto
no puedo yo ni oso,
que siento enflaquecer mi débil canto.

Nemoroso

Corrientes aguas, puras, cristalinas,

doned me; come, if my presence is the only obstacle. You see here a meadow full of green, you see here dense growth, you see here clear water, formerly dear to us, to which I now complain of you with tears. Perhaps here you will find, since I am leaving, him who has taken from me all my happiness; and since I leave him my happiness, it is unimportant that he should have this spot too. Here Salicio put an end to his song, and stressing his final word with a sigh, he gave vent to a deep supply of tears. The mountain, wishing in some way to favor the sad feelings of his grief, echoed and resounded with its heavy voice. Fair Philomena, as though grieved and moved to sympathy, sweetly responds to the weeping sound. What Nemoroso sang after this, say ye, oh Muses, for I neither can nor dare to, feeling my feeble song grow weaker. *Nemoroso:* Running waters, pure and crystalline, trees who

árboles que os estáis mirando en ellas,
verde prado de fresca sombra lleno,
aves que aquí sembráis vuestras querellas,
hiedra que por los árboles caminas,
torciendo el paso por su verde seno:
yo me vi tan ajeno
del grave mal que siento,
que de puro contento
con vuestra soledad me recreaba,
donde con dulce sueño reposaba,
o con el pensamiento discurría
por donde no hallaba
sino memorias llenas de alegría.

Y en este mismo valle, donde agora
me entristezco y me canso en el reposo,
estuve ya contento y descansado.
¡Oh bien caduco, vano y presuroso!
Acuérdome, durmiendo aquí algún hora,
que despertando, a Elisa vi a mi lado.
¡Oh miserable hado!
¡Oh tela delicada,
antes de tiempo dada
a los agudos filos de la muerte!,
más convenible suerte
a los cansados años de mi vida,
que es más que el hierro fuerte,
pues no la ha quebrantado tu partida.

¿Dó están agora aquellos claros ojos
que llevaban tras sí, como colgada,

see yourselves reflected in them, green meadow full of cool shade, birds who here scatter your complaints, ivy climbing up the trees, winding your path through their green bosoms: I once considered myself so far removed from the heavy sadness which I now feel that my perfect happiness caused me to take pleasure in your solitude, where in sweet sleep I rested, or in my imagination I reviewed areas where I found nothing but memories full of joy. And in this same valley, where now I grieve and tire myself as I try to rest, I was once happy and rested. Oh perishable happiness, lightly blown away! I remember, sleeping here one time, that I awoke to find Elisa by my side. Oh wretched fate! Oh delicate fabric, prematurely submitted to the sharp blades of death!, a more fitting fate for the weary years of my life, which is stronger than steel, since your departure has not broken it. Where now are those fair eyes which swept along behind them, as though suspended,

mi alma doquier que ellos se volvían?
¿Dó está la blanca mano delicada,
llena de vencimientos y despojos
que de mí mis sentidos le ofrecían?
Los cabellos que vían
con gran desprecio el oro,
como a menor tesoro,
¿adónde están? ¿Adónde el blando pecho?
¿Dó la coluna que el dorado techo
con presunción graciosa sostenía?
Aquesto todo agora ya se encierra,
por desventura mía,
en la fría, desierta y dura tierra.
¿Quién me dijera, Elisa, vida mía,
cuando en aqueste valle al fresco viento
andábamos cogiendo tiernas flores,
que había de ver con largo apartamiento
venir el triste y solitario día
que diese amargo fin a mis amores?
El cielo en mis dolores
cargó la mano tanto
que a sempiterno llanto
y a triste soledad me ha condenado;
y lo que siento más es verme atado
a la pesada vida y enojosa,
solo, desamparado,
ciego, sin lumbre, en cárcel tenebrosa.
Después que nos dejaste, nunca pace

my soul in whatever direction they turned? Where is the delicate white hand, full of victory over me and spoils surrendered to it by my senses? The hair which looked with scorn on gold as a lesser treasure, where is it now? Where is the soft breast? Where the column which with graceful pride upheld the golden roof? All this is now imprisoned, to my misfortune, beneath the cold, hard, desert earth. Who could have told me, Elisa, my beloved, when in the cool breeze of this valley we were gathering tender flowers, that I was to see with long separation the sad and lonely day come that would put a bitter end to my love? Heaven has dealt me griefs with so heavy a hand that it has sentenced me to everlasting tears and sad solitude; and what I most regret is to find myself tied to life, which is a heavy burden of woes, I alone and abandoned, blind and lightless in a shadowy prison. Since you left us, the cattle never graze their fill any more, nor does the field supply the farmer with generous hand. There is nothing good that doesn't change into evil: weeds choke

en hartura el ganado ya, ni acude
el campo al labrador con mano llena.
No hay bien que en mal no se convierta y mude:
la mala hierba al trigo ahoga, y nace
en lugar suyo la infelice avena;
la tierra, que de buena
gana nos producía
flores con que solía
quitar en sólo vellas mil enojos,
produce agora en cambio estos abrojos,
ya de rigor de espinas intratable;
yo hago con mis ojos
crecer, lloviendo, el fruto miserable.
Como al partir del sol la sombra crece,
y en cayendo su rayo se levanta
la negra escuridad que el mundo cubre,
de do viene el temor que nos espanta
y la medrosa forma en que se ofrece
aquella que la noche nos encubre,
hasta que el sol descubre
su luz pura y hermosa:
tal es la tenebrosa
noche de tu partir, en que he quedado
de sombra y de temor atormentado,
hasta que muerte el tiempo determine
que a ver el deseado
sol de tu clara vista me encamine.
Cual suele el ruiseñor con triste canto
quejarse, entre las hojas escondido,
del duro labrador, que cautamente

the wheat, and in its stead spring up miserable oats; the earth, which willingly used to supply us with flowers, the mere sight of which sufficed to remove a thousand woes, now produces instead these thistles and is so overgrown with thorns that it can't be cultivated; with my eyes, as with rain, I make its wretched fruits grow. As upon the sun's departure shadows lengthen, and when its rays go down there rises the black darkness that covers the world, whence comes the fear that strikes us and the terrible shapes assumed by those which the night conceals from us, until the sun reveals its pure and lovely light: so is the shadowy night of your departure, in which I am left tormented by shadow and fear, until death shall set the time which will take me to see the longed-for sun of your fair sight. As the nightingale is wont with sad song to complain, hidden among the leaves, of the cruel farmer,

le despojó su caro y dulce nido
de los tiernos hijuelos entre tanto
que del amado ramo estaba ausente,
y aquel dolor que siente
con diferencia tanta
por la dulce garganta
despide, y a su canto el aire suena,
y la callada noche no refrena
su lamentable oficio y sus querellas,
trayendo de su pena
al cielo por testigo y las estrellas:
desta manera suelto ya la rienda
a mi dolor, y así me quejo en vano
de la dureza de la muerte airada;
ella en mi corazón metió la mano
y de allí me llevó mi dulce prenda,
que aquél era su nido y su morada.
¡Ay muerte arrebatada!
Por ti me estoy quejando
al cielo y enojando
con importuno llanto al mundo todo:
el desigual dolor no sufre modo.
No me podrán quitar el dolorido
sentir, si ya del todo
primero no me quitan el sentido.
Tengo una parte aquí de tus cabellos,
Elisa, envueltos en un blanco paño,
que nunca de mi seno se me apartan;
descójolos, y de un dolor tamaño

who stealthily has robbed her dear, sweet nest of the tender babes while she was absent from the beloved bough, and the grief that she feels she expresses so differently through her sweet throat, and the air echoes to her song, and silent night does not restrain her offices of lamentation and her complaints, calling upon heaven and the stars to bear witness to her grief: so I give free rein now to my grief and thus lament in vain the harshness of irate death, who thrust her hand within my heart and thence took from me my sweet darling, for that was her nest and her dwelling place. Oh violent death, because of you I am complaining to heaven and annoying with my insistent tears the whole world: my excessive grief permits no moderation. They shall never be able to deprive me of my feeling of grief unless they first deprive me altogether of my feelings. I have here some of your hair, Elisa, wrapped in a white cloth and never separated from my bosom; I take them out and

enternecerme siento que sobre ellos
nunca mis ojos de llorar se hartan.
Sin que de allí se partan,
con sospiros calientes,
más que la llama ardientes,
los enjugo del llanto, y de consuno
casi los paso y cuento uno a uno;
juntándolos, con un cordón los ato.
Tras esto el importuno
dolor me deja descansar un rato.
　Mas luego a la memoria se me ofrece
aquella noche tenebrosa, escura,
que tanto aflige esta ánima mezquina
con la memoria de mi desventura.
Verte presente agora me parece
en aquel duro trance de Lucina;
y aquella voz divina,
con cuyo son y acentos
a los airados vientos
pudieras amansar, que agora es muda,
me parece que oigo, que a la cruda,
inesorable diosa demandabas
en aquel paso ayuda;
y tú, rústica diosa, ¿dónde estabas?
　¿Ibate tanto en perseguir las fieras?
¿Ibate tanto en un pastor dormido?
¿Cosa pudo bastar a tal crueza,
que, conmovida a compasión, oído

feel myself melted by so great a grief that my eyes never get enough of weeping over them. Without removing them, with hot sighs more burning than flame I dry them of tears, and then I review and count them almost one by one; then I tie them together with a ribbon. After this the insistent grief lets me rest awhile. But then there returns to my memory that shadowy dark night which so afflicts my wretched soul with the memory of my misfortune. I seem to see you present now, undergoing Lucina's cruel crisis [i.e., in childbirth]; and your divine voice, with the sound and accents of which you could calm the angry winds, which now is mute, I seem to hear as you called upon that cruel inexorable goddess for aid in your plight; and you, rustic goddess, where were you?

Were you so interested in pursuing beasts? Were you so interested in a sleeping shepherd? What could suffice to cause such cruelty that, moved to

a los votos y lágrimas no dieras
por no ver hecha tierra tal belleza,
o no ver la tristeza
en que tu Nemoroso
queda, que su reposo
era seguir tu oficio, persiguiendo
las fieras por los montes, y ofreciendo
a tus sagradas aras los despojos?
¿Y tú, ingrata, riendo,
dejas morir mi bien ante los ojos?

Divina Elisa, pues agora el cielo
con inmortales pies pisas y mides,
y su mudanza ves, estando queda,
¿por qué de mí te olvidas y no pides
que se apresure el tiempo en que este velo
rompa del cuerpo, y verme libre pueda,
y en la tercera rueda
contigo mano a mano
busquemos otro llano,
busquemos otros montes y otros ríos,
otros valles floridos y sombríos,
donde descanse y siempre pueda verte
ante los ojos míos,
sin miedo y sobresalto de perderte?—

Nunca pusieran fin al triste lloro
los pastores, ni fueran acabadas
las canciones que sólo el monte oía,
si mirando las nubes coloradas,

pity, you gave no ear to her prayers and tears so as not to see such beauty being turned to earth or not to see the sadness in which your Nemoroso is left, whose recreation it was to follow your art, pursuing wild beasts through the mountains and offering their remains at your sacred altars? And you, ungrateful and laughing, let my beloved die before my eyes? Divine Elisa, since now the heavens you tread and measure with immortal feet and see their changes as you stand still, why do you forget me and not pray for the time to be hastened when I shall break the veil of this body and find myself free, and in the third sphere [i.e., the planet Venus] hand in hand with you we can seek another meadow, we can seek other mountains and other rivers, other valleys full of flowers and shade, where I can rest and always see you before my eyes, without the fear and shock of losing you?—The shepherds would never have put an end to their sad lamentations, nor would the songs have ended which only the mountain heard, if looking at the crimson clouds,

al tramontar del sol bordadas de oro,
no vieran que era ya pasado el día.
La sombra se veía
venir corriendo apriesa
ya por la falda espesa
del altísimo monte, y recordando
ambos como de sueño, y acabando
el fugitivo sol, de luz escaso,
su ganado llevando,
se fueron recogiendo paso a paso.

ÉGLOGA III

Aquella voluntad honesta y pura,
ilustre y hermosísima María,
que en mí de celebrar tu hermosura,
tu ingenio y tu valor estar solía,
a despecho y pesar de la ventura
que por otro camino me desvía,
está y estará en mí tanto clavada
cuanto del cuerpo el alma acompañada.
Y aun no se me figura que me toca
aqueste oficio solamente en vida;
mas con la lengua muerta y fría en la boca
pienso mover la voz a ti debida.
Libre mi alma de su estrecha roca,
por el Estigio lago conducida,

embroidered with gold as the sun set behind the mountains, they hadn't seen that the day was now over. The shadows were seen to be running quickly now down the dense slope of the lofty mountain, and as though they both awoke from sleep, and as the fleeing sun, now lacking light, finally left, taking their sheep, they gradually withdrew step by step.

ECLOGUE III: That chaste, pure desire, oh illustrious and most beautiful Maria, which I used to have, to celebrate your beauty, your intellect and your high worth, despite the will of fortune which forces me to follow another road, is and always will be as much a part of me as the soul is accompanied by the body. And I even imagine it will not be my lot to perform this function only in my lifetime, but with my tongue dead and cold in my mouth I intend to stir the voice which I owe to you. My soul, when it is free of its narrow prison and is being ferried over the Stygian Lake, will continue to celebrate you, and that sound will halt the waters of oblivion. But Fortune, not satisfied with my suffering, besets me and takes me from one hardship to

celebrándote irá, y aquel sonido
hará parar las aguas del olvido.
  Mas la fortuna, de mi mal no harta,
me aflige y de un trabajo en otro lleva;
ya de la patria, ya del bien me aparta,
ya mi paciencia en mil maneras prueba;
y lo que siento más es que la carta
donde mi pluma en tu alabanza mueva,
poniendo en su lugar cuidados vanos,
me quita y me arrebata de las manos.
  Pero, por más que en mí su fuerza pruebe,
no tornará mi corazón mudable;
nunca dirán jamás que me remueve
fortuna de un estudio tan loable.
Apolo y las hermanas, todas nueve,
me darán ocio y lengua con que hable
lo menos de lo que en tu ser cupiere,
que esto será lo más que yo pudiere.
  En tanto no te ofenda ni te harte
tratar del campo y soledad que amaste,
ni desdeñes aquesta inculta parte
de mi estilo, que en algo ya estimaste.
Entre las armas del sangriento Marte,
do apenas hay quien su furor contraste,
hurté de el tiempo aquesta breve suma,
tomando ora la espada, ora la pluma.
  Aplica, pues, un rato los sentidos
al bajo son de mi zampoña ruda,

another; now it separates me from my country, now from my love, now tests my patience in a thousand ways; and what I most regret is that the paper on which I am to move my pen in praise of you, replacing it with vain worries, Fortune snatches from my hands. But, no matter how it tests its strength on me, it shall not make my heart become changeable; they will never say that I have been moved by Fortune from so praiseworthy a purpose. Apollo and all nine sisters will give me leisure and a tongue with which to speak the least of the praises of which you are worthy, for this will be the most of which I am capable. Meanwhile, I hope that you're not offended or bored by my writing of the countryside and solitude you loved, and that you don't disdain this rustic aspect of my style, which you once considered worthwhile. From among the weapons of bloodthirsty Mars, where almost no one can withstand his violence, I stole this brief quantity of time, wielding now the sword and now the pen. Apply then for a while your senses to the humble

indina de llegar a tus oídos,
pues de ornamento y gracia va desnuda;
mas a las veces son mejor oídos
el puro ingenio y lengua casi muda,
testigos limpios de ánimo inocente,
que la curiosidad del elocuente.
Por aquesta razón de ti escuchado,
aunque me falten otras, ser merezco.
Lo que puedo te doy, y lo que he dado,
con recibillo tú, yo me enriquezco.
De cuatro ninfas que del Tajo amado
salieron juntas, a cantar me ofrezco:
Filódoce, Dinámene y Climene,
Nise, que en hermosura par no tiene.
Cerca del Tajo en soledad amena,
de verdes sauces hay una espesura,
toda de hiedra revestida y llena,
que por el tronco va hasta el altura,
y así la teje arriba y encadena,
que el sol no halla paso a la verdura;
el agua baña el prado con sonido,
alegrando la hierba y el oído.
Con tanta mansedumbre el cristalino
Tajo en aquella parte caminaba
que pudieran los ojos el camino
determinar apenas que llevaba.
Peinando sus cabellos de oro fino,
una ninfa, del agua do moraba,
la cabeza sacó, y el prado ameno

sound of my crude pipes, unworthy of reaching your ears, for it is naked of adornment and grace; but at times it is better to listen to the simple mind and almost silent tongue, pure witnesses of the innocent soul, than to the sophistication of the rhetorician. Because of this argument I deserve, though I may have no others, to be heard by you. I'm giving you what I can, and your acceptance of what I have given you enriches me. Of four nymphs which together rose up out of our beloved Tagus, I offer to sing: Phyllodoce, Dynamene and Clymene, Nise, who in beauty has no equal. Near the Tagus, in pleasant solitude, there is a thickness of green willows all entwined and covered over in ivy, which climbs up the trunk to the top and so weaves and enchains it above that the sun cannot find its way through the greenness; the water bathes the meadow in sound, making joyful the grass and the ear. So calmly the crystalline Tagus was flowing in that spot that one's eyes could hardly determine in which direction it was moving.

vido de flores y de sombra lleno.
   Movióla el sitio umbroso, el manso viento,
el suave olor de aquel florido suelo.
Las aves en el fresco apartamiento
vió descansar del trabajoso vuelo.
Secaba entonces el terreno aliento
el sol subido en la mitad del cielo.
En el silencio sólo se escuchaba
un susurro de abejas que sonaba.
   Habiendo contemplado una gran pieza
atentamente aquel lugar sombrío,
somorgujó de nuevo su cabeza
y al fondo se dejó calar del río.
A sus hermanas a contar empieza
del verde sitio el agradable frío,
y que vayan les ruega y amonesta
allí con su labor a estar la siesta.
   No perdió en esto mucho tiempo el ruego,
que las tres dellas su labor tomaron,
y en mirando de fuera, vieron luego
el prado, hacia el cual enderezaron.
El agua clara con lacivo juego
nadando dividieron y cortaron,
hasta que el blanco pie tocó mojado,
saliendo de la arena, el verde prado.
   Poniendo ya en lo enjuto las pisadas,
escurrieron del agua sus cabellos,
los cuales esparciendo, cubijadas

Combing her hair of fine gold, a nymph thrust out her head from the water where she lived, and saw the pleasant meadow full of flowers and shade. She was moved by the shady spot, the gentle wind, the sweet odor of that flowery spot. She saw the birds in cool withdrawal resting from the laborious flight. The earthy vapors were at that time being absorbed by the sun, which had climbed to the middle of the sky. In the silence one only heard a murmuring of bees that sounded. Having looked for a long while attentively at that shady spot, she plunged in her head again and let herself drop to the bottom of the river. She then begins to tell her sisters of the green place's pleasant coolness, and she begs and urges them to go and spend the hot afternoon there with their sewing. She didn't waste much time begging them to do this, for the three of them took their sewing and, when they looked out, saw at once the meadow, toward which they headed. The clear water in wanton play they cut through and divided as they swam, until their white feet damply touched the green meadow as they left the sand. Stepping now upon the dryness, they wrung the water out of their hair and, shaking it out,

las hermosas espaldas fueron dellos.
Luego sacando telas delicadas,
que en delgadeza competían con ellos,
en lo más escondido se metieron,
y a su labor atentas se pusieron.

Las telas eran hechas y tejidas
del oro que el felice Tajo envía,
apurado, después de bien cernidas
las menudas arenas do se cría,
y de las verdes hojas, reducidas
en estambre sutil, cual convenía
para seguir el delicado estilo
del oro ya tirado en rico hilo.

La delicada estambre era distinta
de las colores que antes le habían dado
con la fineza de la varia tinta
que se halla en las conchas del pescado.
Tanto artificio muestra en lo que pinta
y teje cada ninfa en su labrado,
cuanto mostraron en sus tablas antes
el celebrado Apeles y Timantes.

Filódoce, que así de aquéllas era
llamada la mayor, con diestra mano
tenía figurada la ribera
de Estrimón, de una parte el verde llano,
y de otra el monte de aspereza fiera,
pisado tarde o nunca de pie humano,

covered with hair their lovely shoulders and backs. Then taking out fine fabrics which in texture competed with their hair, they entered the deepest part of the thicket and began to concentrate upon their handwork. The fabrics were formed and woven of the gold that the fortunate Tagus yields, refined after the tiny sands where it is produced have been sifted out, and of the green leaves, converted into fine yarn as was fitting to accompany the delicate style of the gold, now drawn out into rich threads. The delicate yarn was changed from the colors it had formerly had by the fineness of the varied dye that is found in the shells of fish; each nymph shows as much artistry in what she depicts and weaves in her embroidery as was previously shown in their pictures by the celebrated Apelles and Timanthes. Phyllodoce, for this was the name of the oldest of the nymphs, with dexterous hand had depicted the bank of the Strymon River, on the one hand the green plain and on the other the wild jagged mountain, trodden late or never by human foot,

donde el amor movió con tanta gracia
la dolorosa lengua del de Tracia.
  Estaba figurada la hermosa
Eurídice, en el blanco pie mordida
de la pequeña sierpe ponzoñosa,
entre la hierba y flores escondida;
descolorida estaba como rosa
que ha sido fuera de sazón cogida,
y el ánima, los ojos ya volviendo,
de su hermosa carne despidiendo.
  Figurado se vía estensamente
el osado marido que bajaba
al triste reino de la escura gente,
y la mujer perdida recobraba;
y cómo después desto él, impaciente
por miralla de nuevo, la tornaba
a perder otra vez, y del tirano
se queja al monte solitario en vano.
  Dinámene no menos artificio
mostraba en la labor que había tejido,
pintando a Apolo en el robusto oficio
de la silvestre caza embebecido.
Mudar luego le hace el ejercicio
la vengativa mano de Cupido,
que hizo a Apolo consumirse en lloro
después que le enclavó con punta de oro.
  Dafne, con el cabello suelto al viento,
sin perdonar al blanco pie, corría

where love moved so gracefully the grieving tongue of the Thracian [i.e., Orpheus]. Lovely Eurydice was depicted bitten on her white foot by the small poisonous snake hidden among the grass and flowers; she was pale like a rose that has been plucked out of season and, rolling her eyes back, was already exhaling her soul from her lovely body. One saw depicted at length the daring husband going down to the sad realm of the dark people and regaining his lost wife; and how afterwards he, impatient to see her again, lost her once more, and complains in vain of the tyrant to the solitary mountain. Dynamene showed no less artistry in the handwork that she had woven, painting Apollo as intent upon the robust exercise of forest hunting. Then he is made to change his occupation by the vengeful hand of Cupid, who made Apollo waste away in tears after piercing him with arrowhead of gold. Daphne, with hair flying in the wind, without sparing her white feet, was

por áspero camino tan sin tiento
que Apolo en la pintura parecía
que, porque ella templase el movimiento,
con menos ligereza la seguía.
El va siguiendo, y ella huye como
quien siente al pecho el odioso plomo.
    Mas a la fin los brazos le crecían
y en sendos ramos vueltos se mostraban,
y los cabellos, que vencer solían
al oro fino, en hojas se tornaban;
en torcidas raíces se estendían
los blancos pies, y en tierra se hincaban.
Llora el amante, y busca el ser primero,
besando y abrazando aquel madero.
    Climene, llena de destreza y maña,
el oro y las colores matizando,
iba, de hayas, una gran montaña,
de robles y de peñas, variando.
Un puerco entre ellas, de braveza estraña,
estaba los colmillos aguzando
contra un mozo, no menos animoso,
con su venablo en mano, que hermoso.
    Tras esto, el puerco allí se vía herido
de aquel mancebo, por su mal valiente,
y el mozo en tierra estaba ya tendido,
abierto el pecho del rabioso diente;
con el cabello de oro desparcido
barriendo el suelo miserablemente,

running down a rough road in so headlong a way that it seemed in the painting that Apollo, in order to make her slow down, was following her less speedily. He continues to follow, and she to flee like one who feels in her heart the leaden arrow of hatred. But finally her arms were growing and were seen to have been changed into two branches, and her hair, which used to outshine fine gold, was turning into leaves; as twisted roots her white feet stretched out and thrust themselves into the ground. The lover weeps and seeks her former self as he kisses and embraces that piece of wood. Clymene, very dexterous and skillful, by shading the gold and the colors, was giving variety to a great mountain with beeches, oaks and rocks. Among them a boar of unusual ferocity was sharpening his tusks in preparation for a youth, with spear in hand, no less spirited than handsome. After this, one saw the boar there wounded by the youth, too brave for his own good, and the boy was stretched out already on the ground, his chest cut open by the raging teeth; with his scattered golden hair dragging wretchedly on the ground, the white roses growing around him were changed by his blood into red. One

las rosas blancas por allí sembradas
tornaba con su sangre coloradas.
Adonis éste se mostraba que era,
según se muestra Venus dolorida,
que viendo la herida abierta y fiera,
estaba sobre él casi amortecida.
Boca con boca, coge la postrera
parte del aire que solía dar vida
al cuerpo, por quien ella en este suelo
aborrecido tuvo al alto cielo.
La blanca Nise no tomó a destajo
de los pasados casos la memoria,
y en la labor de su sutil trabajo
no quiso entretejer antigua historia;
antes mostrando de su claro Tajo
en su labor la celebrada gloria,
lo figuró en la parte donde él baña
la más felice tierra de la España.
Pintado el caudaloso río se vía,
que, en áspera estrecheza reducido,
un monte casi alrededor ceñía,
con ímpetu corriendo y con ruído;
querer cercallo todo parecía
en su volver, mas era afán perdido;
dejábase correr, en fin, derecho,
contento de lo mucho que había hecho.
Estaba puesta en la sublime cumbre
del monte, y desde allí por él sembrada,
aquella ilustre y clara pesadumbre,
de antiguos edificios adornada.

could see that he was Adonis by the way that Venus was grieving, who, seeing the fierce, open wound, was almost fainting on top of him. Mouth to mouth, she catches the last bit of air which used to give life to that body for which she on earth had scorned high heaven. Fair Nise did not take as her task the remembering of past episodes, and in the embroidery of her subtle handwork chose not to weave ancient history; revealing instead, in her embroidery, the celebrated glory of her famous Tagus, she depicted it in the region where it bathes the most fortunate land in Spain. One saw painted the mighty river which, hemmed in by jagged narrows, almost surrounded a mountain as it ran impetuously and noisily; it seemed to want to encircle it completely in its circling, but it was wasted effort; finally it allowed itself to run straight on, satisfied with all that it had accomplished. Placed upon the lofty summit of the mountain, and from that point scattered down its slopes, was the illustrious and famous massiveness, with ancient buildings

De allí con agradable mansedumbre
el Tajo va siguiendo su jornada,
y regando los campos y arboledas
con artificio de las altas ruedas.
　En la hermosa tela se veían
entretejidas las silvestres diosas
salir de la espesura, y que venían
todas a la ribera presurosas,
en el semblante tristes, y traían
cestillos blancos de purpúreas rosas,
las cuales esparciendo, derramaban
sobre una ninfa muerta que lloraban.
　Todas con el cabello desparcido
lloraban una ninfa delicada,
cuya vida mostraba que había sido
antes de tiempo y casi en flor cortada.
Cerca del agua, en un lugar florido,
estaba entre la hierba degollada,
cual queda el blanco cisne cuando pierde
la dulce vida entre la hierba verde.
　Una de aquellas diosas, que en belleza,
al parecer, a todas ecedía,
mostrando en el semblante la tristeza
que del funesto y triste caso había,
apartada algún tanto, en la corteza
de un álamo unas letras escrebía,
como epitafio de la ninfa bella,
que hablaban así por parte della:
　"Elisa soy, en cuyo nombre suena
y se lamenta el monte cavernoso,

adorned. From there on, pleasantly calm, the Tagus continues its way, irrigating the fields and groves by the ingenuity of lofty wheels. On the lovely fabric were seen, woven in, woodland goddesses coming out of the forest, and they were all hastening along the bank with sad faces and carrying white baskets of purple roses, which they scattered and poured over a dead nymph for whom they wept. With their hair torn, they all wept for a delicate nymph, whose life had evidently been cut off before its time and almost at its height. Near the water, in a flowery spot, she lay among the grass with severed throat as the white swan lies when he loses his sweet life among the green grasses. One of the goddesses, who in beauty, it seems, exceeded all the rest, showing in her face the sadness which she felt at this sad dire event, standing somewhat to one side, was writing some letters on the bark of a poplar, as an epitaph for the lovely nymph, which spoke thus on her behalf:

testigo del dolor y grave pena
en que por mí se aflige Nemoroso,
y llama 'Elisa'; 'Elisa' a boca llena
responde el Tajo, y lleva presuroso
al mar de Lusitania el nombre mío,
donde será escuchado, yo lo fío."

En fin, en esta tela artificiosa
toda la historia estaba figurada
que en aquella ribera deleitosa
de Nemoroso fué tan celebrada;
porque de todo aquesto y cada cosa
estaba Nise ya tan informada
que llorando el pastor, mil veces ella
se enterneció escuchando su querella.

Y porque aqueste lamentable cuento,
no sólo entre las selvas se contase,
mas, dentro de las ondas, sentimiento
con la noticia desto se mostrase,
quiso que de su tela el argumento
la bella ninfa muerta señalase,
y así se publicase de uno en uno
por el húmido reino de Netuno.

Destas historias tales variadas
eran las telas de las cuatro hermanas,
las cuales, con colores matizadas,
claras las luces, de las sombras vanas
mostraban a los ojos relevadas
las cosas y figuras que eran llanas;

"I am Elisa, at whose name resounds and laments the cavernous mountain, a witness to the pain and heavy grief which for my sake afflicts Nemoroso, and he calls out 'Elisa'; 'Elisa' full-throatedly replies the Tagus, and hastily takes my name to the Lusitanian Sea, where it will be heard, I trust." In sum, upon this artful fabric was depicted the whole story which on that pleasant riverbank had been made so famous by Nemoroso; for Nise was already so well informed of all this and of each detail that, while the shepherd wept, she very often was deeply moved as she listened to his complaint. And in order that this sad story should not only be told among the woods but that also within the waves grief should be felt at this news, she wanted the story on her fabric to show forth the fair nymph's death and so be communicated from one person to another throughout the damp kingdom of Neptune. Of such various stories as these consisted the tapestries of the four sisters, who with shaded colors and bright highlights caused the eye to see standing out in relief from the empty shadows the objects and the figures

tanto que, al parecer, el cuerpo vano
pudiera ser tomado con la mano.
Los rayos ya del sol se trastornaban,
escondiendo su luz, al mundo cara,
tras altos montes, y a la luna daban
lugar para mostrar su blanca cara;
los peces a menudo ya saltaban,
con la cola azotando el agua clara,
cuando las ninfas, la labor dejando,
hacia el agua se fueron paseando.
En las templadas ondas ya metidos
tenían los pies, y reclinar querían
los blancos cuerpos, cuando sus oídos
fueron de dos zampoñas que tañían
suave y dulcemente detenidos
tanto que sin mudarse las oían,
y al son de las zampoñas escuchaban
dos pastores, a veces, que cantaban.
Más claro cada vez el son se oía
de dos pastores que venían cantando
tras el ganado, que también venía
por aquel verde soto caminando,
y a la majada, ya pasado el día,
recogido llevaban, alegrando
las verdes selvas con el son suave,
haciendo su trabajo menos grave.
Tirreno destos dos el uno era,
Alcino el otro, entrambos estimados,
y sobre cuantos pacen la ribera

that were flat, so that apparently the empty body could be seized by the hand. The rays of the sun were now turning away, hiding their light, dear to the world, behind high mountains, and were giving the moon a chance to show her white face; the fish were jumping frequently now, striking the clear water with their tails, when the nymphs, ceasing their work, began to stroll toward the water. In the warm waves they had already put their feet and were about to recline their fair bodies when their ears were so attracted by two pipes playing softly and sweetly that without moving they could hear them, and to the sound of the pipes they listened to two shepherds who were singing alternately. Clearer and clearer the sound was heard of two shepherds who approached singing behind their sheep, which also came walking along through that green meadow and which they were taking to the fold, now that the day was over, making joyful the green woods with the sweet

del Tajo, con sus vacas, enseñados;
mancebos de una edad, de una manera
a cantar juntamente aparejados
y a responder, aquesto van diciendo,
cantando el uno, el otro respondiendo:

Tirreno

Flérida, para mí dulce y sabrosa
más que la fruta del cercado ajeno,
más blanca que la leche y más hermosa
que el prado por abril, de flores lleno:
si tú respondes pura y amorosa
al verdadero amor de tu Tirreno,
a mi majada arribarás primero
que el cielo nos amuestre su lucero.

Alcino

Hermosa Filis, siempre yo te sea
amargo al gusto más que la retama,
y de ti despojado yo me vea
cual queda el tronco de su verde rama,
si más que yo el murciélago desea
la escuridad, ni más la luz desama,
por ver ya el fin de un término tamaño
deste día, para mí mayor que un año.

Tirreno

Cual suele acompañada de su bando
aparecer la dulce primavera

sound and making their work less painful. Tyrrhenus was one of the two and Alzinus the other, both well thought of and better educated than all who take their cattle to graze on the banks of the Tagus; youths well matched in age and manner to sing together and to reply, they go along saying the following, one of them singing and the other replying: *Tyrrhenus:* Flerida, sweeter and more delicious to me than the fruit of another's orchard, whiter than milk and more beautiful than the meadow in April, full of flowers: if you respond pure and loving to the true love of your Tyrrhenus, you will reach my sheepfold before the sky shows us its evening star. *Alzinus:* Lovely Phyllis, may I ever be bitterer to your taste than furze, and may I be bereft of you as the trunk is bereft of its green branch, if the bat desires darkness more than I, or more dislikes the light, wishing to see

cuando Favonio y Céfiro, soplando,
al campo tornan su beldad primera
y van artificiosos esmaltando
de rojo, azul y blanco la ribera:
en tal manera, a mí Flérida mía
viniendo, reverdece mi alegría.

Alcino

¿Ves el furor del animoso viento,
embravecido en la fragosa sierra,
que los antiguos robles ciento a ciento
y los pinos altísimos atierra,
y de tanto destrozo aún no contento,
al espantoso mar mueve la guerra?
Pequeña es esta furia comparada
a la de Filis, con Alcino airada.

Tirreno

El blanco trigo multiplica y crece,
produce el campo en abundancia tierno
pasto al ganado, el verde monte ofrece
a las fieras salvajes su gobierno;
a doquiera que miro me parece
que derrama la copia todo el cuerno:
mas todo se convertirá en abrojos
si dello aparta Flérida sus ojos.

Alcino

De la esterilidad es oprimido
el monte, el campo, el soto y el ganado;

the end of a period as long as this day, for me longer than a year. *Tyrrhenus:* As sweet springtime is wont to appear accompanied by its band when Favonius and Zephyr, blowing, bring back to the fields their former beauty and artfully enamel the bank with red and blue and white: so, when my Flerida returns to me, my joy comes to life again. *Alzinus:* Do you see the madness of the spirited wind, made wild in the steep mountains, which lays low by the hundred ancient oaks and lofty pines, and still not satisfied with so much destruction, wages war against the fearful sea? Such fury is small in comparison with Phyllis's, when angry with Alzinus. *Tyrrhenus:* The white wheat multiplies and grows, the field produces in abundance tender grass for the sheep, the green wood offers to fierce wild beasts its protection; wherever I look, it seems that the horn of plenty is running over: but

la malicia del aire corrompido
hace morir la hierba mal su grado;
las aves ven su descubierto nido,
que ya de verdes hojas fué cercado:
pero si Filis por aquí tornare,
hará reverdecer cuanto mirare.

Tirreno

El álamo de Alcides escogido
fué siempre, y el laurel del rojo Apolo;
de la hermosa Venus fué tenido
en precio y en estima el mirto solo;
el verde sauz de Flérida es querido,
y por suyo entre todos escogiólo;
doquiera que de hoy más sauces se hallen,
el álamo, el laurel y el mirto callen.

Alcino

El fresno por la selva en hermosura
sabemos ya que sobre todos vaya,
y en aspereza y monte de espesura
se aventaja la verde y alta haya,
mas el que la beldad de tu figura
dondequiera mirado, Filis, haya,
al fresno y a la haya en su aspereza
confesará que vence tu belleza.—

Esto cantó Tirreno, y esto Alcino

everything will turn into thistles if Flerida takes her eyes off it. *Alzinus*: By sterility is oppressed the wood, the field, the meadow and the sheep; the evil of corrupt air makes the grass die despite itself; the birds see their nests revealed which were formerly covered by green leaves: but if Phyllis comes back here, she will turn green again everything she sees. *Tyrrhenus:* The poplar was always chosen by Hercules, and the laurel by red Apollo; by lovely Venus was prized and esteemed the myrtle only; the green willow is loved by Flerida, and for her own from among all she chose it; wherever willows are found from now on, let the poplar, the laurel and the myrtle keep silence. *Alzinus:* In the woods the ash's beauty we know already is supreme, and on rough, thick-grown mountains the tall, green beech is superior, but he who has seen anywhere, Phyllis, the beauty of your figure will confess that your loveliness conquers the roughness of the ash and the beech.—Thus Tyrrhenus sang, and thus Alzinus answered him; and having

le respondió; y habiendo ya acabado
el dulce son, siguieron su camino
con paso un poco más apresurado.
Siendo a las ninfas ya el rumor vecino,
todas juntas se arrojan por el vado,
y de la blanca espuma que movieron
las cristalinas ondas se cubrieron.

Gutierre de Cetina

(ca. 1516–ca. 1555)

MADRIGAL I

Ojos claros, serenos,
si de un dulce mirar sois alabados,
¿por qué, si me miráis, miráis airados?
Si cuanto más piadosos,
más bellos parecéis a aquel que os mira,
no me miréis con ira,
porque no parezcáis menos hermosos.
¡Ay tormentos rabiosos!
Ojos claros, serenos,
ya que así me miráis, miradme al menos.

now completed their sweet song, they went on their way with a slightly quickened step. When their sound almost reached the nymphs, the latter plunged together into the shallows, and the white foam that they stirred up covered the crystalline waves.

MADRIGAL I: Fair eyes serene, if you are praised for your sweet glances, why, if you look at me, do you look angrily? If the more kindly you look, the more beautiful you seem to him who looks at you, don't look at me in anger, so that you won't seem less beautiful. Oh maddening torture! Fair eyes serene, since you are looking at me in that way, at least look at me.

MADRIGAL II

Cubrir los bellos ojos
con la mano que ya me tiene muerto
cautela fué por cierto,
que ansí doblar pensastes mis enojos.

Pero de tal cautela
harto mayor ha sido el bien que el daño,
que el resplandor extraño
del sol se puede ver mientras se cela.

Así que, aunque pensastes
cubrir vuestra beldad, única, inmensa,
yo os perdono la ofensa,
pues, cubiertos, mejor verlos dejastes.

SONETO I

¡Ay, sabrosa ilusión, sueño süave!
¿Quién te ha enviado a mí? ¿Cómo viniste?
¿Por dónde entraste al alma? O ¿qué le diste,
a mi secreto por guardar la llave?
¿Quién pudo a mi dolor fiero, tan grave,
el remedio poner que tú pusiste?
Si el ramo tinto en Lete en mí esparciste,
ten la mano al velar, que no se acabe.
Bien conozco que duermo y que me engaño

MADRIGAL II: To cover your lovely eyes with the hand that has already thrilled me to death was indeed a trick, for in this way you intended to double my suffering. But the good caused by this trick has been far greater than the evil, for the unusual gleam of the sun can be seen when it is hidden. Thus, although you intended to cover your loveliness, unique and immense, I forgive you the offence, for, by covering them, you've let them be seen better.

SONNET I: Oh, wonderful illusion, sweet dream! Who has sent you to me? How did you come? How did you get into my soul? Or what bribe did you give for my secret's key? Who else could cure my fierce and serious ailment as you did? If you shook upon me the twig dipped in Lethe's waters, save it,

mientra envuelto en un bien falso, dudoso,
manifiesto mi mal se muestra cierto;
pero, pues excusar no puedo un daño,
hazme sentir, ¡oh sueño pïadoso!,
antes durmiendo el bien que el mal despierto.

SONETO III

Entre armas, guerra, fuego, ira y furores
que al soberbio francés tienen opreso,
cuando el aire es más turbio y más espeso,
allí me aprieta el fiero ardor de amores.
Miro al cielo, los árboles, las flores,
y en ellos hallo mi dolor expreso;
que en el tiempo más frío y más avieso
nacen y reverdecen mis temores.
Digo llorando: « ¡Oh dulce primavera!
¿Cuándo será que a mi esperanza vea,
verde, prestar al alma algún sosiego?»
Mas temo que mi fin mi suerte fiera
tan lejos de mi bien quiere que sea
entre guerra y furor, ira, armas, fuego.

while I'm awake, so that it's not used up. I am well aware that I am asleep and deceive myself when, submerged in a false and dubious happiness, my sadness is indeed obvious; but, since I can not escape suffering, make me aware, oh kind dream, of happiness while sleeping rather than of sadness while awake.

SONNET III: In the midst of arms, war, fire, frenzies and fury which hem in the proud Frenchman, when the air is darkest and thickest, there I am besieged by the fierce ardor of love. I look at the sky, the trees, the flowers, and in them I find my suffering expressed; for in the coldest, most adverse weather my fears sprout and turn green. I say in tears: "Oh sweet springtime, when will I be able to see my hope turn green and bring some peace to my soul?" But I fear that my cruel fate wants me to die this far away from my love, in the midst of war and fury, frenzy, arms, fire.

SONETO V

Horas alegres que pasáis volando,
porque, a vueltas del bien, mayor mal sienta;
sabrosa noche que, en tan dulce afrenta,
el triste despedir me vas mostrando;
importuno reloj que, apresurando
tu curso, mi dolor me representa:
estrellas (con quien nunca tuve cuenta)
que mi partida vais acelerando;
gallo que mi pesar has denunciado,
lucero que mi luz va oscureciendo,
y tu, mal sosegada y moza aurora:
si en vos cabe dolor de mi cuidado,
id poco a poco el paso deteniendo,
si no puede ser más, siquiera un hora.

SONETO VI
Al monte donde fue Cartago

Excelso monte, do el romano estrago
eterna mostrará vuestra memoria;
soberbios edificios, do la gloria
aun resplandece de la gran Cartago;
desierta plaza, que apacible lago
fuiste lleno de triunfos y vitoria;
despedazados mármoles, historia

SONNET V: Happy hours that go flying by, so that in place of happiness I may feel greater sadness; wonderful night that, in so sweet a sorrow, hints at my own sad departure; obnoxious clock that, hastening your course, recalls to my mind my suffering; stars (whom I've never taken into account) that hasten my departure; cock that declares my grief, morning star that darkens my light, and you, unruly young Aurora: if you are capable of sympathizing with my plight, little by little start slowing down, if it can't be any longer, at least for an hour.

SONNET VI: *To the mountain where Carthage once stood:* Lofty mountain, where Roman destruction will forever eternalize your memory; proud buildings, where the glory still gleams of great Carthage; deserted square, which once was a quiet lake full of triumphal victories; shattered marble,

en que se lee cuál es del mundo el pago;
arcos, anfiteatros, baños, templo,
que fuisteis edificios celebrados,
y agora apenas vemos las señales:
gran remedio a mi mal es vuestro ejemplo,
que si del tiempo fuisteis derribados,
el tiempo derribar podrá mis males.

Francisco de la Torre

SONETO V

Sigo, silencio, tu estrellado manto,
de transparentes lumbres guarnecido,
enemiga del Sol esclarecido,
ave noturna de agorero canto.
El falso mago Amor, con el encanto
de palabras quebradas por olvido,
convirtió mi razón y mi sentido,
mi cuerpo no, por deshacelle en llanto.
Tú, que sabes mi mal, y tú, que fuiste
la ocasión principal de mi tormento,
por quien fuí venturoso y desdichado,
oye tú solo mi dolor, que al triste
a quien persigue cielo violento,
no le está bien que sepa su cuidado.

in which one can read the story of the world's rewards; arches, amphitheaters, baths, temple, which once were famous buildings and of which we can now hardly detect the traces: your example is a great cure for my despair, for if by time you have been destroyed, time will be able to destroy my suffering.

SONNET V: I follow, silence, your starry mantle, adorned with bright lights, being the enemy of that bright sun, the nocturnal bird of ominous song. The false magician Love, with the incantation of words broken by oblivion, converted my reason and senses, but not my body, in order to destroy it in tears. You, who know my suffering and were the main cause of my torment, who made me both lucky and unfortunate, you listen alone to my pain, for it is not right that a violent heaven which persecutes a poor man should know of his suffering.

SONETO XX

¡Quántas vezes te me has engalanado.
clara y amiga noche! ¡Quántas, llena
de escuridad y espanto, la serena
mansedumbre del cielo me has turbado!
Estrellas ay que saben mi cuydado
y que se han regalado con mi pena;
que, entre tanta beldad, la más agena
de amor tiene su pecho enamorado.
Ellas saben amar, y saben ellas
que he contado su mal llorando el mío,
embuelto en los dobleces de tu manto.
Tú, con mil ojos, noche, mis querellas
oye y esconde, pues mi amargo llanto
es fruto inútil que al amor embío.

SONETO XXIII

Bella es mi ninfa, si los laços de oro
al apacible viento desordena;
bella, si de sus ojos enagena
el altivo desdén que siempre lloro.
Bella, si con la luz que sola adoro
la tempestad del viento y mar serena;
bella, si a la dureza de mi pena
buelve las gracias del celeste coro.

SONNET XX: How often you have adorned yourself for me, bright, friendly night! And how often, full of darkness and fright, you have upset the peaceful quiet of my heaven! There are stars which know of my suffering and have taken pleasure in my pain; for in the presence of so much beauty, even the one most opposed to love has an enamored heart. They know of love, and they know that I have told of their suffering when bewailing my own, wrapped up in the folds of your mantle. You, of a thousand eyes, night, listen to my plaints and hide them, for my bitter tears are useless fruit which I send to love.

SONNET XXIII: Lovely is my nymph, if she rumples her golden locks in the gentle breeze; lovely, if she exiles from her eyes the proud disdain which I always deplore. Lovely, if with the only light which I adore she calms the tempest of wind and sea; lovely, if upon the harshness of my suffering she

Bella si mansa, bella si terrible;
bella si cruda, bella esquiva, y bella
si buelve grave aquella luz del cielo
cuya beldad humana y apacible
ni se puede saber lo que es sin vella,
ni vista entenderá lo que es el suelo.

ENDECHA II

El pastor más triste
que ha seguido el cielo,
dos fuentes sus ojos
y un fuego su pecho,
llorando caídas
de altos pensamientos,
solo se querella
riberas de Duero.
El silencio amigo,
compañero eterno
de la noche sola,
oye sus tormentos.
Sus endechas llevan
rigurosos vientos,
como su firmeza
mal tenidos zelos.
Solo y pensativo
le halla el claro Febo;
sale su Diana,
y hállale gimiendo.

showers the graces of the heavenly choir. Lovely if gentle, lovely if harsh; lovely if cruel, lovely elusive, and lovely if she turns dark that light of heaven whose kind and gentle beauty cannot be known if she hasn't been seen, nor, once seen, can one understand what the earth is.

LAMENT II: The saddest shepherd ever persecuted by heaven, his eyes two springs and his heart on fire, lamenting the downfall of lofty dreams, all alone complains on the banks of the Duero. Friendly silence, the eternal companion of lonely night, hears his torments. His laments are swept away by harsh winds, as his fidelity is by unjustified jealousy. Alone and pensive the bright sun finds him; his moon comes out and finds him moaning. The heaven which separates him from his great happiness has put him in a state

Cielo que le aparta
de su bien inmenso
le ha puesto en estado
de ningún consuelo.
Tórtola cuytada,
que el montero fiero
le quitó la gloria
de su compañero,
elevada y mustia
del piadoso acento
que oye suspirando
entregar al viento,
porque no se pierdan
suspiros tan tiernos,
ella los recoge,
que se duele dellos.
Y por ser más dulces
que su arrullo tierno,
de su soledad
se quexa con ellos,
que ha de hazer el triste
pierda el sufrimiento,
que tras lo perdido
no cayrá contento.

of disconsolation. A poor turtledove, bereft by fierce hunter of her mate's glory, entranced and saddened by the pitiful tone which she hears him sighingly give to the wind, to keep such tender sighs from being lost, gathers them up, as she feels sorry for them. And since they are sweeter than her own tender coo, she uses them to complain of her loneliness, which will make the sad man lose his endurance, for after what he has lost there will be no happiness.

Hernando de Acuña

(ca. 1520–1580)

SONETO AL REY NUESTRO SEÑOR

Ya se acerca, señor, o es ya llegada
la edad gloriosa en que promete el cielo
una grey y un pastor solo en el suelo,
por suerte a vuestros tiempos reservada.
Ya tan alto principio, en tal jornada,
os muestra el fin de vuestro santo celo
y anuncia al mundo, para más consuelo,
un monarca, un imperio y una espada.
Ya el orbe de la tierra siente en parte,
y espera en todo, vuestra monarquía,
conquistada por vos en justa guerra:
que a quien ha dado Cristo su estandarte
dará el segundo más dichoso día
en que, vencido el mar, venza la tierra.

TO THE KING OUR LORD: There now approaches, sire, or has already arrived, the age of glory in which heaven promises one flock and one shepherd only on the earth, an age fortunately reserved for your time. So great a beginning, in this expedition, gives you signs already of the fulfillment of your holy zeal and announces to the world, as a greater joy, one monarch, one empire and one sword. Already the earthly sphere receives in part, and awaits throughout, your monarchy, won by you in righteous war: for to whom Christ has given his banner, He will also give the second and happier day on which, the sea having been conquered, he will conquer the earth.

Fray Luis de León

(1527–1591)

ODA I
Vida Retirada

¡Qué descansada vida
la del que huye el mundanal ruïdo,
y sigue la escondida
senda por donde han ido
los pocos sabios que en el mundo han sido!
Que no le enturbia el pecho
de los soberbios grandes el estado,
ni del dorado techo
se admira, fabricado
del sabio moro, en jaspes sustentado.
No cura si la fama
canta con voz su nombre pregonera;
no cura si encarama
la lengua lisonjera
lo que condena la verdad sincera.
¿Qué presta a mi contento
si soy del vano dedo señalado,
si en busca de este viento
ando desalentado
con ansias vivas, y mortal cuidado?

ODE I: What a restful life, that of him who flees from worldly noise and follows the hidden path down which have gone the few wise men who have existed in the world! For his heart is not darkened by the status of the great and proud, nor does he stand amazed at gilded ceilings wrought by the skillful Moor, upheld by jasper columns. He does not care whether fame sings out his name with a shouting voice; he does not care whether the flattering tongue extols that which sincere truth condemns. What does it add to my happiness if I am pointed out by the finger of vanity, if in pursuit of this empty wind I run breathlessly, living in anguish and mortal

¡Oh, campo! ¡Oh, monte! ¡Oh, río!
¡Oh, secreto seguro, deleitoso!
Roto casi el navío,
a vuestro almo resposo
huyo de aqueste mar tempestuoso.
Un no rompido sueño,
un día puro, alegre, libre quiero;
no quiero ver el çeño
vanamente severo
del que la sangre sube o el dinero.
Despiértenme las aves
con su cantar süave no aprendido,
no los cuidados graves
de que es siempre seguido
quien al ajeno arbitrio está atenido.
Vivir quiero conmigo;
gozar quiero del bien que debo al cielo,
a solas, sin testigo,
libre de amor, de celo,
de odio, de esperanzas, de recelo.
Del monte en la ladera
por mi mano plantado tengo un huerto,
que con la primavera,
de bella flor cubierto,
ya muestra en esperanza el fruto cierto.
Y como codiciosa
de ver y acrecentar su hermosura,
desde la cumbre airosa
una fontana pura

concern? Oh, field! Oh, woods! Oh, river! Oh, secret refuge of delight! With ship almost destroyed, I flee from this stormy sea to your nourishing repose. An unbroken sleep, a cloudless, happy day of freedom are what I want; I don't want to see the vainly severe frown of him who is exalted by family or wealth. Let the birds awaken me with their sweet unschooled singing, not the grave worries which always plague him who depends on another's will. I want to live by myself; I want to enjoy the blessings that I owe to heaven, all alone, without a witness, free from love, from zeal, from hatred, from hope, from fear. On the slope of the hill, with my own hand I have planted an orchard, which in the springtime, covered with lovely blooms, is already giving hopeful signs of sure fruit. And as though desirous of seeing and increasing its beauty, from the airy hilltop a spring of

hasta llegar corriendo se apresura;
  y luego, sosegada,
el paso entre los árboles torciendo,
el suelo de pasada
de verdura vistiendo,
y con diversas flores va esparciendo.
  El aire el huerto orea,
y ofrece mil olores al sentido;
los árboles menea
con un manso ruïdo,
que del oro y del cetro pone olvido.
  Ténganse su tesoro
los que de un flaco leño se confían;
no es mío ver el lloro
de los que desconfían
cuando el cierzo y el ábrego porfían.
  La combatida antena
cruje, y en ciega noche el claro día
se torna; al cielo suena
confusa vocería,
y la mar enriquecen a porfía.
  A mí una pobrecilla
mesa, de amable paz bien abastada,
me baste; y la vajilla,
de fino oro labrada,
sea de quien la mar no teme airada.
  Y mientras miserable-
mente se están los otros abrasando
con sed insacïable
del no durable mando,

pure water comes hastily running down; and then, more calmly, wending its way among the trees, as it passes, it gradually clothes the ground in green and sprinkles it with different flowers. The breeze flows through the orchard and offers many fragrances to one's senses; it sways the trees with a gentle sound which makes one forget gold and scepters. Let them have their treasures, those who put their faith in frail boats; I won't have to see the tears of those who lose their faith when the north and south winds compete. The straining rigging creaks, and the bright day turns into dark night; a confused sound of voices rises to heaven, and they compete in throwing their riches to the sea. For me, let a humble little table suffice, well supplied with friendly peace; and let the table service, decorated with pure gold, belong to one who does not fear the angry sea. And while others are wretchedly consuming themselves with an insatiable thirst for power which does not

tendido yo a la sombra esté cantando,
  a la sombra tendido,
de yedra y lauro eterno coronado,
puesto el atento oído
al son dulce, acordado,
del plectro sabiamente meneado.

ODA III
A Francisco Salinas
Catedrático de Música de la
Universidad de Salamanca

  El aire se serena
y viste de hermosura y luz no usada,
Salinas, cuando suena
la música extremada,
por vuestra sabia mano gobernada;
  a cuyo son divino
mi alma, que en olvido está sumida,
torna a cobrar el tino
y memoria perdida
de su origen primera esclarecida.
  Y como se conoce,
en suerte y pensamientos se mejora;
el oro desconoce,
que el vulgo ciego adora,
la belleza caduca, engañadora.
  Traspasa el aire todo

last, let me be stretched out singing in the shade, stretched out in the shade, wearing a crown of ivy and eternal laurel, listening attentively to the sweet, well-tuned sound of the strings skilfully plucked.

ODE III: *To Francisco Salinas, Professor of Music at the University of Salamanca:* The air becomes serene and puts on an unusual beauty and light, Salinas, when that exceptional music resounds which is controlled by your skillful hand; at that divine sound my soul, buried in forgetfulness, recovers its bearings and the lost memory of its primeval, noble source. And as it gets to know itself, it betters its condition and thoughts; it forgets gold, which the blind mob worships, and impermament, deceptive beauty. It passes through

hasta llegar a la más alta esfera,
y oye allí otro modo
de no perecedera
música, que es de todas la primera.
 Ve cómo el gran maestro,
a aquesta inmensa cítara aplicado,
con movimiento diestro
produce el son sagrado,
con que este eterno templo es sustentado.
 Y como está compuesta
de números concordes, luego envía
consonante respuesta;
y entrambas a porfía
mezclan una dulcísima armonía.
 Aquí la alma navega
por un mar de dulzura, y finalmente
en él ansí se anega
que ningún accidente
extraño y peregrino oye o siente.
 ¡Oh, desmayo dichoso!
¡Oh, muerte que das vida! ¡Oh, dulce olvido!
¡Durase en tu reposo,
sin ser restituído
jamás a aqueste bajo y vil sentido!
 A aqueste bien os llamo,
gloria del apolíneo sacro coro,
amigos a quien amo
sobre todo tesoro;

the whole atmosphere until it reaches the highest starry sphere, and there it hears another mode of imperishable music, which is the prime source of all musics. It sees how the great Musician, leaning over this immense harp, with dextrous movement produces the sacred sound which sustains this eternal temple. And since it is itself composed of harmonizing elements, it then sends forth a reply in tune; and as they compete, they both compound a very sweet harmony. Here the soul swims in a sea of sweetness, and finally so drowns in this sea that it does not hear or perceive any accidental note which is alien or foreign. Oh, happy swoon! Oh life-giving death! Oh, sweet forgetfulness! If only I could continue in your repose, without ever being restored to this low, inferior mode of feeling! To this delight I summon you, glory of Apollo's sacred choir, friends whom I love more than any

que todo lo demás es triste lloro.
¡Oh! suene de contino,
Salinas, vuestro son en mis oídos,
por quien al bien divino
despiertan los sentidos,
quedando a lo demás amortecidos.

ODA VII
Profecía del Tajo

Folgaba el Rey Rodrigo
con la hermosa Cava en la ribera
del Tajo, sin testigo;
el pecho sacó fuera
el río, y le habló desta manera:
«En mal punto te goces,
injusto forzador; que ya el sonido
y las amargas voces,
y ya siento el bramido
de Marte, de furor y ardor ceñido.
»¡Aquesta tu alegría
¡qué llantos acarrea! Aquesa hermosa,
que vió el sol en mal día,
al Godo, ¡ay!, cuán llorosa,
al soberano cetro, ¡ay! cuán costosa!
»Llamas, dolores, guerras,
muertes, asolamientos, fieros males
entre tus brazos cierras,
trabajos inmortales
a ti y a tus vasallos naturales;

treasure; for everything else is sad tears. Oh, let your music sound forever, Salinas, in my ears, for it awakens to divine delight one's senses and makes them deaf to all else.

ODE VII, *The Tagus River's Prophecy:* King Roderick was taking his pleasure with lovely Cava on the banks of the Tagus, all alone; the river thrust forth his breast and spoke to him as follows: "May you be damned in your pleasure, lawless ravisher; for I already hear the sound and the fierce shouts and the bellowing of Mars, girt in burning madness. How many laments are caused by this enjoyment of yours! How many tears does that beauty, born on a fateful day, cause the Goth, alas, and how costly is she to his sovereign scepter! Flames, suffering, wars, deaths, desolation and fierce ills are what you hold in your arms, and endless labors for you and your natural vassals; for those who in Constantina till the fertile soil, for those bathed by the

» a los que en Constantina
rompen el fértil suelo, a los que baña
el Ebro, a la vecina
Sansueña, a Lusitaña:
a toda la espaciosa y triste España.
»Ya dende Cádiz llama
el injuriado Conde, a la venganza
atento y no a la fama,
la bárbara pujanza,
en quien para tu daño no hay tardanza.
»Oye que al cielo toca
con temeroso son la trompa fiera,
que en Africa convoca
el moro a la bandera
que, al aire desplegada, va ligera.
»La lanza ya blandea
el árabe crüel, y hiere el viento,
llamando a la pelea;
innumerable cuento
de escuadras juntas veo en un momento.
»Cubre la gente el suelo;
debajo de las velas desparece
la mar; la voz al cielo
confusa, incierta, crece;
el polvo roba el día y le escurece.
»¡Ay!, que ya presurosos
suben las largas naves. ¡Ay!, que tienden
los brazos vigorosos
a los remos, y encienden
las mares espumosas por do hienden.
»El Eolo derecho

Ebro River, for nearby Sansueña, for Lusitania, for the whole of sad and spacious Spain. Already from Cádiz the injured count, intent upon vengeance rather than his reputation, summons the barbarian onslaught, in which, unfortunately for you, there is no delay. Listen, the fierce trumpet touches heaven with fearful sound as in Africa it summons the Moor to the flag which flies free, unfurled in the breeze. The cruel Arab is already brandishing his lance and smiting the wind as he calls to battle; I see an innumerable sum of squadrons joined in one moment. People cover the ground; the sea disappears beneath the sails; the noise of vague confusion rises to heaven; dust snatches away daylight and turns it dark. Alas, they are already hastily embarking in the long ships! Alas, they stretch out their vigorous arms to the oars and burn the foaming seas which they cleave. Favorable Eolus swells

hinche la vela en popa, y larga entrada
por el hercúleo Estrecho,
con la punta acerada,
el gran padre Neptuno da a la armada.

»¡Ay, triste! ¿y aun te tiene
el mal dulce regazo? ¿Ni llamado
al mal que sobreviene,
no acorres? ¿Abrazado
con tu calamidad, no ves tu Hado?

»Acude, acorre, vuela,
traspasa la alta sierra, ocupa el llano;
no perdones la espuela,
no des paz a la mano,
menea fulminando el hierro insano.

»¡Ay!, ¡cuánto de fatiga!
¡Ay!, ¡cuánto de sudor está presente
al que viste loriga,
al infante valiente,
a hombres y a caballos juntamente!

»¡Y tú, Betis divino,
de sangre ajena y tuya amancillado,
darás al mar vecino
cuánto yelmo quebrado,
cuánto cuerpo de nobles destrozado!

»El furibundo Marte
cinco luces las haces desordena,
igual a cada parte;

the sail from astern, and with his sharp trident, great father Neptune opens up for the fleet a large entrance through the Straits of Hercules. Alas, doomed man, and are you still held in that deadly sweet embrace? Even when summoned to the overtaking disaster, don't you come running? Embracing your calamity, can't you see your fate? Come running, fly, cross over the high mountains, occupy the plain, spare not the spur, give no rest to your hand, brandish menacingly the mad steel. Alas, how much weariness, alas, how much sweat besets him who wears the breastplate, the brave soldier, men and horses together! And you, divine Betis [the Guadalquivir River], stained by alien and by native blood, how many a broken helmet will you yield to the neighboring sea, how many a crushed nobleman's body! For five days mad Mars breaks up the ordered ranks evenly on

la sexta, ¡ay!, te condena,
¡oh, cara patria! a bárbara cadena.»

ODA VIII
Noche Serena

Cuando contemplo el cielo
de innumerables luces adornado,
y miro hacia el suelo,
de noche rodeado,
en sueño y en olvido sepultado,
el amor y la pena
despiertan en mi pecho un ansia ardiente;
despiden larga vena
los ojos hechos fuente;
la lengua dice al fin con voz doliente:
«Morada de grandeza,
templo de claridad y hermosura:
mi alma que a tu alteza
nació, ¿qué desventura
la tiene en esta cárcel baja, escura?
»¿Qué mortal desatino
de la verdad aleja ansí el sentido,
que de tu bien divino
olvidado, perdido,
sigue la vana sombra, el bien fingido?
»El hombre está entregado
al sueño, de su suerte no cuidando;

either side; on the sixth, alas!, he sentences you, oh dear native land, to the barbarian's chain."

ODE VIII, *Still Night*: When I regard the heavens adorned with innumerable lights, and I look toward the earth, surrounded by night, buried in sleep and oblivion, love and grief awaken within my breast an ardent yearning; my eyes, transformed into a spring, pour out an abundant stream; finally my tongue says, with woeful voice: "Dwelling place of grandeur, temple of brightness and beauty, what curse holds my soul, born for your heights, trapped in this low, dark prison? What mortal error so separates my senses from the truth that, forgetful of your divine treasure, lost, it pursues empty shadows and false treasures? Man surrenders to sleep, taking no thought for

y con paso callado
el cielo, vueltas dando,
las horas del vivir le va hurtando.
»¡Ay!, despertad, mortales!
Mirad con atención en vuestro daño.
¿Las almas inmortales,
hechas a bien tamaño,
podrán vivir de sombra y solo engaño?
»¡Ay!, levantad los ojos
a aquesta celestial eterna esfera:
burlaréis los antojos
de aquesa lisonjera
vida, con cuanto teme y cuanto espera.
»¿Es más que un breve punto
el bajo y torpe suelo, comparado
a aqueste gran trasunto,
do vive mejorado
lo que es, lo que será, lo que ha pasado?
»Quien mira el gran concierto
de aquestos resplandores eternales,
su movimiento cierto,
sus pasos desiguales
y en proporción concorde tan iguales:
»la luna cómo mueve
la plateada rueda, y va en pos de ella
la luz do el saber llueve,
y la graciosa estrella

his destiny; and with silent tread the heavens go round and steal his hours of life. Alas, awaken, mortals! Pay attentive heed to your loss. Can immortal souls, created for so great a blessing, live on shadows and falseness alone? Alas, raise your eyes to this eternal, celestial sphere: you will thus escape the illusions of this seductive life and all that it hopes for and fears. Is the low and graceless earth more than a mere point when compared to this great transfiguration, where in a better state lives what is, what will be, what has been? He who looks at the great concert of these eternal lights, their fixed movements, their footsteps unequal and yet so matched in harmonious proportion: how the moon moves its silver wheel, and behind her follows the light where wisdom pours [Mercury], and the graceful star of Love [Venus] follows it gleaming and beautiful; and how blood-red, irate Mars follows another route, and benign Jupiter, encircled by many blessings, calms the heavens with his beloved rays; at the summit Saturn revolves, the

de Amor la sigue reluciente y bella;
»y cómo otro camino
prosigue el sanguinoso Marte airado,
y el Júpiter benino,
de bienes mil cercado,
serena el cielo con su rayo amado;
»rodéase en la cumbre
Saturno, padre de los siglos de oro;
tras dél la muchedumbre
del reluciente coro
su luz va repartiendo y su tesoro:
»¿quién es el que esto mira
y precia la bajeza de la tierra,
y no gime y suspira
por romper lo que encierra
el alma y de estos bienes la destierra?
»Aquí vive el contento,
aquí reina la paz; aquí, asentado
en rico y alto asiento,
está el Amor sagrado,
de glorias y deleites rodeado.
»Inmensa hermosura
aquí se muestra toda, y resplandece
clarísima luz pura,
que jamás anochece;
eterna primavera aquí florece.
»¡Oh, campos verdaderos!
¡Oh, prados con verdad dulces y amenos!
¡Riquísimos mineros!
¡Oh, deleitosos senos!
¡Repuestos valles, de mil bienes llenos!»

father of the Golden Ages; behind him the throng of the gleaming chorus distributes its light and treasure: who is he that can look at this and still esteem the lowness of the earth, and not groan and sigh to destroy that which traps the soul and keeps it from these blessings? Here lives happiness, here reigns peace; here, seated on a rich and lofty seat, is sacred love, surrounded by glory and delight. Immense beauty is here fully revealed, and there gleams the brightest purest light, which never turns to night; eternal springtime flowers here. Oh, true fields! Oh, meadows pleasant and sweet with truth! Richest deposits of gold! Oh, hollows of delight! Hidden valleys full of countless blessings!"

ODA X

A Felipe Ruiz

¿Cuándo será que pueda,
libre de esta prisión, volar al cielo,
Felipe, y en la rueda
que huye más del suelo,
contemplar la verdad pura, sin velo?
Allí, a mi vida junto,
en luz resplandeciente convertido,
veré, distinto y junto,
lo que es y lo que ha sido,
y su principio propio y ascondido.
Entonces veré cómo
el divino poder echó el cimiento
tan a nivel y plomo,
do estable, eterno asiento
posee el pesadísimo elemento.
Veré las inmortales
columnas do la tierra está fundada,
los lindes y señales
con que a la mar airada
la Providencia tiene aprisionada;
por qué tiembla la tierra,
por qué las hondas mares se embravecen,
dó sale a mover guerra
el cierzo, y por qué crecen
las aguas del Océano y descrecen;
de dó manan las fuentes;

ODE X, *To Felipe Ruiz:* When will I be able, free of this prison, to fly to heaven, Felipe, and in the sphere which flees farthest from earth to contemplate the truth pure and unveiled? There, along with my own life, I shall see, converted into resplendent light, separate yet together, that which is and that which has been, along with its own hidden source of being. Then I shall see how divine power laid the foundations so plumb and true on which the heaviest element is firmly and eternally anchored. I shall see the immortal columns upon which the earth is founded, the limits and lines within which Providence keeps the angry sea imprisoned; why the earth quakes, why the deep seas get rough, whence the north wind sallies to wage war, and why the waters of the Atlantic rise and ebb; whence the springs flow; who

quién ceba y quién bastece de los ríos
las perpetuas corrientes;
de los helados fríos
veré las causas, y de los estíos;
  las soberanas aguas
del aire en la región quién las sostiene;
de los rayos las fraguas,
dó los tesoros tiene
de nieve Dios, y el trueno dónde viene.
  ¿No ves, cuando acontece
turbarse el aire todo en el verano?
El día se ennegrece,
sopla el gallego insano,
y sube hasta el cielo el polvo vano;
  y entre las nubes mueve
su carro Dios, ligero y reluciente;
horrible son conmueve,
relumbra fuego ardiente,
treme la tierra, humíllase la gente;
  la lluvia baña el techo,
envían largos ríos los collados;
su trabajo deshecho,
los campos anegados,
miran los labradores espantados.
  Y de allí levantado
veré los movimientos celestiales,
ansí el arrebatado
como los naturales,

feeds and nourishes the unceasing currents of the rivers; I shall see the causes of the frozen winters and of the summers; who sustains the upper waters in the region of the air; where God keeps the forges of His thunderbolts, His treasuries of snow, and where the thunder comes from. Haven't you seen this when all the air suddenly becomes turbulent in the summer? The sky turns black, the mad northwest wind blows, and the light dust goes up to the sky; and among the clouds God drives his chariot, swift and gleaming; a terrible sound frightens us, blazing fires flash, the earth trembles, the people fall to their knees; rain bathes the roof, the hills send down abundant streams; the terrified farmers gaze at their labor undone and their fields swamped. And rising beyond that point I shall see the movements of the celestial bodies, both the sudden comet and the natural movements, the

las causas de los hados, las señales.
  Quién rige las estrellas
veré, y quién las enciende con hermosas
y eficaces centellas;
por qué están las dos Osas
de bañarse en el mar siempre medrosas.
  Veré este fuego eterno,
fuente de vida y luz, dó se mantiene;
y por qué en el invierno
tan presuroso viene,
por qué en las noches largas se detiene.
  Veré sin movimiento
en la más alta esfera las moradas
del gozo y del contento,
de oro y luz labradas,
de espíritus dichosos habitadas.

ODA XVIII
Morada del Cielo

  Alma región luciente,
prado de bienandanza, que ni al hielo
ni con el rayo ardiente
fallece; fértil suelo,
producidor eterno de consuelo:
  de púrpura y de nieve
florida, la cabeza coronado,
a dulces pastos mueve,
sin honda ni cayado,
el Buen Pastor en ti su hato amado.
  El va, y en pos dichosas
le siguen sus ovejas, do las pace

causes and the indications of one's fate. I shall see who controls the stars and who lights them with beautiful and burning sparks; why the two Bears are always afraid of taking a dip in the sea. I shall see where this eternal fire, the source of light and life, is maintained; and why in the winter it moves so rapidly and delays so during the long nights. I shall see motionless in the highest sphere the dwelling places of joy and happiness, built of gold and light, inhabited by the blessed spirits.

ODE XVIII, *Heavenly Dwelling Place:* Sweet region of light, meadow of blessedness, which neither under ice nor under burning thunderbolt fails; fertile soil eternally producing consolation: with his head crowned in purple and

con inmortales rosas,
con flor que siempre nace,
y cuanto más se goza más renace.
  Ya dentro a la montaña
del alto bien las guía; ya en la vena
del gozo fiel las baña,
y les da mesa llena,
pastor y pasto él solo y suerte buena.
  Y de su esfera, cuando
la cumbre toca altísimo subido
el sol, él sesteando,
de su hato ceñido,
con dulce son deleita el santo oído.
  Toca el rabel sonoro,
y el inmortal dulzor al alma pasa,
con que envilece el oro,
y ardiendo se traspasa,
y lanza en aquel bien libre de tasa.
  ¡Oh, son! ¡Oh, voz! Siquiera
pequeña parte alguna decendiese
en mi sentido, y fuera
de sí la alma pusiese
y toda en ti, ¡oh, Amor!, la convirtiese,
  conocería dónde
sesteas, dulce Esposo; y desatada
de esta prisión adonde
padece, a tu manada
junta, no ya andara perdida, errada.

in flowering snow, without sling or crook the Good Shepherd leads his beloved flock to sweet pastures in you. He goes ahead, and his happy sheep follow after him, where he grazes them on immortal roses, on a flower that always blooms and the more it is enjoyed, the more it blooms again. Now he leads them into the mountain of supreme blessedness; now he bathes them in the stream of faithful joy and feeds them at a bountiful table, he himself being their shepherd and their food and their blessing. And when the sun at its height touches the zenith of its sphere, he at noonday rest, surrounded by his flock, delights their holy ears with sweet music. He plays the sounding rebec, and the immortal sweetness reaches their souls, causing them to scorn gold and in burning rapture to transcend themselves and to plunge into that limitless blessedness. Oh, music! Oh, voice! If only some slight amount would descend into my ears and raise my soul out of itself and turn it wholly into you, oh Love, it would know where you take your noonday rest, sweet Spouse; and freed from this prison where it suffers, together with your flock, it would no longer wander lost.

ODA XIX
En la Ascensión

¡Y dejas, Pastor santo,
tu grey en este valle hondo, escuro,
con soledad y llanto!
Y tú, rompiendo el puro
aire, ¿te vas al inmortal seguro?
Los antes bienhadados,
y los agora tristes y afligidos,
a tus pechos criados,
de ti desposeídos,
¿a dó convertirán ya sus sentidos?
¿Qué mirarán los ojos
que vieron de tu rostro la hermosura,
que no les sea enojos?
Quien oyó tu dulzura,
¿qué no tendrá por sordo y desventura?
Aqueste mar turbado,
¿quién le pondrá ya freno? ¿Quién concierto
al viento fiero, airado?
Estando tú encubierto,
¿qué norte guiará la nave al puerto?
¡Ay!, nube, envidïosa
aun de este breve gozo, ¿qué te aquejas?
¿Dó vuelas presurosa?
¡Cuán rica tú te alejas!
¡Cuán pobres y cuán ciegos, ay, nos dejas!

ODE XIX, *On the Ascension:* And you're abandoning, saintly Shepherd, your flock in this deep, dark valley to be lonely and to weep! And you, yourself, making your way through the upper air, are departing for the refuge of immortality? Those who were formerly fortunate and are now sad and afflicted, having been nourished at your breast and now dispossessed of you, toward what can they now turn their senses? The eyes that have seen the beauty of your face, what can they now look upon that won't be distasteful to them? He who has heard your sweetness, what will he not consider now dull and calamitous? This turbulent sea, who will now hold it in check, or impose order upon the fierce and angry wind? If you are concealed, what North Star will guide the ship to port? Alas, cloud, envious of even this our brief pleasure, why do you hasten? Where are you flying so fast? How wealthy you are as you depart, and how poor and blind, alas, you leave us!

ODA XXII

A Nuestra Señora

Virgen que el sol más pura,
gloria de los mortales, luz del cielo,
en quien la pïedad es cual la alteza:
los ojos vuelve al suelo,
y mira un miserable en cárcel dura,
cercado de tinieblas y tristeza.
Y si mayor bajeza
no conoce, ni igual, juïcio humano,
que el estado en que estoy por culpa ajena,
con poderosa mano
quiebra, Reina del cielo, esta cadena.
Virgen, en cuyo seno
halló la deïdad digno reposo,
do fué el rigor en dulce amor trocado:
si blando al riguroso
volviste, bien podrás volver sereno
un corazón de nubes rodeado.
Descubre el deseado
rostro, que admira el cielo, el suelo adora:
las nubes huïrán, lucirá el día;
tu luz, alta Señora,
venza esta ciega y triste noche mía.
Virgen y madre junto,

ODE XXII, *To Our Lady:* Virgin purer than the sun, glory of mortals, light of heaven, whose pity is as great as your sovereignty: turn your eyes toward earth and look upon a wretch cruelly imprisoned and surrounded by darkness and sadness. And if human judgment knows no lower, or equivalent, depths than the situation that I'm in for others' faults, with your mighty hand, Queen of heaven, break this chain. Virgin in whose bosom deity found a worthy resting place, where harshness was transformed into sweet love: if you softened the harsh, you can easily calm a heart beset by clouds. Reveal your longed-for face, admired by heaven and adored by earth: the clouds will flee, the sun will shine; let your light, sovereign Lady, overcome this dark sad night of mine. Virgin and mother together, the blessed begetter

de tu Hacedor dichosa engendradora,
a cuyos pechos floreció la vida:
mira cómo empeora
y crece mi dolor más cada punto.
El odio cunde, la amistad se olvida;
si no es de ti valida
la justicia y verdad, que tú engendraste,
¿adónde hallarán seguro amparo?
Y pues madre eres, baste
para contigo el ver mi desamparo.
  Virgen, del sol vestida,
de luces eternales coronada,
que huellas con divinos pies la luna:
envidia emponzoñada,
engaño agudo, lengua fementida,
odio crüel, poder sin ley ninguna
me hacen guerra a una;
pues, contra un tal ejército maldito,
¿cuál pobre y desarmado será parte,
si tu nombre bendito,
María, no se muestra por mi parte?
  Virgen, por quien vencida
llora su perdición la sierpe fiera,
su daño eterno, su burlado intento:
miran de la ribera
seguras muchas gentes mi caída,
el agua vïolenta, el flaco aliento;
los unos con contento,

of your Creator, at whose breasts life flourished: see how my suffering grows worse and increases every moment. Hatred thrives, friendship is forgotten; if you do not support justice and truth, which you begot, where will they find sure protection? And since you are a mother, let it suffice for you to see my abandonment. Virgin clothed by the sun, crowned with immortal lights, standing upon the moon with feet divine: poisonous envy, sharp deception, false tongues, cruel hatred, lawless power make war upon me all together; against such a cursed army, what poor unarmed person can prevail if your blessed name, Mary, is not seen to be on my side? Virgin by whom the fierce serpent was vanquished, lamenting his defeat, his eternal loss, his frustrated attempt: many people safe upon the shore observe my fall, the violent current, my weakening breath; some shout with joy, others with terror, the kindest with useless pity. I, keeping my tear-filled eyes upon

los otros con espanto, el más piadoso
con lástima la inútil voz fatiga.
Yo, puesto en ti el lloroso
rostro, cortando voy la onda enemiga.
  Virgen, del Padre Esposa,
dulce Madre del Hijo, templo santo
del inmortal Amor, del hombre escudo:
no veo sino espanto.
Si miro la morada, es peligrosa;
si la salida, incierta; el favor, mudo;
el enemigo, crudo;
desnuda, la verdad; muy proveída
de valedores y armas, la mentira:
la miserable vida
sólo cuando me vuelvo a ti respira.
  Virgen, que al alto ruego
no más humilde «sí» diste que honesto,
en quien los cielos contemplar desean:
como terrero puesto,
los brazos presos, de los ojos ciego,
a cien flechas estoy que me rodean,
que en herirme se emplean.
Siento el dolor, mas no veo la mano;
ni puedo huir, ni me es dado escudarme.
¡Quiera tu soberano
Hijo, Madre de amor, por ti librarme!
  Virgen, lucero amado,
en mar tempestuosa clara guía,

your face, swim through the opposing waves. Virgin, the Father's spouse, the Son's sweet Mother, holy temple of immortal Love, man's shield: all I see is terror. If I observe my dwelling place, it is dangerous; my escape is uncertain; favorable voices are silent; the enemy is cruel; truth is naked; falsehood is well provided with supporters and arms: only when I turn to you does my wretched life catch its breath. Virgin whose consent to the supreme request was no less pure than it was humble, whom the heavens desire to contemplate: with my arms tied and my eyes blindfolded, I am set like a target for a hundred arrows that surround me and that are used to wound me. I feel the pain, but do not see the hand; neither can I flee, nor am I permitted to protect myself. May your sovereign Son, Mother of love, for your sake consent to set me free! Virgin, beloved star, bright guide on the

a cuyo santo rayo calla el viento:
mil olas a porfía
hunden en el abismo un desarmado
leño de vela y remo, que sin tiento
el húmedo elemento
corre; la noche carga, el aire truena;
ya por el suelo va, ya el cielo toca;
gime la rota entena.
¡Socorre, antes que embista en cruda roca!
   Virgen, no inficionada
de la común mancilla y mal primero,
que al humano linaje contamina:
bien sabes que en ti espero
dende mi tierna edad; y si malvada
fuerza, que me venció, ha hecho indina
de tu guarda divina
mi vida pecadora, tu clemencia
tanto mostrará más su bien crecido,
cuanto es más la dolencia,
y yo merezco menos ser valido.
   Virgen, el dolor fiero
añuda ya la lengua, y no consiente
que publique la voz cuanto desea;
mas oye tú al doliente
ánimo, que contino a ti vocea.

stormy sea, at whose holy gleam the wind becomes still: a thousand waves compete to sink into the depths an unarmed galley which headlong rushes through the water; the night is heavy, the atmosphere thunders; now it touches the bottom, now the sky; the broken rigging groans. Help, before it runs upon the cruel rocks! Virgin uninfected by the universal stain and primal evil which contaminates the human race: you know well that I have put my hope in you since childhood; and if the power of evil, which has conquered me, has made my sinful life unworthy of your divine protection, your mercy will be all the more abundant, the greater my suffering and the less I deserve to be helped. Virgin, cruel pain now ties my tongue and keeps my voice from declaring all it wishes to; but you please listen to the suffering spirit which continually calls upon you.

DÉCIMA
Al salir de la cárcel

Aqui la envidia y mentira
me tuvieron encerrado.
Dichoso el humilde estado
del sabio que se retira
de aqueste mundo malvado,
y con pobre mesa y casa,
en el campo deleitoso
con sólo Dios se compasa,
y a solas su vida pasa,
ni envidiado ni envidioso.

Baltasar del Alcázar

(1530–1606)

CANCIÓN I

Tres cosas me tienen preso
de amores el corazón:
la bella Inés, y jamón,
y berenjenas con queso.
Una Inés, amantes, es
quien tuvo en mí tal poder
que me hizo aborrecer
todo lo que no era Inés.
Trájome un año sin seso,
hasta que en una ocasión

DECIMA, *Upon Leaving Prison:* Here envy and falsehood kept me imprisoned. Happy is the humble estate of the wise man who withdraws from this evil world and with simple table and house, in the pleasant countryside, is at harmony only with God and spends his life alone, neither envied nor envious.

SONG I: Three things have captured my heart with love: *lovely Inez, and ham, and eggplant with cheese.* A certain Inez, lovers, is the person who exerted upon me such power that she made me hate everything that wasn't Inez. She kept me madly in love for a year, until one day *she gave me, for*

me dió a merendar jamón
y berenjenas con queso.
  Fué de Inés la primer palma;
pero ya juzgarse ha mal
entre todos ellos cuál
tiene más parte en mi alma.
En gusto, medida y peso
no les hallo distinción:
ya quiero Inés, ya jamón,
ya berenjenas con queso.
  Alega Inés su beldad;
el jamón, que es de Aracena;
el queso y la berenjena,
su andaluz antigüedad.
Y está tan en fil el peso
que, juzgado sin pasión,
todo es uno: Inés, jamón
y berenjenas con queso.
  Servirá este nuevo trato
destos mis nuevos amores
para que Inés sus favores
nos los venda más barato,
pues tendrá por contrapeso,
si no hiciere razón,
una lonja de jamón
y berenjenas con queso.

SONETO

  Yo acuerdo revelaros un secreto
en un soneto, Inés, bella enemiga;
mas, por buen orden que yo en éste siga,

lunch, ham and eggplant with cheese. Inez won the first prize; but now it would be hard to judge, among the three, which holds greater sway over my heart. In taste, measure and weight I find no difference between them: *one moment I love Inez, the next ham, the next eggplant with cheese.* Inez asserts her beauty; the ham, that it's from Aracena; the cheese and eggplant assert their Andalusian ancestry. And the scales are so evenly balanced that, judged dispassionately, *it's all the same: Inez, ham, and eggplant with cheese.* This new acquaintance with my new loves will have the advantage of making Inez sell us her favors more cheaply, for she'll have, to offset her, if she isn't nice to me, *a slice of ham and eggplant with cheese.*

SONNET: I agree to tell you a secret in a sonnet, Inez, lovely enemy; but no

no podrá ser en el primer cuarteto.
   Venidos al segundo, yo os prometo
que no se ha de pasar sin que os lo diga;
mas estoy hecho, Inés, una hormiga,
que van fuera ocho versos del soneto.
   Pues ved, Inés, qué ordena el duro hado,
que teniendo el soneto ya en la boca
y el orden de decillo ya estudiado,
   conté los versos todos y he hallado
que, por la cuenta que a un soneto toca,
ya este soneto, Inés, es acabado.

Fernando de Herrera

(ca. 1534–1597)

CANCION EN ALABANZA DE LA DIVINA MAJESTAD POR LA VICTORIA DEL SEÑOR DON JUAN

   Cantemos al Señor, que en la llanura
venció del mar al enemigo fiero.
Tú, Dios de las batallas, tú eres diestra,
salud, y gloria nuestra.
Tú rompiste las fuerças y la dura
frente de Faraón, feroz guerrero.
Sus escogidos príncipes cubrieron
los abissos del mar, y decendieron

matter how I try in this one, it cannot be in the first quatrain. Now that we're in the second, I promise you it won't come to an end without my telling you; but I'll be darned, Inez, if eight lines of the sonnet haven't gone by. Now look, Inez, at the cruel dictates of fate, for after having already begun the sonnet and having worked out its composition, I have counted all the lines and find that, by the rules of the sonnet, this sonnet, Inez, is now finished.

HYMN IN PRAISE OF GOD'S MAJESTY FOR THE VICTORY OF SIR JOHN [AT LEPANTO]: Let us sing unto the Lord, who on the plains of the sea conquered the fierce enemy. You, God of battles, You are our right arm, salvation and glory. You broke the power and stubborn brow of Pharaoh, the ferocious warrior. His chosen princes covered the abysses of the sea, and they went

qual piedra en el profundo; y tu ira luego
los tragó, como arista seca el fuego.
El sobervio tirano, confiado
en el grande aparato de sus naves,
que de los nuestros la cerviz cativa
y las manos aviva
al ministerio de su duro estado,
derribó con los braços suyos graves
los cedros más ecelsos de la cima
y el árbol que más yerto se sublima,
bebiendo agenas aguas, y pisando
el más cerrado y apartado vando.
Temblaron los pequeños confundidos
del ímpio furor suyo; alçó la frente
contra ti, Señor Dios, y enfurecido
ya contra ti se vido,
con los armados brazos estendidos,
el arrogante cuello del potente.
Cercó su coraçón de ardiente saña
contra las dos Esperias que el mar baña,
porque en ti confiadas le resisten,
y de armas de tu fe y amor se visten.
Dixo aquel, insolente y desdeñoso:
"¿No conocen mis iras estas tierras,
y de mis padres los ilustres hechos?
¿o valieron sus pechos

down like stones to the depths; and Your wrath then swallowed them up, as fire does the dry chaff. The proud tyrant, putting his trust in the grandiose show of his ships, which the captive necks and hands of our people drive forward in the service of his cruel government, chopped down with his own heavy arms the loftiest cedars of the peak and the tree which rises straightest, drinking foreign waters and treading upon the best defended and most distant areas. The small ones trembled in consternation at his impious madness; he raised his head against You, Lord God, and in anger against You was seen, with armed hands extended, the arrogant neck of the powerful one. He encircled his heart with burning wrath against the two sea-bathed Hesperias [Italy and Spain] because, putting their trust in You, they resist him and arm themselves with Your faith and love. He said, insolently and disdainfully: "Aren't these lands acquainted with my wrath and the illustrious deeds of my ancestors? Were their breasts able to stand against them with the hesitant Hungarian or in the wars of Dalmatia and

contra ellos, con el úngaro dudoso,
y de Dalmacia y Rodas en las guerras?
¿pudo su Dios librallos de sus manos?
¡Que Dios salvó a los de Austria y los Germanos!
¿por ventura podrá su Dios aora
guardallos de mi diestra vencedora?
"Su Roma, temerosa y umillada,
sus canciones en lágrimas convierte;
ella y sus hijos mi furor esperan,
quando vencidos mueran.
Francia está con discordia quebrantada,
y en España amenaza orrible muerte
quien onra de la luna las vanderas;
y aquellas gentes en la guerra fieras
ocupadas están en su defensa:
y aunque no, ¿quién podrá hazerme ofensa?
"Los poderosos pueblos me obedecen,
y con su daño el yugo an consentido,
y me dan por salvarse ya la mano;
y su valor es vano,
que sus luzes muriendo se escurecen.
Sus fuertes en batalla an perecido,
sus vírgenes están en cativerio,
su gloria a buelto al cetro de mi imperio.
Del Nilo a Eufrátes y al Danubio frío,
quanto el sol alto mira, todo es mío."
Tú, Señor, que no sufres que tu gloria
usurpe quien confía en su grandeza,

Rhodes? Could their God liberate them from their hands? So God saved the Austrians and the Germans! Can their God now protect them from my conquering right hand? Their Rome, fearful and dishonored, turns her hymns into tears; she and her children await my wrath, when they will be conquered and die. France is rent by discords, and in Spain dreadful butchery is promised by him who honors the crescent flags; and those nations fierce in war are busy defending themselves: and even if they weren't, who could wage offensive war on me? The powerful nations obey me, and have accepted my yoke to their loss, and now to save themselves they help me; and their bravery is vain, for their lights grow dim and die. Their strong men have perished in battle, their maidens are in captivity, their glory has turned to my imperial scepter. From the Nile to the Euphrates and the cold Danube, everything viewed by the lofty sun is mine." You, Lord, who do not permit Your glory to be usurped by him who trusts in

prevaleciendo en vanidad y en ira,
a este sobervio mira,
que tus templos afea en su vitoria
y tus hijos oprime con dureza,
y en sus cuerpos las fieras bravas ceva,
y en su esparcida sangre el odio prueva;
y hecho ya su oprobio, dize: "¿Dónde
el Dios déstos está? ¿de quién se esconde?"
¡Por la gloria devida de tu nombre,
por la vengança de tu muerta gente,
y de los presos por aquel gemido,
buelve el braço tendido
contra aquel, que aborrece ya ser ombre,
y las onras que a ti se dan consiente,
y tres y quatro vezes su castigo
dobla con fortaleza al enemigo;
y la injuria a tu nombre cometida
sea el duro cuchillo de su vida!
Levantó la cabeça el poderoso
que tanto odio te tiene, en nuestro estrago
juntó el consilio, y contra nos pensaron
los que en él se hallaron.
"¡Venid! dixeron: y en el mar undoso
hagamos de su sangre un grande lago;
deshagamos a estos de la gente,
y el nombre de su Cristo juntamente,
y, dividiendo d'ellos los despojos,
hártense en muerte suya nuestros ojos."

his own grandeur, excelling in vanity and wrath, look upon this proud man who profanes Your temples with his victory and harshly oppresses Your children and feeds the wild beasts on their bodies and proves his hatred by shedding their blood; and having completed his profanation, he says: "Where is these men's God? From whom is He hiding?" For the honor due to Your name, for the vengeance of Your slaughtered people, and for the groaning of those prisoners, stretch out Your arm against him, who is tired now of being a mere man, and give Your consent to the honors rendered You, and double three and four times over in vigor the enemy's punishment; and let the injury which he did to Your name be the blade that cuts off his life! The powerful one who so hates You raised his head, summoned a council for your destruction, and against us schemed those who were present at the council. "Come," they said, "and in the wavy sea let us make a great lake of their blood; let us destroy them as a nation, together with the name of their Christ, and dividing their spoils, let us feast our eyes upon

Vinieron de Asia y de la antigua Egito
los árabes y fieros Africanos,
y los que Grecia junta mal con ellos,
con levantados cuellos,
con gran potencia y número infinito.
Y prometieron con sus duras manos
encender nuestros fines, y dar muerte
con hierro a nuestra juventud más fuerte,
nuestros niños prender y las donzellas,
y la gloria ofender y la luz dellas.

Ocuparon del mar los largos senos,
en silencio y temor puesta la tierra,
y nuestros fuertes súbito cessaron
y medrosos callaron;
hasta que a los feroces Agarenos,
el Señor eligiendo nueva guerra,
se opuso el joven de Austria valeroso
con el claro Español y belicoso;
que Dios no sufre en Babilonia viva
su querida Sión siempre cativa.

Qual león a la presa apercibido,
esperavan los ímpios confiados
a los que tú, Señor, eras escudo;
que el coraçón desnudo
de temor, y de fe todo vestido,
de tu espíritu estavan confortados.
Sus manos a la guerra compusiste,
y a sus braços fortíssimos pusiste

their death." There came from Asia and ancient Egypt the Arabs and fierce Africans, and those whom Greece treacherously joined with them, with haughty necks, great power and infinite number. And with their cruel hands they promised to set fire to our lands and to put to the sword our strongest young men, to capture our children and maidens, and to defile their beauty and glory. They filled the great gulfs of the sea, the earth falling into silence and fright, and our strong men suddenly ceased and became quiet in fear; until, the Lord choosing to wage a new war, the fierce sons of Hagar were opposed by the valiant young man of Austria, accompanied by the illustrious and warlike Spaniard; for God does not permit his beloved Zion to live forever captive in Babylon. Like a lion ready for the prey, the confident infidels were waiting for those whose shield, Lord, You are; for their hearts, stripped of fear and all clad in faith, were strengthened by Your spirit. You prepared their hands for war, and You made their arms as strong

como el arco azerado, y con la espada
mostraste en su favor la diestra armada.
Turbáronse los grandes, los robustos
rindiéronse temblando y desmayaron,
y tú pusiste, Dios, como la rueda,
como la arista queda
al ímpetu del viento, a estos injustos,
que mil huyendo de uno se pasmaron.
Qual fuego abrasa selvas, y qual llama
que en las espesas cumbres se derrama,
tal en tu ira y tempestad seguiste
y su faz de inominia confundiste.
Quebrantaste al dragón fiero, cortando
las alas de su cuerpo temerosas
y sus braços terribles no vencidos,
que con hondos gemidos
se retira a su cueva silvos dando,
y tiembla con sus sierpes venenosas,
lleno de miedo torpe sus entrañas,
de tu león temiendo las hazañas;
que, saliendo de España, dió un rugido
que con espanto lo dexó atordido.
Oy los ojos se vieron umillados
del sublime varón y su grandeza,
y tú solo, Señor, fuiste exaltado;
que tu día es llegado,
Señor de los ejércitos armados,
sobre la alta cerviz y su dureza,
sobre derechos cedros y estendidos,

as bows of steel, and You revealed in support of them Your right hand armed with the sword. The great men were dismayed, the strong surrendered, trembling, and fainted, and You made these unrighteous men like the wheel and the chaff driven by the wind, for they were terrified, a thousand of them fleeing before one man. As fire burns the forests and as flame pours over the thick-grown mountaintops, so You pursued them in tempestuous wrath and confounded their faces with shame. You destroyed the fierce dragon, cutting the fearful wings from his body and his terrible unvanquished arms, and with deep groans he withdraws hissing to his cave and trembles with his poisonous snakes, his entrails full of paralyzing fright, afraid of the deeds of Your lion, which came out of Spain and gave a roar which left him

sobre empinados montes y crecidos,
sobre torres y muros, y las naves
de Tiro, que a los tuyos fueron graves.
  Babilonia y Egito amedrentada
del fuego y asta temblará sangrienta,
y el humo subirá a la luz del cielo,
y, faltos de consuelo,
con rostro oscuro y soledad turbada
tus enemigos llorarán su afrenta.
Y tú, Grecia, concorde a la esperança
de Egito, y gloria de su confiança
triste, que a ella pareces, no temiendo
a Dios, y en tu remedio no atendiendo:
  porque ingrata tus hijas adornaste
en adulterio con tan ímpia gente,
que desseava profanar tus frutos,
y con ojos enxutos
sus odiösos passos imitaste,
su aborrecible vida y mal presente,
por esso Dios se vengará en tu muerte;
que llega a tu cerviz su diestra fuerte
la aguda espada. ¿Quién será que pueda
tener su mano poderosa queda?
  Mas tú, fuerça del mar, tú, ecelsa Tiro,
que en tus naves estavas gloriösa,

stunned with terror. Today the eyes and grandeur of the proud man were humiliated, and You alone, Lord, were exalted; for Your day is come, Lord of the armies, upon the proud neck and its stiffness, upon the tall, straight cedars, upon the steep, high mountains, upon towers and walls, and the ships of Tyre, which oppressed Your people. Babylon and Egypt will tremble in fear of the fire and bloody spear, and smoke will rise to the light of heaven and, hopeless, with their faces dark and their solitude disturbed, Your enemies will lament their dishonor. And you, Greece, agreeing with Egypt's hope and the glory of her ill-fated confidence, which you resemble, neither fearing God nor attending to your own welfare: because ungratefully you adorned your daughters for adultery with such godless people, who desired to profane your offspring, and with dry eyes you followed their hateful footsteps, their abhorrent life and present disaster, because of that God will take vengeance in your death; for His strong right arm puts the sharp sword to your neck. Who can possibly restrain His powerful hand? But you, power of the seas, you, proud Tyre, who gloried in your ships and frightened the

y el término espantavas de la tierra,
y si hazías guerra,
de temor la cubrías con suspiro,
¿cómo acabaste fiera y orgullosa?
¿quién pensó a tu cabeça daño tanto?
Dios, para convertir tu gloria en llanto
y derribar tus ínclitos y fuertes,
te hizo perecer con tantas muertes.

Llorad, naves del mar, que es destruída
toda vuestra sobervia y fortaleza.
¿Quién ya tendrá de ti lástima alguna,
tú, que sigues la luna,
Asia adúltera, en vicios sumergida?
¿quién mostrará por ti alguna tristeza?
¿quién rogará por ti? Que Dios entiende
tu ira, y la sobervia que te ofende;
y tus antiguas culpas y mudança
an buelto contra ti a pedir vengança.

Los que vieren tus braços quebrantados
y de tus pinos ir el mar desnudo,
que sus ondas turbaron y llanura,
viendo tu muerte oscura,
dirán, de tus estragos espantados:
"¿Quién contra la espantosa tanto pudo?"
El Señor, que mostró su fuerte mano,
por la fe de su príncipe cristiano
y por el nombre santo de su gloria,
a España le concede esta vitoria.

limits of the earth and, if you waged war, covered it with fearful sighs, to what end did you come in your ferocity and pride? Who ever thought that your head would suffer such destruction? God, to turn your glory into tears and to bring low your great strong men, made you perish in so many different ways. Weep, ships of the sea, for all your power and pride is destroyed. Who will feel pity for you any longer, you who follow the moon, adulterous Asia, submerged in sinfulness? Who will show any sadness for you, who will pray for you? For God understands your wrath and the pride from which you suffer; and your ancient sins and inconstancy have turned upon you seeking vengeance. Those who shall see your arms broken and the sea empty of your pine ships which stirred up its waves and flatness, seeing your dark death, will ask, frightened by your destruction: "Who was able to do so much against the fearful one?" The Lord, who showed His strong hand, for the sake of the faith of His Christian prince and for the holy name of His own glory, gives this victory to Spain.

Bendita, Señor, sea tu grandeza,
que después de los daños padecidos,
después de nuestras culpas y castigo,
rompiste al enemigo
de la antigua sobervia la dureza.
Adórante, Señor, tus escogidos;
confiesse quanto cerca el ancho cielo
tu nombre, o nuestro Dios, nuestro consuelo,
y la cerviz rebelde, condenada,
padesca en bravas llamas abrasada.
A ti solo la gloria
por siglos de los siglos, a ti damos
la onra, y umillados te adoramos.

SONETO I

Osé i temí: mas pudo la osadía
tanto que desprecié el temor cobarde;
subí a do el fuego más m' enciende i arde
cuanto más la esperança se desvía.
Gasté en error la edad florida mía;
aora veo el daño, pero tarde,
que ya mal puede ser qu' el seso guarde
a quien s' entrega ciego a su porfía.
Tal vez pruevo (mas ¿qué me vale?) alçarme
del grave peso que mi cuello oprime;
anque falta a la poca fuerça el hecho.

Blessed, Lord, be Your greatness, for after the destruction suffered, after our sins and punishment, You broke the enemy's stiffness and ancient pride. Your chosen ones adore You, Lord; let everything enclosed by the width of heaven confess Your name, oh our God, our consolation, and let the rebellious neck be condemned to suffer and burn in fierce flames. You alone we glorify for ever and ever, You we honor, and You we humbly adore.

SONNET I: I dared and was afraid: but my daring was so powerful that I scorned cowardly fear; I climbed up to where the fire ignites and burns me all the more, the further I am removed from hope. I have wasted in error my youth; now I see the damage, but it is too late, for good sense can hardly protect any longer him who blindly yields himself to obstinate persistence. Sometimes I try (but what good does it do me?) to rise above the heavy weight which bears down upon my neck; but my lack of strength can-

Sigo al fin mi furor, porque mudarme
no es onra ya, ni justo que s' estime
tan mal de quien tan bien rindió su pecho.

SONETO XIV

"¿Dó vas? ¿dó vas, crüel, dó vas?; refrena,
refrena el pressuroso passo, en tanto
que de mi dolor grave el largo llanto
a abrir comiença esta honda vena;
oye la voz de mil suspiros llena,
i de mi mal sufrido el triste canto,
que no podrás ser fiera i dura tanto
que no te mueva esta mi acerba pena;
buelve tu luz a mí, buelve tus ojos,
antes que quede oscuro en ciega niebla",
dezía en sueño, o en ilusión perdido.
Bolví, halléme solo i entre abrojos,
i en vez de luz, cercado de tiniebla,
i en lágrimas ardientes convertido.

SONETO XVIII

Flaca esperança en todas mis porfías,
vano desseo en desigual tormento,
i inútil fruto del dolor que siento,
lágrimas sin descanso i ansias mías:
un' ora alegre en tantos tristes días

not achieve this. So I finally give in to my madness, for it would no longer be to my credit to change, nor is it just that one should have so low a reputation who has so fully sacrificed his heart.

SONNET XIV: "Where are you going, cruel one, where?; restrain, restrain your hasty steps, while my prolonged weeping begins to tap the deep wellspring of my woeful suffering; listen to a voice filled with innumerable sighs and to the sad song of the misfortune I suffer, for you can't be so fiercely callous as not to be moved by my harsh grief; turn your light upon me, turn your eyes, before I'm left in the dark of a dense mist," I said in my sleep, or lost in an illusion. I came back to my senses and found myself alone among thorns, and instead of light I was surrounded by darkness, and weltering in fiery tears.

SONNET XVIII: Oh hope which is weak in all my persistent efforts, fruitless desire outweighed by torment, and vain outcome of the pain I feel, ceaseless tears and anguishes mine: allow a sad wretch to have one happy hour in so

sufrid que tenga un triste descontento,
i que pueda sufrir tal vez contento
la gloria de fingidas alegrías;
no es justo, no, que siempre quebrantado
me oprima el mal, i me deshaga el pecho
nueva pena d' antiguo desvarío.
Mas ¡ô! que temo tanto el dulce estado
que (como al bien no esté enseñado i hecho)
abraço ufano el grave dolor mío.

SONETO XXI

Como en la cumbre ecelsa de Mimante,
do en eterna prisión arde, i procura
alçar la frente airada, i guerra oscura
mover de nuevo al cielo el gran gigante,
se nota de las nuves, que delante
buelan i encima, en órrida figura
la calidad de tempestad futura,
qu' amenaza con áspero semblante:
assí de mis suspiros i tristeza,
del grave llanto i grande sentimiento
se muestra el mal qu' encierra el duro pecho.
Por esso no os ofenda mi flaqueza,
bella Estrella d' Amor; que mi tormento
no cabe bien en vaso tan estrecho.

many sad days, and let him occasionally bear happily the glory of feigned happiness; it is not at all just that I should always be oppressed and crushed by misfortune and that my heart should be rent by new sufferings caused by an old madness. But, alas, I am so afraid of happiness that, not having been trained and accustomed to good fortune, I proudly embrace my painful suffering.

SONNET XXI: As on the lofty mountain peak of Mimas, where the great giant burns in eternal prison and tries to raise his angry forehead and wage dark war once more against heaven, one sees in the fearful shapes of the clouds which fly before and over it the sort of coming storm which threatens with fierce aspect: so by my sighs and sadness, by my heavy tears and deep suffering, is revealed the pain enclosed within my enduring breast. Therefore, don't let my weakness offend you, beautiful Star of Love, for my torment cannot be contained within so narrow a vessel.

SONETO XXVI

Subo con tan gran peso quebrantado
por esta alta, empinada, aguda sierra,
que aún no llego a la cumbre, cuando ierra
el pie, i trabuco al fondo despeñado.
Del golpe i de la carga maltratado,
me alço a pena, i a mi antigua guerra
buelvo; mas ¿qué me vale? que la tierra
mesma me falta al curso acostumbrado.
Pero aunqu' en el peligro desfallesco,
no desamparo el passo; qu' antes torno
mil vezes a cansarm' en este engaño.
Crece el temor, i en la porfía cresco;
i sin cessar, cual rueda buelve en torno,
assí rebuelvo a despeñarm' al daño.

SONETO XXXVIII

Serena Luz, en quien presente espira
divino amor, qu' enciende i junto enfrena
el noble pecho, qu' en mortal cadena
al alto Olimpo levantars' aspira;
ricos cercos dorados, do se mira
tesoro celestial d' eterna vena;
armonía d' angélica Sirena,
qu' entre las perlas i el coral respira:
¿cuál nueva maravilla, cuál exemplo
de la immortal grandeza nos descubre
aquessa sombra del hermoso velo?

SONNET XXVI: Staggering under so great a weight I climb up this high, steep, sharp mountain that I have yet to reach the summit when my foot slips and I tumble down the cliff to the bottom. Bruised by the blows and the load, I can hardly rise, and I go back to my old struggle; but what good does it do me?, for the ground itself fails me on my accustomed route. But, although I faint at the danger, I do not give up the trail; rather, I tire myself out again and again in this self-deception. As fear grows, I grow in persistence; and unceasingly, as a wheel turns around and around, so I return to plunge down the cliff to my own hurt.

SONNET XXXVIII: Serene Light, in whom breathes the presence of divine love, which inflames and at the same time restrains the noble heart, which in its mortal chains aspires to rise to lofty Olympus; precious ringlets of gold, in which one sees the heavenly treasure of the eternal lode; angelic mermaid's music, which wafts among pearls and coral: what new wonder, what image of immortal grandeur is revealed to us by the shadow of your lovely body?

Que yo en essa belleza que contemplo
(aunqu' a mi flaca vista ofende i cubre),
la immensa busco, i voi siguiendo al cielo.

SONETO XL

Viví gran tiempo en confusión perdido,
i todo de mí mesmo enagenado,
desesperé de bien, qu' en tal estado
perdí la mejor luz de mi sentido.
Mas cuando de mí tuve más olvido,
rompió los duros lazos al cuidado
d' Amor el enemigo más onrado,
i ante mis pies lo derribó vencido.
Aora que procuro mi provecho,
puedo dezir que vivo, pues soi mío,
libre, ageno d' Amor i de sus daños.
Pueda el desdén, Antonio, en vuestro pecho
acabar semejante desvarío,
antes que prevalescan sus engaños.

SONETO LXV

Ya el rigor importuno i grave ielo
desnuda los esmaltes i belleza
de la pintada tierra, i con tristeza
s' ofende en niebla oscura el claro cielo.
Mas, Pacheco, este mesmo órrido suelo
reverdece i pomposo su riqueza

For I, in that beauty which I contemplate (although it dazzles and blinds my weak vision), seek the beauty without limits, and follow along that road to heaven.

SONNET XL: I lived for a long time lost in confusion, and wholly deprived of myself, I despaired of happiness, for in this state I lost the brightest powers of my intellect. But when I forgot myself most completely, the harsh bonds of my preoccupation were broken by Love's most respectable enemy, and he struck him down, conquered, before my feet. Now that I seek my own interests, I can say that, since I belong to myself, I live in freedom, far from Love and his harms. I hope that disdain, Antonio, can bring to an end a similar madness in your heart before his deceptions prevail.

SONNET LXV: Now the vigorous onslaught and stiff ice strips the colors and beauty from the painted earth, and sadly a dark mist obscures the bright sky. And yet, Pacheco, this same frozen soil turns green again and leafily shows forth its riches, and Favonius' warm breath dissolves the marble-white hardness. But the sweet color and beauty of our human life, when it leaves, does

muestra, i del blanco mármol la dureza
desata de Favonio el tibio buelo.
Pero el dulce color i hermosura
de nuestra umana vida, cuando huye,
no torna: ¡ô mortal suerte!, ¡ô breve gloria!
Mas sola la virtud nos assegura,
qu' el tiempo avaro, aunqu' esta flor destruye,
contra ella nunca osó intentar vitoria.

Francisco de Aldana

(1537–1578)

SONETO XIII

De sus hermosos ojos dulcemente
un tierno llanto Filis despedía
que por el rostro amado parecía
claro y precioso aljófar trasparente;
en brazos de Damón, con baja frente,
triste, rendida, muerta, helada y fría,
estas palabras breves le decía,
creciendo a su llorar nueva corriente:
"¡Oh pecho duro, oh alma dura y llena
de mil durezas! ¿Dónde vas huyendo?
¿Dó vas con ala tan ligera y presta?"
Y él, soltando de llanto amarga vena,
della las dulces lágrimas bebiendo,
besóla, y sólo un ¡ay! fué su respuesta.

not return: oh mortal fate, oh brief glory! Yet virtue alone protects us, for grasping time, although it destroys the flower of this life, has never dared try to conquer that.

SONNET XIII: Sweetly from her lovely eyes Phyllis let fall soft tears which on her dear cheeks looked like bright pearly dew transparent; in Damon's arms, with lowered forehead, sad, exhausted, slain, frozen and cold, she said these brief words to him, as she added another flood to her tears: "Oh hard heart, oh soul hard and filled with hardness, where are you running away to? Where are you going on wing so swift, so fast?" And he, giving way to a bitter flood of lamentation, drinking her sweet tears, kissed her, and "Alas!" was his only reply.

SONETO XVII

Mil veces digo, entre los brazos puesto
de Galatea, que es más que el sol hermosa;
luego ella, en dulce vista desdeñosa,
me dice, "Tirsis mío, no digas esto."
Yo lo quiero jurar, y ella de presto
toda encendida de un color de rosa
con un beso me impide y presurosa
busca atapar mi boca con su gesto.
Hágole blanda fuerza por soltarme,
y ella me aprieta más y dice luego:
"No lo jures, mi bien, que yo te creo."
Con esto de tal fuerza a encadenarme
viene que Amor, presente al dulce juego,
hace suplir con obras mi deseo.

SONETO XXX

Otro aquí no se ve que, frente a frente,
animoso escuadrón moverse guerra,
sangriento humor teñir la verde tierra,
y tras honroso fin correr la gente;
éste es el dulce son que acá se siente:
"¡España, Santïago, cierra, cierra!",
y por süave olor, que el aire atierra,
humo de azufre dar con llama ardiente;
el gusto envuelto va tras corrompida

SONNET XVII: I say a thousand times, while held in Galatea's arms, that she is more beautiful than the sun; then she, with a sweetly disdainful look, tells me, "Tyrsis mine, don't say that." I try to swear it, and she, suddenly inflamed with a rosy color, stops me with a kiss and hastily seeks to cover my mouth with her face. I struggle gently against her to free myself, and she holds me more tightly and then says, "Don't swear, my love, for I believe you." Thereupon she so entwines me that Cupid, witnessing our sweet game, causes my desires to be fulfilled.

SONNET XXX: Nothing else is seen here except, face to face, vigorous squadrons attacking one another, bloody liquid staining the green grass, and people pursuing an honorable end; this is the sweet sound which here is heard: "Spain, St. James, attack, attack!," and as a pleasant smell, to confound the air, sulfur smoke exploding with blazing flames; one's sense of taste, con-

agua, y el tacto sólo apalpa y halla
duro trofeo de acero ensangrentado,
   hueso en astilla, en él carne molida,
despedazado arnés, rasgada malla:
¡oh solo de hombres digno y noble estado!

SONETO XXXIV
Reconocimiento de la vanidad del mundo

   En fin, en fin, tras tanto andar muriendo,
tras tanto varïar vida y destino,
tras tanto de uno en otro desatino
pensar todo apretar, nada cogiendo,
   tras tanto acá y allá yendo y viniendo
cual sin aliento inútil peregrino,
¡oh Dios!, tras tanto error del buen camino,
yo mismo de mi mal ministro siendo,
   hallo, en fin, que ser muerto en la memoria
del mundo es lo mejor que en él se asconde,
pues es la paga dél muerte y olvido,
   y en un rincón vivir con la vitoria
de sí, puesto el querer tan sólo adonde
es premio el mismo Dios de lo servido.

fused, seeks corrupt water, and one's touch strokes only the hard trophy of bloody steel, splintered bone, flesh ground upon bone, fragments of armor, torn mail: oh sole noble state worthy of men!

SONNET XXXIV, *Recognition of the World's Vanity:* At last, at last, after so long a time suffering, after so many changes of life and career, after so many attempts, between one madness and another, to seize everything, but catching nothing, after so much coming and going hither and yon like a breathless, useless pilgrim, oh God!, after wandering so often from the right road, I myself being the executor of my own evil, at last I find that to be dead in the world's memory is the best thing the world has to offer, for its wages are death and oblivion, and to live in a corner with one's victory over oneself, putting one's love in that place alone where God himself is the reward for one's service.

SONETO XXXVII
Al Cielo

Clara fuente de luz, nuevo y hermoso,
rico de luminarias, patrio Cielo,
casa de la verdad sin sombra o velo,
de inteligencias ledo, almo reposo:
¡oh cómo allá te estás, cuerpo glorioso,
tan lejos del mortal caduco velo,
casi un Argos divino alzado a vuelo,
de nuestro humano error libre y piadoso!
¡Oh patria amada!, a ti sospira y llora
esta en su cárcel alma peregrina,
llevada errando de uno en otro instante;
esa cierta beldad que me enamora
suerte y sazón me otorgue tan benina
que, do sube el amor, llegue el amante.

Anónimo

SONETO A CRISTO CRUCIFICADO

No me mueve, mi Dios, para quererte
el cielo que me tienes prometido;
ni me mueve el infierno tan temido
para dejar por eso de ofenderte.
Tú me mueves, señor; muéveme el verte

SONNET XXXVII, *To Heaven:* Bright source of light, new and beautiful, filled with luminaries, our native Heaven, the home of truth without shadow or veil, the happy, strengthening repose of intelligences: oh how distant you are, substance of glory, so far from the mortal, dying body, like a divine Argos poised in flight, free from our human error and merciful! Oh beloved native land!, to you this wandering soul in its prison sends sighs and tears, driven on in error from one moment to another; may that true beauty which draws my love grant me fortune and occasion so favorable that, whither love rises, there the lover may arrive.

TO THE CRUCIFIED CHRIST: I am not moved, my God, to love You by the heaven that You have promised me; nor am I moved by fearful hell to cease for that reason to offend You. You are what moves me, Lord; it moves me

clavado en una cruz y escarnecido;
muéveme ver tu cuerpo tan herido;
muévenme tus afrentas y tu muerte.
Muéveme, en fin, tu amor, y en tal manera
que aunque no hubiera cielo, yo te amara,
y aunque no hubiera infierno, te temiera.
No tienes que me dar porque te quiera,
pues aunque cuanto espero no esperara,
lo mismo que te quiero te quisiera.

San Juan de la Cruz

(1542–1591)

CANCIÓN I: CÁNTICO ESPIRITUAL
Canciones
Entre el alma y el esposo

Esposa

1. ¿Adónde te escondiste,
amado, y me dejaste con gemido?
Como el ciervo huiste,
habiéndome herido;
salí tras ti, clamando, y eras ido.

2. Pastores, los que fuerdes
allá, por las majadas, al otero,
si por ventura vierdes
aquel que yo más quiero,

to see You nailed to a cross and made fun of; it moves me to see Your body so wounded; I am moved by the insults and death that You undergo. I am moved, in sum, by love for You, and so greatly that, even if there were no heaven, I would love You, and even if there were no hell, I would fear You. You do not have to give me anything to make me love You, for even if I did not hope for what I do hope for, I would love You the same as I do love You.

SONG I: SPIRITUAL CANTICLE, *Songs of the Soul and the Bridegroom: Bride:* 1. Where have you hidden yourself, my love, and left me moaning? Like

decidle que adolezco, peno y muero.

3. Buscando mis amores,
iré por esos montes y riberas;
ni cogeré las flores,
ni temeré las fieras,
y pasaré los fuertes y fronteras.

(*Pregunta a las Criaturas*)

4. ¡Oh bosques y espesuras,
plantadas por la mano del amado!
¡Oh prado de verduras,
de flores esmaltado,
decid si por vosotros ha pasado!

Respuesta de las Criaturas

5. Mil gracias derramando,
pasó por estos sotos con presura,
y yéndolos mirando,
con sola su figura
vestidos los dejó de hermosura.

Esposa

6. ¡Ay, quién podrá sanarme!
Acaba de entregarte ya de vero;
no quieras enviarme
de hoy más ya mensajero,
que no saben decirme lo que quiero.

7. Y todos cuantos vagan,
de ti me van mil gracias refiriendo.
Y todos más me llagan,

the stag you have fled, having wounded me; I came out, crying, after you, and you had gone away. 2. Shepherds, you who are going there to the hill for your flocks, if by any chance you see him whom I love most dearly, tell him that I am suffering, mourning, dying. 3. In search of my love I will cross those mountains and river banks; I will neither pick the flowers nor fear the beasts, and I will pass forts and frontiers. *(She asks the creatures):* 4. Oh woods and thickets, planted by the hand of my beloved, oh green meadow bedecked with flowers, tell me whether he has passed near you! *The creatures' reply:* 5. Shedding countless graces, he passed hastily through these thickets, and as he passed, looking at them, by the mere sight of him left them clothed in beauty. *Bride:* 6. Alas, who can heal me! Yield yourself

y déjame muriendo
un no sé qué que quedan balbuciendo.

8. Mas ¿cómo perseveras,
oh vida, no viviendo donde vives,
y haciendo, porque mueras,
las flechas que recibes,
de lo que del amado en ti concibes?

9. ¿Por qué, pues has llagado
aqueste corazón, no le sanaste?
Y pues me le has robado,
¿por qué así le dejaste,
y no tomas el robo que robaste?

10. Apaga mis enojos,
pues que ninguno basta a deshacellos,
y véante mis ojos,
pues eres lumbre dellos,
y sólo para ti quiero tenellos.

11. ¡Oh cristalina fuente,
si en esos tus semblantes plateados,
formases de repente
los ojos deseados,
que tengo en mis entrañas dibujados!

12. ¡Apártalos, amado,
que voy de vuelo!

Esposo

Vuélvete, paloma,

to me fully and truly now; don't send me any more messengers after today, for they cannot tell me what I want to know. 7. And all the wanderers keep telling me of your countless graces. And they all wound me more deeply, and I am left dying by something mysterious which they keep murmuring. 8. But how can you continue, my life, when you are living far away from your source of life and making for yourself suicidal arrows out of your own inner conceptions of the beloved? 9. Why, since you have wounded my heart, have you not healed it? And since you have stolen it from me, why have you abandoned it thus and not taken away what you have stolen? 10. Cool my madness, for no one can destroy it, and let my eyes see you, for you

que el ciervo vulnerado
por el otero asoma,
al aire de tu vuelo, y fresco toma.

Esposa

13. ¡Mi amado, las montañas,
los valles solitarios nemorosos,
las ínsulas extrañas,
los ríos sonorosos,
el silbo de los aires amorosos;

14. la noche sosegada,
en par de los levantes de la aurora,
la música callada,
la soledad sonora,
la cena que recrea y enamora;

15. nuestro lecho florido,
de cuevas de leones enlazado,
en púrpura tendido,
de paz edificado,
de mil escudos de oro coronado!

16. A zaga de tu huella,
las jóvenes discurren al camino;
al toque de centella,
al adobado vino,
emisiones de bálsamo divino.

17. En la interior bodega

are their light, and for you alone I wish to have them. 11. Oh crystal spring, if only in your silvery face you would suddenly let take shape the eyes I long for, which I have engraved in my heart! 12. Take them away, beloved, for I am soaring! *Bridegroom:* Come back, dove, for the wounded stag shows himself on the hill, in the breeze of your flight, and cools himself. *Bride:* 13. My beloved, the mountains, the solitary wooded valleys, the distant isles, the sounding rivers, the whistling of the loving breezes; 14. the quiet night, near the break of dawn, the silent music, the sounding solitude, the supper of recreation and love; 15. our bed of flowers, woven of lion caves, stretched out upon purple, built of peace, surmounted by countless golden shields. 16. Following your footsteps the young maidens run wildly out to the road; at the touch of the spark and the taste of the spiced wine, there are waves of divine balm. 17. In my beloved's inner wine cellar I

de mi amado bebí, y cuando salía,
por toda aquesta vega,
ya cosa no sabía,
y el ganado perdí que antes seguía.

18. Allí me dió su pecho,
allí me enseñó ciencia muy sabrosa,
y yo le di de hecho
a mí, sin dejar cosa;
allí le prometí de ser su esposa.

19. Mi alma se ha empleado,
y todo mi caudal, en su servicio;
ya no guardo ganado,
ni ya tengo otro oficio,
que ya sólo en amar es mi ejercicio.

20. Pues ya si en el ejido
de hoy más no fuere vista ni hallada,
diréis que me he perdido;
que andando enamorada,
me hice perdidiza, y fuí ganada.

21. De flores y esmeraldas,
en las frescas mañanas escogidas,
haremos las guirnaldas,
en tu amor florecidas,
y en un cabello mío entretejidas:

22. en sólo aquel cabello
que en mi cuello volar consideraste;
mirástele en mi cuello,
y en él preso quedaste,
y en uno de mis ojos te llagaste.

drank, and when I came out, all the way down the meadow I was no longer aware of anything, and I lost the sheep that I had been following before. 18. There he gave me his breast, there he taught me very pleasant knowledge, and I gave him myself indeed, holding nothing back; there I promised him to be his wife. 19. My soul and all my possessions have been used in his service; I no longer herd sheep or have any other job, for my only occupation now is love. 20. So now, if I'm not seen or found again in the pasture after today, you will say that I've let myself be lost; that being in love, I wandered and strayed, and I was won. 21. Of blossoms and

23. Cuando tú me mirabas,
tu gracia en mí tus ojos imprimían;
por eso me adamabas,
y en eso merecían
los míos adorar lo que en ti vían.

24. No quieras despreciarme,
que si color moreno en mí hallaste,
ya bien puedes mirarme,
después que me miraste,
que gracia y hermosura en mí dejaste.

25. Cogednos las raposas,
que está ya florecida nuestra viña,
en tanto que de rosas
hacemos una piña,
y no parezca nadie en la montiña.

26. Deténte, cierzo muerto;
ven, austro, que recuerdas los amores,
aspira por mi huerto,
y corran sus olores,
y pacerá el amado entre las flores.

Esposo

27. Entrado se ha la esposa
en el ameno huerto deseado,
y a su sabor reposa,
el cuello reclinado

emeralds, gathered on cool mornings, we shall make garlands, flowery with your love and woven together with one of my hairs: 22. with only that hair which you watched being wafted on my neck; you looked at it on my neck, and you became imprisoned in it, and you were wounded by one of my eyes. 23. While you were looking at me, your eyes imprinted upon me your grace; that is why you loved me, and for that reason my eyes were worthy of adoring what they saw in you. 24. Don't despise me, for though you found me to be dark in color, you may well look at me now, after you have looked upon me, for you thereby left grace and beauty in me. 25. Catch the foxes for us, for our vineyard is in bloom, while we make a cluster of roses, and let no onc appcar upon the mountain. 26. Restrain yourself, deadly north wind; come, west wind, with memories of love, and breathe through my garden, and let its fragrance flow, and my beloved will graze among the flowers. *Bridegroom:* 27. The bride has entered into the pleasant garden we've desired, and she rests pleasantly, reclining her neck upon the

sobre los dulces brazos del amado.

28. Debajo del manzano,
allí conmigo fuiste desposada,
allí te di la mano,
y fuiste reparada
donde tu madre fuera violada.

29. A las aves ligeras,
leones, ciervos, gamos saltadores,
montes, valles, riberas,
aguas, aires, ardores
y miedos de las noches veladores,

30. por las amenas liras
y canto de serenas os conjuro
que cesen vuestras iras
y no toquéis al muro,
porque la esposa duerma más seguro.

Esposa

31. Oh ninfas de Judea,
en tanto que en las flores y rosales
el ámbar perfumea,
morá en los arrabales,
y no queráis tocar nuestros umbrales.

32. Escóndete, carillo,
y mira con tu haz a las montañas,
y no quieras decillo;
mas mira las compañas
de la que va por ínsulas extrañas.

beloved's sweet arms. 28. Under the apple tree, there you were first betrothed to me, there I gave you my hand, and you were redeemed where your mother was raped. 29. Swift birds, lions, deer, leaping harts, mountains, valleys, river banks, waters, airs, wakeful warmths and fears of the night. 30. by the pleasant harp and songs of the mermaids I beseech you to lay aside your wraths and not to touch the wall, so that the bride may more soundly sleep. *Bride:* 31. Oh nymphs of Judea, so long as amber perfumes the flowers and rose bushes, stay in the dwellings on the edge of town, and do not try to reach our threshold. 32. Hide yourself, my darling, and look with your face upon the mountains, and keep our secret; but look upon the companions of her who travels through the distant isles. *Bridegroom:* 33.

Esposo

33. La blanca palomica
al arca con el ramo se ha tornado,
y ya la tortolica
al socio deseado
en las riberas verdes ha hallado.

34. En soledad vivía,
y en soledad ha puesto ya su nido,
y en soledad la guía
a solas su querido,
también en soledad de amor herido.

Esposa

35. Gocémonos, amado,
y vámonos a ver en tu hermosura
al monte o al collado
do mana el agua pura;
entremos más adentro en la espesura.

36. Y luego a las subidas
cavernas de la piedra nos iremos,
que están bien escondidas,
y allí nos entraremos,
y el mosto de granadas gustaremos.

37. Allí me mostrarías
aquello que mi alma pretendía,
y luego me darías
allí tú, vida mía,
aquello que me diste el otro día:

38. el aspirar del aire,

The little white dove has come back to the ark with the branch, and now the little turtledove has found her longed-for mate on the green river banks. 34. In solitude she lived, and in solitude she has laid her nest, and in solitude she is guided all alone by her lover, who was also wounded in solitude by love. *Bride:* 35. Let us enjoy one another, beloved, and let us see ourselves in your beauty, going to the mountain or the hill where the pure water gushes up; let us go deeper into the thicket. 36. And then we will go away to the high rock caverns, which are well hidden, and there we shall enter and taste the juice of pomegranates. 37. There you would show me that thing which my soul was seeking, and then you would give me there, my love, that

el canto de la dulce filomena,
el soto y su donaire,
en la noche serena
con llama que consume y no da pena;

39. que nadie lo miraba,
Aminadab tampoco parecía,
y el cerco sosegaba,
y la caballería
a vista de las aguas descendía.

CANCIÓN II: LA NOCHE OSCURA
Canciones
De el alma que se goza de haber llegado al alto estado de la perfección, que es la unión con Dios, por el camino de la negación espiritual.

1. En una noche oscura,
con ansias en amores inflamada,
¡oh dichosa ventura!,
salí sin ser notada,
estando ya mi casa sosegada:

2. a escuras y segura,
por la secreta escala disfrazada,
¡oh dichosa ventura!,
a escuras y en celada,
estando ya mi casa sosegada;

thing which you gave me the other day: 38. the breathing of the air, the song of the sweet nightingale, the woods and its charm, in the quiet night of flame which destroys and causes no regrets; 39. for no one saw it, nor did Aminadab appear, and the siege was relaxed, and at the sight of the water the horsemen descended.

SONG II, *The Dark Night: Songs of the soul rejoicing at having reached the highest state of perfection, which is union with God, by means of spiritual self-denial.* 1. On a dark night, inflamed with the passions of love, oh favoring fortune!, I went out unnoticed, after my house had been set to rest: 2. in the dark and safely sure, by the secret stair disguised, oh favoring fortune!, in the dark and concealed, after my house had been set to rest; 3. in the fortunate night, in secret, for no one saw me, nor did I see anything, with no other light or guide than that which was burning in my heart. 4. This light guided me more surely than that of noonday to where he was wait-

3. en la noche dichosa,
en secreto, que nadie me veía,
ni yo miraba cosa,
sin otra luz y guía
sino la que en el corazón ardía.

4. Aquésta me guïaba
más cierto que la luz del mediodía,
a donde me esperaba
quien yo bien me sabía,
en parte donde nadie parecía.

5. ¡Oh noche que guiaste!,
¡oh noche amable más que el alborada!,
¡oh noche que juntaste
amado con amada,
amada en el amado transformada!

6. En mi pecho florido,
que entero para él solo se guardaba,
allí quedó dormido,
y yo le regalaba;
y el ventalle de cedros aire daba.

7. El aire de la almena,
cuando yo sus cabellos esparcía,
con su mano serena
en mi cuello hería,
y todos mis sentidos suspendía.

8. Quedéme y olvidéme,
el rostro recliné sobre el amado,
cesó todo, y dejéme,
dejando mi cuidado
entre las azucenas olvidado.

ing for me, I know well who, in a place where no one was to be seen. 5. Oh night which guided me, oh night more friendly than the dawn, oh night that joined lover to beloved, the beloved being transformed into the lover! 6. On my flowery breast, kept wholly for himself alone, there he went to sleep, and I caressed him, and the fanning of the cedars made a breeze. 7. The breeze from the battlements, while I spread out his hair, with its gentle hand struck my neck and suspended all my senses. 8. I stood still and forgot myself, I leaned my face over the lover, everything stopped and I abandoned myself, leaving my cares forgotten among the lilies.

CANCIÓN III: LLAMA DE AMOR VIVA

Canciones
Del alma en la íntima comunicación
de unión de amor de Dios.

1. ¡Oh llama de amor viva
que tiernamente hieres
de mi alma en el más profundo centro!,
pues ya no eres esquiva,
acaba ya si quieres,
rompe la tela de este dulce encuentro.

2. ¡Oh cauterio suave!,
¡oh regalada llaga!,
¡oh mano blanda!, ¡oh toque delicado
que a vida eterna sabe,
y toda deuda paga!
Matando, muerte en vida la has trocado.

3. ¡Oh lámparas de fuego,
en cuyos resplandores
las profundas cavernas del sentido,
que estaba oscuro y ciego,
con extraños primores
calor y luz dan junto a su querido!

4. ¡Cuán manso y amoroso
recuerdas en mi seno,
donde secretamente solo moras;
y en tu aspirar sabroso,
de bien y gloria lleno,
cuán delicadamente me enamoras!

SONG III, *Living flame of Love: Songs of the soul in the intimate communion of union with God's love.* 1. Oh living flame of love which tenderly wounds the deepest center of my soul, since you no longer avoid me, have done now, if you will, and break the fabric of this sweet encounter. 2. Oh gentle cautery, oh caressing blow of the soft hand, oh delicate touch which tastes of eternal love and pays all debts! By killing, you have turned death into life. 3. Oh lamps of fire in whose gleam the deep caverns of sense, formerly dark and blind, give forth light and warmth, together with unknown delights, to their beloved! 4. How peacefully and lovingly you awaken in my breast, where you dwell alone in secret; and with your delicious breath, redolent of heavenly glory, how delicately you win my love!

COPLA I
Coplas hechas sobre un extasi de harta contemplación

Entréme donde no supe,
y quedéme no sabiendo,
toda sciencia trascendiendo.

Yo no supe dónde entraba,
pero cuando allí me vi,
sin saber dónde me estaba,
grandes cosas entendí.
No diré lo que sentí,
que me quedé no sabiendo,
toda sciencia trascendiendo.

De paz y de piedad
era la sciencia perfecta,
en profunda soledad,
entendida vía recta;
era cosa tan secreta
que me quedé balbuciendo,
toda sciencia trascendiendo.

Estaba tan embebido,
tan absorto y ajenado,
que se quedó mi sentido
de todo sentir privado,
y el espíritu, dotado
de un entender no entendiendo,
toda sciencia trascendiendo.

VERSE I, *Verses upon a highly contemplative ecstasy:* I entered where I never knew, and I was left without knowing, transcending all knowledge. I never knew where I was entering, but when I found myself there, without knowing where I was, I understood important matters. I don't say what I felt, for I was left without knowing, transcending all knowledge. It was the perfect knowledge of peace and piety, a straight road well understood in deep solitude; it was something so secret that I was left babbling, transcending all knowledge. I was so drawn into it, so absorbed and taken out of myself, that my feeling was left devoid of all feeling, and my mind was endued with an understanding by not understanding, transcending all knowledge.

El que allí llega de vero,
de sí mismo desfallesce;
cuanto sabía primero
mucho bajo le paresce;
y su sciencia tanto cresce
que se queda no sabiendo,
toda sciencia trascendiendo.

Cuanto más alto se sube,
tanto menos se entendía
qué es la tenebrosa nube
que a la noche esclarecía;
por eso quien la sabía
queda siempre no sabiendo,
toda sciencia trascendiendo.

Este saber no sabiendo
es de tan alto poder
que los sabios arguyendo
jamás le pueden vencer;
que no llega su saber
a no entender entendiendo,
toda sciencia trascendiendo.

Y es de tan alta excelencia
aqueste sumo saber
que no hay facultad ni sciencia
que le puedan emprender;
quien se supiere vencer
con un no saber sabiendo,
irá siempre trascendiendo.

Y si lo queréis oír,

He who really reaches that point faints away from himself; he scorns all that he formerly knew; and his knowledge increases so much that he is left without knowing, transcending all knowledge. The higher one rises, the less one understands what the shadowy cloud is which brightens the night; therefore he who knows it remains ever unknowing, transcending all knowledge. This unknowing knowledge is of such great power that the scholars can never overcome it by arguing; for their knowledge does not extend to this non-understanding by understanding, transcending all knowledge. And this highest way of knowing is so completely superior that there is no uni-

consiste esta suma sciencia
en un subido sentir
de la divinal esencia;
es obra de su clemencia
hacer quedar no entendiendo,
toda sciencia trascendiendo.

COPLA II: QUE MUERO PORQUE NO MUERO

Coplas del alma que
pena por ver a Dios

Vivo sin vivir en mí,
y de tal manera espero
que muero porque no muero.

En mí yo no vivo ya,
y sin Dios vivir no puedo;
pues sin él y sin mí quedo,
este vivir ¿qué será?
Mil muertes se me hará,
pues mi misma vida espero,
muriendo porque no muero.

Esta vida que yo vivo
es privación de vivir;
y así, es contino morir
hasta que viva contigo;
oye, mi Dios, lo que digo:
que esta vida no la quiero,
que muero porque no muero.

versity or science that can attempt it; he who can overcome himself by a knowing non-knowing will always be transcending. And if you want to listen, this highest knowledge consists of a heightened perception of the Divine Essence; it is a result of His mercy to leave one not understanding, transcending all knowledge.

VERSE II, FOR I'M DYING BECAUSE I DO NOT DIE, *Verses of the soul painfully yearning to see God:* I live without living in myself, and my hopes are so high that I'm dying because I do not die. I no longer live in myself, and without God I cannot live; since I'm left without Him and without myself, what can my present life be? It will become for me a thousand deaths, for I'm longing for my own life, dying because I do not die. This life that I live is the absence of living; and so it is to die constantly until I live with You; listen, God, to what I'm saying: I don't want this life, for I'm dying because I do

Estando absente de ti,
¿qué vida puedo tener
sino muerte padescer,
la mayor que nunca vi?
Lástima tengo de mí,
pues de suerte persevero
que muero porque no muero.

El pez que del agua sale
aun de alivio no caresce,
que en la muerte que padesce
al fin la muerte le vale.
¿Qué muerte habrá que se iguale
a mi vivir lastimero,
pues si más vivo, más muero?

Cuando me pienso aliviar
de verte en el Sacramento,
háceme más sentimiento
el no te poder gozar;
todo es para más penar,
por no verte como quiero,
y muero porque no muero.

Y si me gozo, Señor,
con esperanza de verte,
en ver que puedo perderte
se me dobla mi dolor;
viviendo en tanto pavor,
y esperando como espero,
muérome porque no muero.

not die. Absent from You, what kind of life can I lead but to suffer death, the cruelest death I've ever known? I'm sorry for myself, for I so persevere that I'm dying because I do not die. Even the fish taken out of water does not lack relief, for in the death which he suffers, death finally comes to his rescue. What death can there be to equal my pitiful life, for the more I live, the more I die? When I expect relief by contemplating You in the Sacrament, I am made to suffer more by not being able to possess You; it all contributes to further pain because I cannot contemplate You as I wish, and I'm dying because I do not die. And if I take joy, Lord, in the hope of contemplating You, when I realize that I can lose you, my grief is doubled; living in such fear, and hoping as I do, I'm dying because I do not die. Take me out of this death, God, and give me life; don't keep me tied down by such strong

Sácame de aquesta muerte,
mi Dios, y dame la vida;
no me tengas impedida
en este lazo tan fuerte;
mira que peno por verte,
y mi mal es tan entero
que muero porque no muero.

Lloraré mi muerte ya,
y lamentaré mi vida
en tanto que detenida
por mis pecados está.
¡Oh mi Dios! ¿Cuándo será
cuando yo diga de vero:
vivo ya porque no muero?

COPLA III
Otras coplas a lo Divino

Tras de un amoroso lance,
y no de esperanza falto,
volé tan alto, tan alto,
que le di a la caza alcance.

Para que yo alcance diese
a aqueste lance divino,
tanto volar me convino
que de vista me perdiese;
y con todo, en este trance,
en el vuelo quedé falto;
mas el amor fué tan alto
que le di a la caza alcance.

bonds; consider that I'm painfully yearning to see You, and my suffering is so complete that I'm dying because I do not die. I shall grieve for my death, and I shall regret my life so long as it is prolonged because of my sins. Oh my God, when will it be that I can really say: I'm living now because I do not die?

VERSE III, *More verses rewritten in a religious sense:* After an amorous encounter, and one not lacking in hope, I flew so very, very high that I managed to attain the prey. In order for me to attain this divine encounter, I had to fly so high that I was lost from sight; and nevertheless, in this encounter, my power of flight did not suffice; but love rose so high that I managed to

Cuando más alto subía,
deslumbróseme la vista,
y la más fuerte conquista
en escuro se hacía;
mas por ser de amor el lance,
di un ciego y oscuro salto,
y fuí tan alto, tan alto,
que le di a la caza alcance.

Cuanto más alto llegaba
de este lance tan subido,
tanto más bajo y rendido
y abatido me hallaba.
Dije: ¡No habrá quien alcance!
Y abatíme tanto, tanto,
que fuí tan alto, tan alto,
que le di a la caza alcance.

Por una extraña manera
mil vuelos pasé de un vuelo,
porque esperanza de cielo
tanto alcanza cuanto espera;
esperé sólo este lance,
y en esperar no fuí falto,
pues fuí tan alto, tan alto,
que le di a la caza alcance.

attain the prey. When I was rising highest, my sight was dazzled, and the most difficult conquest took place in the dark; but since it was an encounter of love, I took a dark, blind leap, and I rose so very, very high that I managed to attain the prey. The higher I reached in this encounter so lofty, the lower and more tired and defeated I felt. I said: "No one can reach it!" And I went down so very, very low that I rose so very, very high that I managed to attain the prey. In some strange way I surpassed countless flights in a single flight, for hope of heaven attains all that it hopes for; I hoped only for this encounter, and in hoping I was not deficient, for I rose so very, very high that I managed to attain the prey.

CANCIÓN IV: EL PASTORCICO
Otras canciones a lo Divino,
de Cristo y el alma

Un pastorcico solo está penado,
ajeno de placer y de contento,
y en su pastora puesto el pensamiento,
y el pecho del amor muy lastimado.

No llora por haberle amor llagado,
que no le pena verse así afligido,
aunque en el corazón está herido;
mas llora por pensar que está olvidado,

que sólo de pensar que está olvidado
de su bella pastora, con gran pena
se deja maltratar en tierra ajena,
el pecho del amor muy lastimado.

Y dice el pastorico: ¡Ay desdichado
de aquel que de mi amor ha hecho ausencia,
y no quiere gozar la mi presencia,
y el pecho por su amor muy lastimado!

Y a cabo de un gran rato se ha encumbrado
sobre un árbol, do abrió sus brazos bellos,
y muerto se ha quedado, asido de ellos,
el pecho del amor muy lastimado.

SONG IV, THE LITTLE SHEPHERD, *More songs rewritten in a religious sense, of Christ and the soul:* A little shepherd is suffering alone, bereft of joy and happiness, thinking of his shepherdess, with his heart deeply wounded by love. He doesn't weep because love has wounded him, for it doesn't grieve him to be so afflicted, although he is wounded in the heart; but he weeps when he considers that he has been forgotten. Just because he considers that he has been forgotten by his lovely shepherdess, with great suffering he lets himself be abused in an alien land, with his heart deeply wounded by love. And the little shepherd says: "Alas for him who has separated himself from my love, and does not want to enjoy my presence, with my heart deeply wounded by love for him!" And after a long while, he climbed up a tree where he opened wide his lovely arms, and there he died, fastened by his arms, with his heart deeply wounded by love.

CANTAR: AUNQUE ES DE NOCHE

Cantar de la alma que se huelga
de conoscer a Dios por fe

Que bien sé yo la fonte que mana y corre,
aunque es de noche.

Aquella eterna fonte está ascondida,
que bien sé yo dó tiene su manida,
aunque es de noche.

Su origen no lo sé, pues no le tiene,
mas sé que todo origen della viene,
aunque es de noche.

Sé que no puede ser cosa tan bella,
y que cielos y tierra beben de ella,
aunque es de noche.

Bien sé que suelo en ella no se halla,
y que ninguno puede vadealla,
aunque es de noche.

Su claridad nunca es escurecida,
y sé que toda luz de ella es venida,
aunque es de noche.

Sé ser tan caudalosos sus corrientes
que infiernos, cielos riegan, y las gentes,
aunque es de noche.

SONG, ALTHOUGH IT IS NIGHT, *Song of the soul which rejoices in knowing God by faith:* For I well know the fountain that wells up and flows, although it is night. That eternal fountain is hidden, for I well know where it has its source, although it is night. I don't know its origin, for it doesn't have one, but I know that every origin comes from it, although it is night. I know that nothing can be so beautiful, and that heaven and earth drink from it, although it is night. I well know that it has no bottom, and that no one can wade across it, although it is night. Its brightness is never obscured, and I know that all light has come from it, although it is night. I know that its currents are so abundant that they supply hell, heaven and the nations, although

El corriente que nace de esta fuente,
bien sé que es tan capaz y omnipotente,
aunque es de noche.

El corriente que de estas dos procede
sé que ninguna de ellas le precede,
aunque es de noche.

Aquesta eterna fonte está escondida
en este vivo pan por darnos vida,
aunque es de noche.

Aquí se está llamando a las criaturas,
y de esta agua se hartan, aunque a escuras,
porque es de noche.

Aquesta viva fuente, que deseo,
en este pan de vida yo la veo,
aunque de noche.

It is night. The current which has its source in this fountain, I well know that it is powerful, omnipotent, although it is night. The current which proceeds from the two of them, I know is preceded by neither of them, although it is night. This eternal fountain is hidden in this living bread to give us life, although it is night. Here the creatures are summoned, and they fill themselves with this water, even in the dark, because it is night. This living fountain, which I desire, I see in this bread of life, although it is night.

Baroque Poets

Lupercio L. de Argensola

(1559–1613)

Bartolomé L. de Argensola

(1562–1631)

SONETO I
A una muger que se
afeitaba y estaba hermosa

Yo os quiero confesar, don Juan, primero:
que aquel blanco y color de doña Elvira
no tiene de ella más, si bien se mira,
que el haberle costado su dinero.
Pero tras eso confesaros quiero
que es tanta la beldad de su mentira
que en vano a competir con ella aspira
belleza ygual de rostro verdadero.
Mas, ¿qué mucho que yo perdido ande
por un engaño tal, pues que sabemos
que nos engaña así Naturaleza?
Porque ese cielo azul que todos vemos
ni es cielo ni es azul: ¡Lástima grande
que no sea verdad tanta belleza!

SONNET I, ***To a woman who used cosmetics and looked beautiful:*** **I want to confess to you, Sir John, first of all: that those whites and reds of Mistress Elvira's complexion are only hers, if one considers it closely, in that they have cost her her money. But in the second place I want to confess to you that her falsified beauty is so great that in vain can the similar beauty of a real face aspire to compete with it. Yet what's so surprising if I should be deceived by such a trick, for we know that Nature herself tricks us in this way? Because that blue sky which we all see is neither sky nor blue: what a pity that so much beauty should be so false!**

SONETO II
Al sueño

Imagen espantosa de la muerte,
sueño cruel, no turbes más mi pecho,
mostrándome cortado el nudo estrecho,
consuelo solo de mi adversa suerte.
Busca de algún tyrano el muro fuerte,
de jaspe las paredes, de oro el techo;
o el rico avaro en el angosto lecho
haz que temblando con sudor despierte.
El uno vea el popular tumulto
romper con furia las herradas puertas,
o al sobornado siervo el hierro oculto;
el otro, sus riquezas descubiertas
con llave falsa o con violento insulto:
i déxale al Amor sus glorias ciertas.
[*Lupercio*]

SONETO III

No fueron tus divinos ojos, Ana,
los que al yugo amoroso me han rendido;
ni los rosados labios, dulce nido
del ciego niño, donde néctar mana;
ni las mexillas de color de grana;
ni el cabello, que al oro es preferido;

SONNET II, *To sleep:* Fearful image of death, cruel sleep, disturb my heart no more by making me think that the tight knot has been cut, the sole consolation for my adverse fortune. Seek out some tyrant's mighty fortress, its walls of jasper, its ceiling of gold; or the rich miser in his narrow bed, make him wake up in a trembling sweat. Let the former see the angry mob storm in a fury his iron gates, or the bribed slave's hidden knife; let the latter see his wealth made public by a counterfeit key or by violent assault: and leave to Love his glories secure. [*Lupercio*]

SONNET III: Your divine eyes, Anne, are not what submitted me to love's yoke; nor your rosy lips, the blind boy's [Cupid's] sweet nest, where nectar springs; nor your red cheeks nor your hair, brighter than gold; nor your

ni las manos, que a tantos han venzido;
ni la voz, que está en duda si es humana.
Tu alma, que en tus obras se trasluze,
es la que sugetar pudo la mía,
porque fuesse inmortal su cautiverio.
Assí todo lo dicho se reduze
a solo su poder, porque tenía
por ella cada cual su ministerio.

[*Lupercio*]

SONETO IV

Tras importunas lluvias amaneze,
coronando los montes, el sol claro;
salta del lecho el labrador avaro,
que las horas ociosas aborreze.
La torva frente al duro yugo ofreze
el animal que a Europa fué tan caro;
sale, de su familia firme amparo,
i los surcos solícito enrriqueze.
Vuelve de noche a su muger honesta,
que lumbre, mesa y lecho le apercibe,
i el enjambre de hijuelos le rodea.
Fáciles cosas cena con gran fiesta,
el sueño sin enbidia le recibe:
¡o Corte, o confusión!, ¿quién te dessea?

[*Lupercio*]

hands, which have conquered so many; nor your voice, which seems more than human. It was your soul, visible in your deeds, which was able to subject mine, so that its captivity would last beyond death. Thus everything that has been mentioned can be reduced simply to the power of your soul, for by its commission each member performed its ministry.

SONNET IV: After persistent rains the bright sun dawns, crowning the mountains; the thrifty farmer leaps from his bed, hating to see time wasted. To the cruel yoke the bull offers his fierce horns, the animal which Europa so loved; he goes out, his family's strong defender, and eagerly sows the furrows. At night he returns to his good woman, who prepares for him warmth, table and bed, and their swarm of children surround him. He dines cheaply with great happiness, an envyless slumber overcomes him: oh city's confusion, who wants you?

SONETO V

"Dime, Padre común, pues eres justo,
¿por qué ha de permitir tu providencia,
que, arrastrando prisiones la innocencia,
suba la fraude a tribunal augusto?
¿Quién da fuerzas al brazo, que robusto
haze a tus leyes firme resistencia,
i que el zelo, que más las reverencia,
gima a los pies del venzedor injusto?
Vemos que vibran vitoriosas palmas
manos inicas, la virtud gimiendo
del triunfo en el injusto regocijo."
Esto dezía yo, cuando, riendo,
celestial nimfa aparezió, i me dijo:
"¡Ciego!, ¿es la tierra el centro de las almas?"

[*Bartolomé*]

SONETO VI

A un caballero y una dama que se criaban juntos desde niños y siendo mayores de edad perseveraron en la misma conversación

Firmio, en tu edad ningún peligro hay leve;
porque nos hablas ya con voz escura,
i, aunque dudoso, el bozo a tu blancura
sobre esse labio superior se atreve.

SONNET V: "Tell me, Father of all, since you are righteous, why does your providence permit innocence to wear heavy chains and fraud to occupy the court of law? Who strengthens the arm that powerfully offers your laws firm resistance, and drives piety, which most reveres them, to groan at the feet of the unrighteous conqueror? We see iniquitous hands waving the palms of victory, virtue groaning under the triumphal celebration of the unrighteous." This is what I was saying when, smiling, a heavenly nymph appeared and said to me: "Fool, is earth the element of souls?"

SONNET VI: *To a gentleman and a lady who had been raised together since childhood and, being now older, persisted in the same casual relationship:* Firmio, at your age no danger is a slight one, for you speak to us now in a husky voice and, although almost invisible, a fuzz breaks the smoothness of your upper lip. And in your case, Drusila, your breast is suddenly revealing the subtle outline of two curves, and on the white summit of each one a living ruby marks a tiny center. Let your friendship be restrained by stricter

I en ti, o Drusila, de sutil relieve
el pecho sus dos bultos apresura,
i en cada cual sobre la cumbre pura
vivo forma un rubí su centro breve.
Sienta vuestra amistad leyes mayores;
que siempre Amor para el primer veneno
busca la inadvertencia más sencilla.
Si astuto el áspid se escondió en lo ameno
de un campo fértil, ¿quién se maravilla
de que pierdan el crédito sus flores?
[*Bartolomé*]

Luis de Góngora

(1561–1627)

SONETO LIII

(moral)

Infiere, de los achaques de la vejez,
cercano el fin, a que católico se alienta

En este occidental, en este, oh Licio,
climatérico lustro de tu vida,
todo mal afirmado pie es caída,
toda fácil caída es precipicio.
¿Caduca el paso? Ilústrese el jüicio.
Desatándose va la tierra unida;
¿qué prudencia del polvo prevenida
la rüina aguardó del edificio?

rules, for Love's first poison needs only the simplest carelessness. If the sly snake has hidden himself in the pleasantest part of a fertile field, who can be surprised that flowers have lost their good reputation?

SONNET LIII (MORAL), *He infers, from the ailments of old age, that death is near, and as a Catholic takes courage:* In this sunset, this climacteric period, oh Licio, of your life, every shaky footstep is a fall, every easy fall is precipitous. Is your stride failing? Illuminate your judgment. The soil [i.e., your body], once united, is beginning to fall to pieces; what prudent person, warned by the dust, ever waited for the collapse of the building? The poi-

La piel, no sólo, sierpe venenosa,
mas con la piel los años se desnuda,
y el hombre, no. ¡Ciego discurso humano!
¡Oh aquel dichoso, que la ponderosa
porción depuesta en una piedra muda,
la leve da al zafiro soberano!
[1623]

SONETO LIV

(moral)

De la brevedad engañosa de la vida

Menos solicitó veloz saeta
destinada señal, que mordió aguda;
agonal carro por la arena muda
no coronó con más silencio meta,
que presurosa corre, que secreta,
a su fin nuestra edad. A quien lo duda,
fiera que sea de razón desnuda,
cada Sol repetido es un cometa.
¿Confiésalo Cartago, y tú lo ignoras?
Peligro corres, Licio, si porfías
en seguir sombras y abrazar engaños.
Mal te perdonarán a ti las horas:
las horas que limando están los días,
los días que royendo están los años.
[1623]

sonous snake sheds, not only his skin, but with his skin the years, and man does not. Blind human reason! Oh happy he who, laying aside his heavy part [body] upon a mute stone, gives his light part [soul] to sovereign sapphire [heaven]!

SONNET LIV (MORAL), *Concerning the deceptive brevity of life:* Less swiftly did the arrow seek the destined mark [target], into which it sharply bit; the competing chariot upon the mute sand did not round more quietly the column than hastily and secretly runs to its end our life. For him who doubts it, even a brute bereft of reason, each repeated sun [day] is a warning comet. Carthage confesses this, and you ignore it? You run a risk, Licio, if you insist on pursuing shadows and embracing deceptions. You will hardly be pardoned by the hours: the hours which are trimming down the days, the days which are gnawing away the years.

SONETO LXIX

(fúnebre)

Inscripción para el sepulcro de Domínico Greco

Esta en forma elegante, oh peregrino,
de pórfido luciente dura llave,
el pincel niega al mundo más süave,
que dio espíritu a leño, vida a lino.
Su nombre, aún de mayor aliento dino
que en los clarines de la Fama cabe,
el campo ilustra de ese mármol grave:
venéralo y prosigue tu camino.
Yace el Griego. Heredó Naturaleza
Arte; y el Arte, estudio. Iris, colores.
Febo, luces—si no sombras, Morfeo—.
Tanta urna, a pesar de su dureza,
lágrimas beba, y cuantos suda olores
corteza funeral de árbol sabeo.
[1615]

SONETO LXXXII

(amoroso)

La dulce boca que a gustar convida
un humor entre perlas destilado,
y a no invidiar aquel licor sagrado

SONNET LXIX (FUNEREAL), *Inscription for the tomb of Dominico Greco* [El Greco]: This elegantly formed, hard key, oh pilgrim, of shining porphyry denies to the world the softest brush which ever gave breath to wood, life to linen [canvas]. His name, worthy of even greater blasts than Fame's trumpets are capable of, illuminates the surface of this solemn marble: venerate it and continue your journey. Here lies the Greek. Nature has inherited his Art; and Art, his skill. The rainbow, his colors. Phoebus [the sun], his lights—or his shadows, Morpheus [sleep, dreams]—. Let this great urn, despite its hardness, absorb our tears and the odors sweated by the funereal bark of the Arabian tree [myrrh].

SONNET LXXXII (LOVE): The sweet mouth that invites one to taste a liquid distilled among pearls [teeth], and not to covet that sacred liquor which

que a Júpiter ministra el garzón de Ida,
   amantes, no toquéis, si queréis vida,
porque entre un labio y otro colorado
Amor está, de su veneno armado,
cual entre flor y flor sierpe escondida.
   No os engañen las rosas que, a la Aurora,
diréis que aljofaradas y olorosas
se le cayeron del purpúreo seno:
   manzanas son de Tántalo, y no rosas,
que después huyen del que incitan ahora;
y sólo del amor queda el veneno.

[1584]

SONETO LXXXVI

(amoroso)

   De pura honestidad templo sagrado
cuyo bello cimiento y gentil muro
de blanco nácar y alabastro duro
fue por divina mano fabricado;
   pequeña puerta de coral preciado,
claras lumbreras de mirar seguro,
que a la esmeralda fina el verde puro
habéis para viriles usurpado;
   soberbio techo, cuyas cimbrias de oro,
al claro sol, en cuanto en torno gira,
ornan de luz, coronan de belleza;

Ida's youth [Ganymede] serves to Jupiter [i.e., divine nectar], don't touch it, lovers, if you want to live, because between one red lip and another is Love, armed with his poison, like a serpent hidden between two flowers. Don't be fooled by the roses which you may say have fallen, dew-pearled and fragrant, from Dawn's purple bosom: they are Tantalus's apples, and not roses, later fleeing from him whom they now provoke; and all that is left of love is the poison.

SONNET LXXXVI (LOVE): Sacred temple of pure chastity, whose beautiful foundation and refined wall were built, by a divine hand, of white nacre and hard alabaster; small door of precious coral, bright windows of steady gaze, which from the fine emerald have usurped its pure green for your panes of glass; superb roof, whose golden moldings, while the bright sun revolves around, adorn it with light, crown it with beauty; beautiful idol,

ídolo bello, a quien humilde adoro:
oye piadoso al que por ti suspira,
tus himnos canta y tus virtudes reza.
[1582]

SONETO CIII

(amoroso)

De un caminante enfermo que
se enamoró donde fue hospedado

Descaminado, enfermo, peregrino,
en tenebrosa noche, con pie incierto
la confusión pisando del desierto,
voces en vano dio, pasos sin tino.
Repetido latir, si no vecino,
distinto, oyó de can siempre despierto,
y en pastoral albergue mal cubierto,
piedad halló, si no halló camino.
Salió el Sol, y entre armiños escondida,
soñolienta beldad con dulce saña
salteó al no bien sano pasajero.
Pagará el hospedaje con la vida;
más le valiera errar en la montaña
que morir de la suerte que yo muero.
[1594]

whom I humbly adore: hear with pity him who sighs for you, sings your hymns, and recites your virtues.

SONNET CIII (LOVE), *Concerning a sick wayfarer who fell in love where he was lodged:* Lost and sick, a wanderer, in the shadowy night, with uncertain foot treading the confusion of the wilds, gave shouts in vain, took aimless steps. The repeated barking, if not nearby, at least distinct, he heard of an always wakeful dog, and in a shepherd's shelter, poorly thatched, he found kindness, if not his way. The sun came up; and concealed among ermines, a sleepy beauty with sweet cruelty assaulted the hardly well traveler. He will pay for his lodging with his life; it would have been better for him to wander in the mountains than to die in the way that I am dying [i.e., of love].

SONETO CIX

(amoroso)

De una dama que, quitándose una sortija,
se picó con un alfiler

Prisión del nácar era articulado
(de mi firmeza un émulo luciente)
un dïamante, ingenïosamente
en oro también él aprisionado.
Clori, pues, que su dedo apremïado
de metal, aun precioso, no consiente,
gallarda un día, sobre impacïente,
lo redimió del vínculo dorado.
Mas, ay, que insidïoso latón breve
en los cristales de su bella mano
sacrílego divina sangre bebe:
púrpura ilustró menos indïano
marfil; invidïosa, sobre nieve
claveles deshojó la Aurora en vano.
[1620]

SONETO CLXV

Ilustre y hermosísima María,
mientras se dejan ver a cualquier hora
en tus mejillas la rosada Aurora,
Febo en tus ojos y en tu frente el día,
y mientras con gentil descortesía

SONNET CIX (LOVE), *Concerning a lady who, taking off a ring, pricked herself with a pin:* A shackle for the jointed mother-of-pearl (a gleaming competitor of my own constancy) was a diamond, itself also ingeniously shackled in gold. Clori, then, who does not consent that her finger be oppressed by metal, however precious, one day elegantly, as well as impatiently, redeemed it from the golden bond. But, alas, a little piece of insidious brass among the crystals of her lovely hand sacrilegiously drinks divine blood: purple dye was less brilliant upon Indian ivory; enviously, upon snow the Dawn shattered carnations in vain.

SONNET CLXV: Illustrious and most beautiful Maria, while one may still see at any time in your cheeks the rosy Dawn, Phoebus [the sun] in your eyes and on your forehead the day, and while with gentle discourtesy the wind

mueve el viento la hebra voladora
que la Arabia en sus venas atesora
y el rico Tajo en sus arenas cría;
antes que, de la edad Febo eclipsado
y el claro día vuelto en noche obscura,
huya la Aurora del mortal nublado;
antes que lo que hoy es rubio tesoro
venza a la blanca nieve su blancura:
goza, goza el color, la luz, el oro.
[1583]

SONETO CLXVI

Mientras por competir con tu cabello,
oro bruñido al sol relumbra en vano;
mientras con menosprecio en medio el llano
mira tu blanca frente el lilio bello;
mientras a cada labio, por cogello,
siguen más ojos que al clavel temprano;
y mientras triunfa con desdén lozano
del luciente cristal tu gentil cuello:
goza cuello, cabello, labio y frente,
antes que lo que fue en tu edad dorada
oro, lilio, clavel, cristal luciente,
no sólo en plata o vïola troncada
se vuelva, mas tú y ello juntamente
en tierra, en humo, en polvo, en sombra, en nada.
[1582]

blows the flying threads which Arabia treasures in its veins and the rich Tagus produces in its sands; before, Phoebus being eclipsed by time and the bright day changed into dark night, the Dawn flees from the deadly cloud; before that which is a golden treasure today vanquishes white snow with its whiteness: enjoy, enjoy, the color, the light, the gold.

SONNET CLXVI: While, to compete with your hair, gold burnished in the sun gleams in vain; while with scorn, in the midst of the plain, your white brow regards the lily fair; while each lip is pursued by more eyes than follow the early carnation; and while with proud disdain your neck triumphs over bright crystal: enjoy neck, hair, lips, and brow, before what was in your golden youth gold, lily, carnation, crystal bright, not only turns into silver or a crushed violet, but you and all of it together into earth, smoke, dust, shadow, nothingness.

FÁBULA DE POLIFEMO Y GALATEA

Al conde de Niebla

1

Estas que me dictó rimas sonoras,
culta sí, aunque bucólica, Talía
—¡oh excelso conde!—, en las purpúreas horas
que es rosas la alba y rosicler el día,
ahora que de luz tu Niebla doras,
escucha, al son de la zampoña mía,
si ya los muros no te ven, de Huelva,
peinar el viento, fatigar la selva.

2

Templado, pula en la maestra mano
el generoso pájaro su pluma,
o tan mudo en la alcándara, que en vano
aun desmentir al cascabel presuma;
tascando haga el freno de oro, cano,
del caballo andaluz la ociosa espuma;
gima el lebrel en el cordón de seda.
Y al cuerno, al fin, la cítara suceda.

3

Treguas al ejercicio sean robusto,
ocio atento, silencio dulce, en cuanto

FABLE OF POLYPHEMUS AND GALATEA, *To the Count of Niebla:* 1. These resounding rhymes which were dictated to me by the cultured, yet bucolic, Thalia, [the Muse of pastoral poetry]—oh excellent Count!—, during the purple hours when the dawn is roses and the day is rosy, now that you are gilding your "mist" with light [i.e., are in your village of Niebla], listen to them [these rhymes], sung to the sound of my pipes, if the walls of Huelva no longer see you combing the wind and beating the forest [hunting]. 2. Well conditioned, let the noble bird [falcon] preen his feathers upon the master's hand, or upon his perch, so quietly that he may try, in vain, to belie the bell [tied to his foot]; by champing, let the Andalusian horse make hoary his golden bit with his idle foam; let the hound whine upon his silken leash. And, finally, let the hunter's horn yield to the poet's harp. 3. Respite from that robust exercise be your attentive leisure and sweet silence while under august canopy you listen to the brutish song of the musical giant. Replace with the Muses today your sports; for if my Muse is capable of blowing such a trumpet (second to none of Fame's), your name will be

debajo escuchas de dosel augusto,
del músico jayán el fiero canto.
Alterna con las Musas hoy el gusto;
que si la mía puede ofrecer tanto
clarín (y de la Fama no segundo),
tu nombre oirán los términos del mundo.

4

Donde espumoso el mar sicilïano
el pie argenta de plata al Lilibeo
(bóveda o de las fraguas de Vulcano,
o tumba de los huesos de Tifeo),
pálidas señas cenizoso un llano
—cuando no del sacrílego deseo—
del duro oficio da. Allí una alta roca
mordaza es a una gruta, de su boca.

5

Guarnición tosca de este escollo duro
troncos robustos son, a cuya greña
menos luz debe, menos aire puro
la caverna profunda, que a la peña;
caliginoso lecho, el seno obscuro
ser de la negra noche nos lo enseña
infame turba de nocturnas aves,
gimiendo tristes y volando graves.

6

De este, pues, formidable de la tierra
bostezo, el melancólico vacío
a Polifemo, horror de aquella sierra,

heard to the ends of the earth. 4. Where foamily the sea of Sicily silvers the foot of Mt. Lilybaeum (either the vault of Vulcan's forges, or the tomb of Typhaeus' bones), an ashy plain gives pale indications—if not of the sacrilegious desire [of the giant Typhaeus]—of the difficult occupation [of the blacksmith]. There a high rock serves as gag to a grotto's mouth. 5. A crude adornment [or fortification] for this harsh crag are robust trunks, to whose matted hair the deep cavern owes less light and fresh air than to the cliff itself; that the obscure recess is black night's caliginous bed is demonstrated to us by an infamous mob of nocturnal fowls, moaning sadly and flying heavily. 6. The melancholy emptiness, then, of this formidable yawning of the earth serves Polyphemus, the terror of that mountain, as a bar-

bárbara choza es, albergue umbrío
y redil espacioso donde encierra
cuanto las cumbres ásperas cabrío
de los montes, esconde: copia bella
que un silbo junta y un peñasco sella.

7

Un monte era de miembros eminente
este (que, de Neptuno hijo fiero,
de un ojo ilustra el orbe de su frente,
émulo casi del mayor lucero)
cíclope, a quien el pino más valiente,
bastón, le obedecía, tan ligero,
y al grave peso junco tan delgado,
que un día era bastón y otro cayado.

8

Negro el cabello, imitador undoso
de las obscuras aguas del Leteo,
al viento que lo peina proceloso,
vuela sin orden, pende sin aseo;
un torrente es su barba impetüoso,
que (adusto hijo de este Pirineo)
su pecho inunda, o tarde, o mal, o en vano
surcada aun de los dedos de su mano.

9

No la Trinacria en sus montañas, fiera
armó de crüeldad, calzó de viento,

baric hut, a shadowy shelter, and a spacious fold where he encloses all the goats which hide the rough peaks of the mountains: a beautiful abundance which one whistle brings together and one boulder seals in. 7. A lofty mountain of limbs was this (fierce son of Neptune, illuminating the orb of his forehead with one eye, which almost competes with the greatest star) cyclops, to whom the most valiant pine tree was obedient as a cane so light, and so slender a reed under his heavy weight, that one day it was a cane and the next a crook. 8. His black hair, wavily imitating the dark waters of Lethe, in the wind that stormily combs it flies disorderly, hangs unkempt; an impetuous torrent is his beard, which (the burnt offspring of this Pyrenee) inundates his breast, [his beard which is] either too lately, or badly, or vainly plowed even by the fingers of his hand. 9. Trinacria [Sicily] in its mountains has never armed a beast with ferocity or shod it with the wind to fiercely

que redima feroz, salve ligera,
su piel manchada de colores ciento:
pellico es ya la que en los bosques era
mortal horror al que con paso lento
los bueyes a su albergue reducía,
pisando la dudosa luz del día.

10

Cercado es (cuanto más capaz, más lleno)
de la fruta, el zurrón, casi abortada,
que el tardo otoño deja al blando seno
de la piadosa hierba, encomendada:
la serba, a quien le da rugas el heno;
la pera, de quien fue cuna dorada
la rubia paja, y—pálida tutora—
la niega avara, y pródiga la dora.

11

Erizo es el zurrón, de la castaña,
y (entre el membrillo o verde o datilado)
de la manzana hipócrita, que engaña,
a lo pálido no, a lo arrebolado,
y, de la encina (honor de la montaña,
que pabellón al siglo fue dorado)
el tributo, alimento, aunque grosero,
del mejor mundo del candor primero.

12

Cera y cáñamo unió (que no debiera)

redeem or swiftly save its skin, marked with a hundred colors: a jacket of skins is already that [beast] which in the woods was a deadly terror for him who with slow step led the oxen back to his shelter, treading the dubious light of day [twilight]. 10. A fenced-in orchard for the fruit (the more capacious, the fuller) is his shepherd's pouch, on the verge of miscarriage, [fruit] which the late autumn entrusts to the soft bosom of the tender grass: the sorb-apple, wrinkled by the hay; the pear, whose golden cradle was the blond straw, which—as a pale guardian—stingily keeps the pear and prodigally gilds it. 11. The pouch is the burr [husk] of the chestnut, and (among quinces either green or date-colored) of the hypocritical apple, which is deceptive, not because it's pale, but because it's rouged, and for the oak tree's (the mountain's glory, which was a tent for the Golden Age) tribute, [which was] food, though coarse, for the better world of primitive innocence. 12. Wax and hemp joined (which it shouldn't have) a hundred

cien cañas, cuyo bárbaro rüído,
de más ecos que unió cáñamo y cera
albogues, duramente es repetido.
La selva se confunde, el mar se altera,
rompe Tritón su caracol torcido,
sordo huye el bajel a vela y remo:
¡tal la música es de Polifemo!

13

Ninfa, de Doris hija, la más bella,
adora, que vio el reino de la espuma.
Galatea es su nombre, y dulce en ella
el terno Venus de sus Gracias suma.
Son una y otra luminosa estrella
lucientes ojos de su blanca pluma:
si roca de cristal no es de Neptuno,
pavón de Venus es, cisne de Juno.

14

Purpúreas rosas sobre Galatea
la Alba entre lilios cándidos deshoja:
duda el Amor cuál más su color sea,
o púrpura nevada, o nieve roja.
De su frente la perla es, eritrea,
émula vana; el ciego dios se enoja,
y, condenado su esplendor, la deja
pender en oro al nácar de su oreja.

15

Invidia de las ninfas y cuidado

canes, whose barbarous noise is harshly repeated by more echoes than the number of Pan-pipes joined by hemp and wax. The forest is confounded, the sea is disturbed, Triton breaks his twisted conch, deafened flees the ship by sail and oar: such is the music of Polyphemus! 13. He adores a nymph, the most beautiful daughter of Doris seen by the kingdom of foam. Galatea is her name, and sweetly Venus unites in her the triad of her Graces. Her two bright stars are shining eyes in her white plumage: if she is not Neptune's crystal rock, she is Venus' peacock, Juno's swan [i.e., is white, but has eye-shaped markings]. 14. Purple roses upon Galatea the Dawn shatters among white lilies: Love wonders which is more her color, snowy purple or red snow. The Eritrean pearl is a vain rival of her brow; the blind god [Cupid, Love] is angered and, condemning its brilliance, lets it hang in gold from the nacre of her ear. 15. She was the envy of the nymphs and the

de cuantas honra el mar deidades era;
pompa del marinero niño alado
que sin fanal conduce su venera.
Verde el cabello, el pecho no escamado,
ronco sí, escucha a Glauco la ribera
inducir a pisar la bella ingrata,
en carro de cristal, campos de plata.

16

Marino joven, las cerúleas sienes,
del más tierno coral ciñe Palemo,
rico de cuantos la agua engendra bienes,
del Faro odioso al promontorio extremo;
mas en la gracia igual, si en los desdenes
perdonado algo más, que Polifemo,
de la que, aún no le oyó, y, calzada plumas,
tantas flores pisó como él espumas.

17

Huye la ninfa bella; y el marino
amante nadador, ser bien quisiera,
ya que no áspid a su pie divino,
dorado pomo a su veloz carrera;
mas, ¿cuál diente mortal, cuál metal fino
la fuga suspender podrá ligera
que el desdén solicita? ¡Oh cuánto yerra
delfín que sigue en agua corza en tierra!

amorous concern of all the deities honored by the sea; the glory of the winged sailor boy [Cupid] who lanternless pilots his Venus-shell [scallop]. With his green hair and his chest, not scaly, but hoarse, the shore listens to Glaucus persuading the ungrateful beauty to ride, in a crystal chariot, upon fields of silver [the sea]. 16. A marine youth, Palemon binds his sea-green temples with the tenderest coral, being wealthy in all the goods engendered by the water, from the fearful Lighthouse [at Messina] to the distant promontory [of Lilybaeum, at the opposite end of Sicily]; but in her favors [he is] the same as Polyphemus, though in her scorn perhaps somewhat more spared, by her who hardly heard him when, with feathers on her feet, she trod as many flowers as he did bubbles. 17. The lovely nymph flees; and the marine lover, swimming, would like very much to be, if not an asp to bite her divine foot [*cf.* Eurydice], a golden apple in the midst of her swift race [*cf.* Atalanta]; but what deadly tooth or precious metal can suspend the fast flight motivated by scorn? Oh how mistaken is the dolphin that pursues in the water a deer on land! 18. Sicily, with all that it hides and

18

Sicilia, en cuanto oculta, en cuanto ofrece,
copa es de Baco, huerto de Pomona:
tanto de frutas ésta la enriquece,
cuanto aquél de racimos la corona.
En carro que estival trillo parece,
a sus campañas Ceres no perdona,
de cuyas siempre fértiles espigas
las provincias de Europa son hormigas.

19

A Pales su viciosa cumbre debe
lo que a Ceres, y aún más, su vega llana;
pues si en la una granos de oro llueve,
copos nieva en la otra mil de lana.
De cuantos siegan oro, esquilan nieve,
o en pipas guardan la exprimida grana,
bien sea religión, bien amor sea,
deidad, aunque sin templo, es Galatea.

20

Sin aras, no: que el margen donde para
del espumoso mar su pie ligero,
al labrador, de sus primicias ara,
de sus esquilmos es al ganadero;
de la Copia—a la tierra, poco avara—
el cuerno vierte el hortelano, entero,
sobre la mimbre que tejió, prolija,
si artificiosa no, su honesta hija.

all that it proffers, is a wineglass of Bacchus and an orchard of Pomona: the latter endows it with as much fruit as the former crowns it with grape clusters. In a chariot which looks like a summer thresher, Ceres gives no rest to its fields, for whose ever productive heads of grain the provinces of Europe are ants. 19. To Pales [goddess of sheep-raising] its luxuriant highland yields as much as, and even more than, its flat lowland does to Ceres; for if upon the one it rains golden grains, upon the other it snows innumerable flakes of wool. For all those who reap gold, shear snow, or store in casks the pressed-out purple, either because of religion or because of love, Galatea, though temple-less, is a deity. 20. But not altar-less: for the edge of the foaming sea where she detains her swift foot is to the farmer an altar for his firstfruits, for his shearings to the shepherd; the horn of plenty—hardly stingy to this land—the fruit grower pours entire upon the wicker woven, slowly, if not artfully, by his chaste daughter. 21. Youth is on fire, and the

21

Arde la juventud, y los arados
peinan las tierras que surcaron antes,
mal conducidos, cuando no arrastrados
de tardos bueyes, cual su dueño errantes;
sin pastor que los silbe, los ganados
los crujidos ignoran resonantes
de las hondas, si, en vez del pastor pobre,
el céfiro no silba, o cruje el robre.

22

Mudo la noche el can, el día, dormido,
de cerro en cerro y sombra en sombra yace.
Bala el ganado; al mísero balido,
nocturno el lobo de las sombras nace.
Cébase; y fiero, deja humedecido
en sangre de una lo que la otra pace.
¡Revoca, Amor, los silbos, o a su dueño
el silencio del can siga, y el sueño!

23

La fugitiva ninfa, en tanto, donde
hurta un laurel su tronco al sol ardiente,
tantos jazmines cuanta hierba esconde
la nieve de sus miembros, da a una fuente.
Dulce se queja, dulce le responde
un ruiseñor a otro, y dulcemente
al sueño da sus ojos la armonía,
por no abrasar con tres soles el día.

plows which formerly made furrows now comb the earth, poorly guided, if not dragged along by slow oxen as errant as their masters; without a shepherd to whistle at them, the flocks forget the noisy creaking of the slings, unless, instead of the poor shepherd, the west wind whistles or the oak tree creaks. 22. The dog, mute by night and by day asleep, lies around from hill to hill and from shade to shade. The flock bleats; at the wretched bleat the nocturnal wolf is born of the shadows. He gluts himself; and fiercely he leaves dampened with the blood of one what another grazes upon. Recall, oh Love, the shepherd's whistling, or let the dog's silence and sleep go the way of his master! 23. The fleeing nymph, meanwhile, where a bay tree steals its own trunk from the burning sun, yields to a spring as many jasmines [her white skin] as grass is hidden by the snow of her limbs. Sweetly complains and sweetly responds one nightingale to another, and sweetly the harmony takes her eyes to sleep, so as not to burn the day with three suns.

24

Salamandria del Sol, vestido estrellas,
latiendo el Can del cielo estaba, cuando
(polvo el cabello, húmidas centellas,
si no ardientes aljófares, sudando)
llegó Acis; y, de ambas luces bellas
dulce Occidente viendo al sueño blando,
su boca dio, y sus ojos cuanto pudo,
al sonoro cristal, al cristal mudo.

25

Era Acis un venablo de Cupido,
de un fauno, medio hombre, medio fiera,
en Simetis, hermosa ninfa, habido:
gloria del mar, honor de su ribera.
El bello imán, el ídolo dormido,
que acero sigue, idólatra venera,
rico de cuanto el huerto ofrece pobre,
rinden las vacas y fomenta el robre.

26

El celestial humor recién cuajado
que la almendra guardó entre verde y seca,
en blanca mimbre se lo puso al lado,
y un copo, en verdes juncos, de manteca;
en breve corcho, pero bien labrado,
un rubio hijo de una encina hueca,
dulcísimo panal, a cuya cera
su néctar vinculó la primavera.

24. The sun's salamander [thought to live in fire], clothed in stars, the sky's Dog [constellation] was barking when (his hair dust, sweating damp sparks, if not burning drops) Acis arrived; and, seeing the sweet sunset of both lovely lights in gentle sleep, he applied his mouth, and his eyes as much as possible, to the sounding crystal [water] and the mute [her body], respectively. 25. Acis was one of Cupid's arrows, begotten by a faun, half man, half beast, on Symaethis, a lovely nymph: glory of the sea, adornment of its shore. The beautiful magnet, the sleepy idol, which he follows like steel, he idolatrously venerates, wealthy in everything offered by a simple orchard, yielded by cows and nurtured by the oak [honey]. 26. The heavenly liquid recently coagulated, stored in the half-green, half-dry almond, on white wicker he placed beside her, and a pat, in green reeds, of butter; upon a small but well shaped piece of cork the blond offspring of a hollow oak, sweetest honeycomb, to whose wax springtime has bonded its

27

Caluroso, al arroyo da las manos,
y con ellas las ondas a su frente,
entre dos mirtos que, de espuma canos,
dos verdes garzas son de la corriente.
Vagas cortinas de volantes vanos
corrió Favonio lisonjeramente
a la (de viento cuando no sea) cama
de frescas sombras, de menuda grama.

28

La ninfa, pues, la sonorosa plata
bullir sintió del arroyuelo apenas
cuando, a los verdes márgenes ingrata,
segur se hizo de sus azucenas.
Huyera; mas tan frío se desata
un temor perezoso por sus venas,
que a la precisa fuga, al presto vuelo,
grillos de nieve fue, plumas de hielo.

29

Fruta en mimbres halló, leche exprimida
en juncos, miel en corcho, mas sin dueño;
si bien al dueño debe, agradecida,
su deidad culta, venerado el sueño.
A la ausencia mil veces ofrecida,
este de cortesía no pequeño
indicio la dejó—aunque estatua helada—
más discursiva y menos alterada.

nectar. 27. Hot, he puts his hands in the brook, and with them its waves on his brow, between two myrtles which, white with foam, are two green herons in the stream. Favonius [the breeze] caressingly drew vague curtains with vain frills around the bed, if not of wind [hammock?], of cool shade and fine grass. 28. The nymph, then, hardly heard bubble the sounding silver [the water] of the brook when, ungrateful to its green banks, she converted herself into a sickle of her own lilies [white limbs]. She would have fled; but so cold a sluggish fear runs through her veins that it was, to her urgent escape, to her swift flight, shackles of snow, feathers of ice. 29. She found fruit on wicker, pressed-out milk on reeds, honey on cork, but ownerless; although, in gratitude, she owes the owner the devotion paid to her divinity, the veneration paid to her sleep. Many times on the verge of absence [flight], this not small indication of courtesy left her—although a frozen statue—more discursive and less perturbed. 30. She doesn't, of

30

No al Cíclope atribuye, no, la ofrenda;
no a sátiro lascivo, ni a otro feo
morador de las selvas, cuya rienda
el sueño aflija, que aflojó el deseo.
El niño dios, entonces, de la venda,
ostentación gloriosa, alto trofeo
quiere que al árbol de su madre sea
el desdén hasta allí de Galatea.

31

Entre las ramas del que más se lava
en el arroyo, mirto levantado,
carcaj de cristal hizo, si no aljaba,
su blanco pecho, de un arpón dorado.
El monstro de rigor, la fiera brava
mira la ofrenda ya con más cuidado,
y aun siente que a su dueño sea, devoto,
confuso alcaide más, el verde soto.

32

Llamáralo, aunque muda, mas no sabe
el nombre articular que más querría;
ni lo ha visto, si bien pincel süave
lo ha bosquejado ya en su fantasía.
Al pie—no tanto ya, del temor, grave—
fía su intento; y, tímida, en la umbría
cama de campo y campo de batalla,
fingiendo sueño al cauto garzón halla.

course, attribute to the Cyclops this offering; nor to a lascivious satyr or any other ugly inhibitant of the forests, whose restraints are destroyed by sleep [i.e., the sight of a sleeping woman], which have already been loosened by desire. Then the child god with the blindfold [Cupid] wants for a glorious display, a supreme trophy for his mother's tree [Venus's myrtle], the hitherto scornful attitude [toward men] of Galatea. 31. From among the boughs of the lofty myrtle most washed by the brook, he made a crystal quiver, if not a case, out of her white breast for a golden arrow. The cruel monster, the fierce wild beast now looks at the offering more carefully, and even regrets that its devout owner should still be vaguely imprisoned by the green thicket. 32. Although silent, she would call him, but she doesn't know how to articulate the name which she would most like to; nor has she seen him, although a soft brush has already sketched him in her fantasy. To her foot—no longer so heavy with fear—she entrusts her attempt; and timidly, in the shady field-bed and battlefield, she finds the

33

El bulto vio, y, haciéndolo dormido,
librada en un pie toda sobre él pende
(urbana al sueño, bárbara al mentido
retórico silencio que no entiende):
no el ave reina, así, el fragoso nido
corona inmóvil, mientras no desciende
—rayo con plumas—al milano pollo
que la eminencia abriga de un escollo,

34

como la ninfa bella, compitiendo
con el garzón dormido en cortesía,
no sólo para, mas el dulce estruendo
del lento arroyo enmudecer querría.
A pesar luego de las ramas, viendo
colorido el bosquejo que ya había
en su imaginación Cupido hecho
con el pincel que le clavó su pecho,

35

de sitio mejorada, atenta mira,
en la disposición robusta, aquello
que, si por lo süave no la admira,
es fuerza que la admire por lo bello.
Del casi tramontado sol aspira
a los confusos rayos, su cabello;
flores su bozo es, cuyas colores,
como duerme la luz, niegan las flores.

cunning boy feigning sleep. 33. She saw his figure and, supposing him asleep, she, balanced on one foot, hangs completely over him (kind to his sleep, uncouth with respect to the mendacious rhetorical silence which she doesn't understand): not so motionless does the queen of birds [the eagle] hover over the craggy nest, before she plunges down—a feathered thunderbolt—upon the kite's nestling which the peak of a rock protects, 34. as the lovely nymph, competing in courtesy with the sleeping boy, not only stands still, but would like to silence the sweet noise of the slow-moving brook. Then, despite the branches seeing colored the sketch which Cupid had already made in her imagination with the brush which had pierced her breast, 35. having improved her position, she attentively looks, in his robust lines, at that which, if it doesn't amaze her because of its delicacy, necessarily amazes her because of its beauty. His hair competes with the vague rays of the sun which has almost set; his downy lip is like flowers, whose colors, since the light

36

En la rústica greña yace oculto,
el áspid, del intonso prado ameno,
antes que del peinado jardín culto
en el lascivo, regalado seno:
en lo viril desata de su vulto
lo más dulce el Amor, de su veneno;
bébelo Galatea, y da otro paso
por apurarle la ponzoña al vaso.

37

Acis—aún más de aquello que dispensa
la brújula del sueño vigilante—,
alterada la ninfa esté o suspensa,
Argos es siempre atento a su semblante,
lince penetrador de lo que piensa,
cíñalo bronce o múrelo diamante:
que en sus paladïones Amor ciego,
sin romper muros, introduce fuego.

38

El sueño de sus miembros sacudido,
gallardo el joven la persona ostenta,
y al marfil luego de sus pies rendido,
el coturno besar dorado intenta.
Menos ofende el rayo prevenido,
al marinero, menos la tormenta
prevista le turbó o pronosticada:
Galatea lo diga, salteada.

39

Más agradable y menos zahareña,

sleeps, are withheld by the flowers. 36. In the rustic tangle of the pleasantly unkempt meadow the asp lies hidden rather than in the lasciviously delightful bosom of the well-combed cultivated garden: in the virile aspects of his face Love releases the sweetest of his venom; Galatea drinks it, and takes another step to drain the cup of poison. 37. Acis—even more than is allowed by the peephole of his vigilant sleep—whether the nymph is disturbed or hesitant, is always an Argos intent upon her face, a lynx who penetrates her thoughts, whether she girds them with bronze or walls them in with diamond: for in his Trojan horses blind Love, without destroying walls, smuggles fire in. 38. Shaking the sleep from his limbs, the youth

al mancebo levanta venturoso,
dulce ya concediéndole y risueña,
paces no al sueño, treguas sí al reposo.
Lo cóncavo hacía de una peña
a un fresco sitïal dosel umbroso,
y verdes celosías unas hiedras,
trepando troncos y abrazando piedras.

40

Sobre una alfombra, que imitara en vano
el tirio sus matices (si bien era
de cuantas sedas ya hiló, gusano,
y, artífice, tejió la Primavera)
reclinados, al mirto más lozano,
una y otra lasciva, si ligera,
paloma se caló, cuyos gemidos
—trompas de Amor—alteran sus oídos.

41

El ronco arrullo al joven solicita;
mas, con desvíos Galatea suaves,
a su audacia los términos limita,
y el aplauso al concento de las aves.
Entre las ondas y la fruta, imita
Acis al siempre ayuno en penas graves:
que, en tanta gloria, infierno son no breve,
fugitivo cristal, pomos de nieve.

elegantly displays himself and then, prostrated at the ivory of her feet, he tries to kiss her golden boot. The foreseen thunderbolt frightens the sailor less, the storm anticipated or prognosticated disturbs him less: let Galatea say so, thus assaulted. 39. More pleasant and less untractable, she raises the lucky lad, sweetly now and smilingly granting him, not peace for sleep, but a truce in his rest. The hollowness of a cliff served a cool spot as a shady canopy, and as green blinds served some ivy, climbing trunks and embracing rocks. 40. They having reclined upon a carpet whose colors the Tyrian would imitate in vain (although it was made only of the silks spun by Springtime as a worm and woven by her as an artisan), upon the leafiest myrtle first one and then another dove, lasciviously if swiftly, alights, and their moans—Love's trumpets—disturb their ears. 41. The hoarse cooing excites the youth; but Galatea, with gentle evasion, sets limits to his audacity and limits his applause to the birds' harmony. Caught between the waves and the fruit, Acis imitates him who was always hungry in great torment [Tantalus]: for, in such a heaven, no slight hell is fleeing crystal and snowy

42

No a las palomas concedió Cupido
juntar de sus dos picos los rubíes,
cuando al clavel el joven atrevido
las dos hojas le chupa carmesíes.
Cuantas produce Pafo, engendra Gnido,
negras vïolas, blancos alhelíes,
llueven sobre el que Amor quiere que sea
tálamo de Acis ya y de Galatea.

43

Su aliento humo, sus relinchos fuego,
si bien su freno espumas, ilustraba
las columnas Etón que erigió el griego,
do el carro de la luz sus ruedas lava,
cuando, de amor el fiero jayán ciego,
la cerviz oprimió a una roca brava,
que a la playa, de escollos no desnuda,
linterna es ciega y atalaya muda.

44

Arbitro de montañas y ribera,
aliento dio, en la cumbre de la roca,
a los albogues que agregó la cera,
el prodigioso fuelle de su boca;
la ninfa los oyó, y ser más quisiera
breve flor, hierba humilde, tierra poca,
que de su nuevo tronco vid lasciva,
muerta de amor, y de temor no viva.

apples. 42. Hardly did Cupid permit the doves to join the rubies of their two beaks when the daring youth sucks the carnation's two red petals. All the dark violets and the white gilliflowers produced by Paphos and begotten by Gnidos [cities sacred to Venus] rain down upon what Love wants now to be a bridal couch for Acis and Galatea. 43. His breath smoke and his whinnying fire, though his bit was foam, Aethon [one of the Sun's horses] was illuminating the columns erected by the Greek [Hercules], where light's chariot washes its wheels, when the fierce giant, blind with love, oppresses the neck of a wild rock, which for the beach, which is not bereft of crags, is a blind lighthouse and a mute watchtower. 44. The arbiter he of mountains and shore, on the top of the rock, the prodigious bellows of his mouth gave breath to the pipes joined by wax; the nymph heard them, and she would rather be a small flower, a humble plant, a little earth than on her new tree trunk a lascivious vine, dying with love and not alive for fear. 45. But—her

45

Mas—cristalinos pámpanos sus brazos—
amor la implica, si el temor la anuda,
al infelice olmo que pedazos
la segur de los celos hará aguda.
Las cavernas en tanto, los ribazos,
que ha prevenido la zampoña ruda,
el trueno de la voz fulminó luego:
¡referidlo, Pïérides, os ruego!

46

«¡Oh bella Galatea, más süave
que los claveles que tronchó la aurora;
blanca más que las plumas de aquel ave
que dulce muere y en las aguas mora;
igual en pompa al pájaro que, grave,
su manto azul de tantos ojos dora
cuantas el celestial zafiro estrellas!
¡Oh tú, que en dos incluyes las más bellas!:

47

»deja las ondas, deja el rubio coro
de las hijas de Tetis, y el mar vea,
cuando niega la luz un carro de oro,
que en dos la restituye Galatea.
Pisa la arena, que en la arena adoro
cuantas el blanco pie conchas platea,
cuyo bello contacto puede hacerlas,
sin concebir rocío, parir perlas.

arms being tendrils of crystal—love entwines her, if fear ties her tight, to the unfortunate elm tree which will be hacked to bits by the sharp sickle of jealousy. Meanwhile the caverns and the hills, which the crude pipes had warned, were subsequently blasted by the thunder of his voice: tell it, oh Muses, I beg you! 46. "Oh lovely Galatea, more delicate than the carnations shattered by dawn; whiter than the feathers of that bird which dies sweetly and dwells in the water [the swan]; equal in splendor to the bird which solemnly gilds its blue mantle with as many eyes as stars [gild] the sapphire of heaven! Oh you who, in your two stars [eyes], possess the most beautiful ones!: 47. "leave the waves, leave the blonde chorus of Thetis's daughters, and let the sea behold how, when one golden chariot withholds light, Galatea restores it with two. Tread the sand, for on the sand I adore all the shells silvered by your white foot, whose lovely touch can make them, without dew's conception, give birth to pearls. 48. "Deaf daughter of the sea,

48

»Sorda hija del mar, cuyas orejas
a mis gemidos son rocas al viento:
o dormida te hurten a mis quejas
purpúreos troncos de corales ciento,
o al disonante número de almejas
—marino, si agradable no, instrumento—
coros tejiendo estés, escucha un día
mi voz, por dulce, cuando no por mía.

49

»Pastor soy, mas tan rico de ganados,
que los valles impido más vacíos,
los cerros desparezco levantados
y los caudales seco de los ríos;
no los que, de sus ubres desatados,
o derivados de los ojos míos,
leche corren y lágrimas; que iguales
en número a mis bienes son mis males.

50

»Sudando néctar, lambicando olores,
senos que ignora aun la golosa cabra,
corchos me guardan, más que abeja flores
liba inquïeta, ingenïosa labra;
troncos me ofrecen árboles mayores,
cuyos enjambres, o el abril los abra,
o los desate el mayo, ámbar distilan
y en ruecas de oro rayos del sol hilan.

whose ears to my moans are rocks in the wind: whether in sleep you are stolen from my complaints by a hundred purple coral trunks, or whether to the dissonant rhythm of clams—a marine, if not agreeable, instrument—you are weaving dance figures, listen for once to my voice, because it's sweet, if not because it's mine. 49. "I am a shepherd, but so rich in flocks that I obstruct the emptiest valleys, I conceal the lofty hills, and I dry up the rivers' streams; but not those which flow from their udders or spring from my eyes; for equal in number to my possessions are my griefs. 50. "Sweating forth nectar, distilling fragrances, corners yet unknown to the greedy goat conceal for me more cork hives than the flowers that the bee restlessly sips and ingeniously elaborates; the larger trees offer me trunks whose hives, whether broken open by April or allowed to swarm by May, exude amber and on distaffs of gold spin sunbeams. 51. "I'm a son of the

51

»Del Júpiter soy hijo, de las ondas,
aunque pastor; si tu desdén no espera
a que el monarca de esas grutas hondas,
en trono de cristal te abrace nuera,
Polifemo te llama, no te escondas;
que tanto esposo admira la ribera
cual otro no vio Febo, más robusto,
del perezoso Volga al Indo adusto.

52

»Sentado, a la alta palma no perdona
su dulce fruto mi robusta mano;
en pie, sombra capaz es mi persona
de innumerables cabras el verano.
¿Qué mucho, si de nubes se corona
por igualarme la montaña en vano,
y en los cielos, desde esta roca, puedo
escribir mis desdichas con el dedo?

53

»Marítimo alcïón roca eminente
sobre sus huevos coronaba, el día
que espejo de zafiro fue luciente
la playa azul, de la persona mía.
Miréme, y lucir vi un sol en mi frente,
cuando en el cielo un ojo se veía:
neutra el agua dudaba a cuál fe preste,
o al cielo humano, o al cíclope celeste.

Jupiter of the waves [Neptune], although a shepherd; if your scornfulness is not waiting for the monarch of those deep grottos on his crystal throne to embrace you as his daughter-in-law, Polyphemus is calling you, don't hide; for the seashore is admiring such a bridegroom that Phoebus has never seen a more robust one, from the sluggish Volga to the scorched Indus. 52. "Seated, my robust hand does not spare the lofty palmtree its sweet fruit; standing, my body is a shade sufficient for innumerable goats in summer. What wonder, if the mountain crowns itself with clouds in vain to equal me, and on the heavens, from this rock, I can write my misfortunes with my finger? 53. "The maritime halcyon upon his eggs crowned a high cliff on the day that [i.e., during halcyon days, calm weather] the blue beach was a gleaming sapphire mirror of my figure. I looked at myself, and I saw a sun shining on my brow: the water, undecided, was doubtful which to put its faith in, the human heaven or the heavenly cyclops. 54. "On other doors the

54

»Registra en otras puertas el venado
sus años, su cabeza colmilluda
la fiera cuyo cerro levantado,
de helvecias picas es muralla aguda;
la humana suya el caminante errado
dio ya a mi cueva, de piedad desnuda,
albergue hoy, por tu causa, al peregrino,
do halló reparo, si perdió camino.

55

»En tablas dividida, rica nave
besó la playa miserablemente,
de cuantos vomitó riquezas, grave,
por las bocas del Nilo el Orïente.
Yugo aquel día, y yugo bien süave,
del fiero mar a la sañuda frente
imponiéndole estaba (si no al viento
dulcísimas coyundas) mi instrumento,

56

»cuando, entre globos de agua, entregar veo
a las arenas ligurina haya,
en cajas los aromas del Sabeo,
en cofres las riquezas de Cambaya:
delicias de aquel mundo, ya trofeo
de Escila, que, ostentado en nuestra playa,
lastimoso despojo fue dos días
a las que esta montaña engendra arpías.

deer registers his years [i.e., by his antlers], his long-tusked head is registered by the beast whose high ridge [spine] is a sharp wall of Swiss pikes [i.e., the boar]; the wandering wayfarer once yielded his human head to my cave, bereft of pity, now a shelter, because of you, for the pilgrim, where he has found refreshment, if he has lost his way. 55. "Broken up into boards, a rich ship kissed the beach in misery, loaded with all the riches which the Orient vomits through the mouths of the Nile. A yoke that day, and a very gentle yoke, was being imposed upon the fierce sea's angry brow (if not sweetest yoke-straps upon the wind) by my instrument, 56. "when, amidst globes of water, I see the Ligurian beechtree surrender to the sands in boxes the Sheban's perfumes, in coffers the riches of Cambay: the former delights of that world, now Scylla's trophy, which, displayed upon our beach, was for two days the pitiable spoil of the harpies engendered by this mountain. 57. "A second lifesaving board to a Genoese

57

»Segunda tabla a un ginovés mi gruta
de su persona fue, de su hacienda;
la una reparada, la otra enjuta,
relación del naufragio hizo horrenda.
Luciente paga de la mejor fruta
que en hierbas se recline, en hilos penda,
colmillo fue del animal que el Ganges
sufrir muros le vio, romper falanges:

58

»arco, digo, gentil, bruñida aljaba,
obras ambas de artífice prolijo,
y de Malaco rey a deidad Java
alto don, según ya mi huésped dijo.
De aquél la mano, de ésta el hombro agrava;
convencida la madre, imita al hijo:
serás a un tiempo en estos horizontes
Venus del mar, Cupido de los montes.»

59

Su horrenda voz, no su dolor interno,
cabras aquí le interrumpieron, cuantas
—vagas el pie, sacrílegas el cuerno—
a Baco se atrevieron en sus plantas.
Mas, conculcado el pámpano más tierno
viendo el fiero pastor, voces él tantas,
y tantas despidió la honda piedras,
que el muro penetraron de las hiedras.

was my grotto, for his body and for his possessions; when the former had been rested and the latter dried out, he told the terrifying story of the shipwreck. The gleaming payment for the best fruit resting in straw, hanging from strings, was a tusk of the animal which the Ganges saw bearing walls and breaking squadrons: 58. "a fine bow, I mean, a burnished quiver, both of them the work of a careful artisan and, as my guest told me, the gift of a Moluccan king to a Javanese deity. Weigh down with the former your hand, with the latter your shoulder; having convinced the mother [Venus], imitate the son [Cupid]: you will be simultaneously in these regions a Venus of the sea, a Cupid of the mountains." 59. His awful voice, but not his inner suffering, was at this point interrupted by all the goats which, with wandering foot and sacrilegious horn, had dared to violate Bacchus's plants. But the fierce shepherd, seeing the tenderest shoots trampled, sent out so many yells and stones from his sling that they pierced the wall of ivy.

60

De los nudos, con esto, más süaves,
los dulces dos amantes desatados,
por duras guijas, por espinas graves
solicitan el mar con pies alados:
tal, redimiendo de importunas aves
incauto meseguero sus sembrados,
de liebres dirimió copia, así, amiga,
que vario sexo unió y un surco abriga.

61

Viendo el fiero jayán, con paso mudo
correr al mar la fugitiva nieve
(que a tanta vista el líbico desnudo
registra el campo de su adarga breve)
y al garzón viendo, cuantas mover pudo
celoso trueno, antiguas hayas mueve:
tal, antes que la opaca nube rompa,
previene rayo fulminante trompa.

62

Con vïolencia desgajó infinita,
la mayor punta de la excelsa roca,
que al joven, sobre quien la precipita,
urna es mucha, pirámide no poca.
Con lágrimas la ninfa solicita
las deidades del mar, que Acis invoca:
concurren todas, y el peñasco duro
la sangre que exprimió, cristal fue puro.

60. The two sweet lovers, loosed by this from the most pleasant knots, over harsh pebbles and painful thorns seek the sea with winged feet: thus the careless farmer, saving his wheat fields from insistent birds, has separated in this way a friendly pair of rabbits, joined by their different sexes and sheltered by a furrow. 61. The fierce giant, seeing the fugitive snow [Galatea] run with muted step toward the sea (for to such sharp vision the naked Libyan reveals the limited area of his shield) and, seeing the boy, stirs as many aged beechtrees as could be stirred by jealous thunder: thus, before the dark cloud breaks, a blasting trumpet warns of the thunderbolt. 62. With infinite violence he tore loose the greatest peak of the lofty rock, which for the youth, upon whom he hurls it down, is large for an urn, not small for a pyramid. With tears the nymph calls upon the deities of the sea, which Acis too invokes: they all respond, and the blood crushed out by the harsh boulder was turned into pure crystal. 63. Hardly were his limbs lam-

63

Sus miembros lastimosamente opresos
del escollo fatal fueron apenas,
que los pies de los árboles más gruesos
calzó el líquido aljófar de sus venas.
Corriente plata al fin sus blancos huesos,
lamiendo flores y argentando arenas,
a Doris llega, que, con llanto pío,
yerno lo saludó, lo aclamó río.

[1613]

LETRILLA XIX

(sacra)

Oveja perdida, ven
sobre mis hombros, que hoy
no sólo tu pastor soy,
sino tu pasto también.

Por descubrirte mejor
cuando balabas perdida,
dejé en un árbol la vida,
donde me subió el amor;
si prenda quieres mayor,
mis obras hoy te la den.
Oveja perdida, ven
sobre mis hombros, que hoy
no sólo tu pastor soy,
sino tu pasto también.

Pasto al fin hoy tuyo hecho,
¿cuál dará mayor asombro,

entably oppressed by the fatal rock when the feet of the biggest trees were shod in the liquid pearls of his veins. Finally, his white bones converted into flowing silver, lapping the flowers and silvering the sands, he reached Doris, who, with pitying tears, greeted him as a son-in-law, acclaimed him as a river.

SONG XIX (SACRED): *Lost sheep, come upon my shoulders, for today I am not only your shepherd, but your fodder as well.* The better to find you when you were lost and bleating, I left my life on a tree which love had helped me climb; if you want more of a pledge, let my deeds today give it to you. *Lost sheep,* etc. Finally converted today into your fodder, which will be more

o el traerte yo en el hombro,
o el traerme tú en el pecho?
Prendas son de amor estrecho
que aun los más ciegos las ven.
Oveja perdida, ven
sobre mis hombros, que hoy
no sólo tu pastor soy,
sino tu pasto también.

[1609]

LETRILLA XXIII

(sacra)

Al nacimiento de Cristo nuestro Señor

Caído se le ha un clavel
hoy a la Aurora del seno:
¡qué glorioso que está el heno,
porque ha caído sobre él!

Cuando el silencio tenía
todas las cosas del suelo,
y coronada del yelo
reinaba la noche fría,
en medio la monarquía
de tiniebla tan crüel,
caído se le ha un clavel
hoy a la Aurora del seno:
¡qué glorioso que está el heno,
porque ha caído sobre él!

De un solo clavel ceñida
la Virgen, aurora bella,
al mundo se le dio, y ella
quedó cual antes florida;

amazing, for me to carry you on my shoulder or for you to carry me in your heart? These are pledges of such intimate love that even the blindest see them. *Lost sheep,* etc.

SONG XXIII (SACRED), *On the birth of Christ our Lord: Today a carnation has fallen from Dawn's bosom: how glorious the hay looks, because it has fallen upon it!* When silence held all the things of earth, and crowned with ice the cold night reigned, in the midst of the rule of such cruel darkness,

a la púrpura caída
sólo fue el heno fiel.
Caído se le ha un clavel
hoy a la Aurora del seno:
¡qué glorioso que está el heno,
porque ha caído sobre él!

El heno, pues, que fue dino,
a pesar de tantas nieves,
de ver en sus brazos leves
este rosicler divino,
para su lecho fue lino,
oro para su dosel.
Caído se le ha un clavel
hoy a la Aurora del seno:
¡qué glorioso que está el heno,
porque ha caído sobre él!
[1621]

LETRILLA XLVIII

(burlesca)

Ándeme yo caliente
y ríase la gente.

Traten otros del gobierno
del mundo y sus monarquías,
mientras gobiernan mis días
mantequillas y pan tierno,
y las mañanas de invierno
naranjada y aguardiente,
y ríase la gente.

Coma en dorada vajilla
el Príncipe mil cuidados,

today a carnation has fallen, **etc. Adorned with a single carnation the Virgin, beautiful dawn, gave it to the world, and she was left as flower-clad as before; to the fallen purple, only the hay was faithful.** ***Today a carnation has fallen,*** **etc. The hay, then, which was worthy, despite so much snow, to behold in its soft arms this divine rose of dawn, was linen for his bed, gold for his canopy.** ***Today a carnation has fallen,*** **etc.**

SONG XLVIII (BURLESQUE): ***Let me be wildly enthusiastic, and let the people***

como píldoras dorados;
que yo en mi pobre mesilla
quiero más una morcilla
que en el asador reviente,
y ríase la gente.

Cuando cubra las montañas
de blanca nieve el enero,
tenga yo lleno el brasero
de bellotas y castañas,
y quien las dulces patrañas
del Rey que rabió me cuente,
y ríase la gente.

Busque muy en hora buena
el mercader nuevos soles;
yo conchas y caracoles
entre la menuda arena,
escuchando a Filomena
sobre el chopo de la fuente,
y ríase la gente.

Pase a media noche el mar,
y arda en amorosa llama,
Leandro por ver su dama;
que yo más quiero pasar
del golfo de mi lagar
la blanca o roja corriente,
y ríase la gente.

Pues Amor es tan cruel
que de Píramo y su amada

laugh. Let others deal with governing the world and its monarchies, while my time is spent on butter and soft bread, and on winter mornings orangeade and brandy, *and let the people laugh.* Let the Prince eat on golden plate a thousand cares, like gilded pills; for I at my poor table prefer a black sausage bursting on the spit, *and let the people laugh.* When January covers the mountains with white snow, let me have my brasier full of acorns and chestnuts, and someone to tell me the old stories of the king who went mad, *and let the people laugh.* Let the merchant, with my best wishes, seek new suns; I'll look for seashells and snails in the fine sand, listening to the nightingale on the poplar by the spring, *and let the people laugh.* Let Leander

hace tálamo una espada,
do se junten ella y él,
sea mi Tisbe un pastel
y la espada sea mi diente,
y ríase la gente.
[1581]

ROMANCE XVII

(amoroso)

Angélica y Medoro

1. En un pastoral albergue
que la guerra entre unos robres
lo dejó por escondido
o lo perdonó por pobre,
2. do la paz viste pellico
y conduce entre pastores
ovejas del monte al llano
y cabras del llano al monte,
3. mal herido y bien curado,
se alberga un dichoso joven,
que sin clavarle Amor flecha,
lo coronó de favores.
4. Las venas con poca sangre,
los ojos con mucha noche,
lo halló en el campo aquella
vida y muerte de los hombres.

pass over the sea at midnight, burning with amorous flame, to see his lady; for I prefer to pass from the gulf of my winepress, the white or red stream, *and let the people laugh*. Since Love is so cruel that for Pyramus and his beloved he makes a wedding bed out of a sword, on which he and she are united, let my Thisbe be a cake and the sword be my tooth, *and let the people laugh.*

BALLAD XVII (LOVE), *Angelica and Medoro:* 1. In a shepherd's shelter among some oaks which the war had missed because it was hidden or had reprieved because poor, 2. where peace wears a rustic jacket and, among the shepherds, drives sheep from the mountain to the plain and goats from the plain to the mountain, 3. badly wounded and well treated, is lodged a lucky youth who, without Cupid's piercing him with an arrow, was crowned with Love's favors. 4. His veins almost empty of blood, his eyes full of night, he was found on the field by that life and death of men [a beautiful woman]. 5. She gets

5. Del palafrén se derriba,
no porque al moro conoce,
sino por ver que la hierba
tanta sangre paga en flores.
6. Límpiale el rostro, y la mano
siente al Amor que se esconde
tras las rosas, que la muerte
va violando sus colores.
7. Escondióse tras las rosas
porque labren sus arpones
el diamante del Catay
con aquella sangre noble.
8. Ya le regala los ojos,
ya le entra, sin ver por dónde,
una piedad mal nacida
entre dulces escorpiones.
9. Ya es herido el pedernal,
ya despide el primer golpe
centellas de agua. ¡Oh, piedad,
hija de padres traidores!
10. Hierbas aplica a sus llagas,
que si no sanan entonces,
en virtud de tales manos
lisonjean los dolores.
11. Amor le ofrece su venda,
mas ella sus velos rompe
para ligar sus heridas:
los rayos del sol perdonen.
12. Los últimos nudos daba

down from her palfrey, not because she knows the Moor, but because she sees the grass paying for so much blood with flowers. 6. She bathes his face, and her hand perceives Love hiding behind the roses, for death is doing violence to his color. 7. Love hid behind the roses so that his arrows might work the diamond of Cathay [Angelica's hard heart] with that noble blood. 8. Now he regales her eyes, now there enters her, no one sees how, a sympathy base-born among sweet scorpions. 9. Now the flint is struck, now the first blow yields liquid sparks [tears]. Oh sympathy, the daughter of traitorous parents! 10. She applies herbs to his wounds, and if they don't heal immediately, by virtue of such hands the pains are pleasant. 11. Love offers her his blindfold, but she tears up her veils to bind his wounds: may

cuando el cielo la socorre
de un villano en una yegua
que iba penetrando el bosque.
13. Enfrénanle de la bella
las tristes piadosas voces,
que los firmes troncos mueven
y las sordas piedras oyen;
14. y la que mejor se halla
en las selvas que en la corte,
simple bondad al pío ruego
cortésmente corresponde.
15. Humilde se apea el villano,
y sobre la yegua pone
un cuerpo con poca sangre,
pero con dos corazones;
16. a su cabaña los guía,
que el sol deja su horizonte
y el humo de su cabaña
les va sirviendo de norte.
17. Llegaron temprano a ella,
do una labradora acoge
un mal vivo con dos almas,
y una ciega con dos soles.
18. Blando heno en vez de pluma
para lecho les compone,
que será tálamo luego
do el garzón sus dichas logre.

the sun's rays forgive [her eyes' competition]! 12. She was tying the last knots when heaven aids her with a villager on a mare who was going through the woods. 13. He is curbed by the sad piteous cries of the beauty, which move the firm tree trunks and which the deaf stones hear; 14. and what is more easily found in the wilds than at court, simple kindness courteously responds to the pitiful plea. 15. The villager humbly dismounts, and on his mare he places a body with little blood, but two hearts; 16. to his cabin he leads them, for the sun is leaving the horizon and the smoke from his cabin serves them as a North Star. 17. They soon reached it, where a farmer's wife takes in a man hardly alive with two souls and a woman blind with two suns [eyes]. 18. Soft hay instead of feathers for a bed she fixes them, which will later be a wedding bed on which the boy will enjoy

19. Las manos, pues, cuyos dedos
de esta vida fueron dioses,
restituyen a Medoro
salud nueva, fuerzas dobles,
20. y le entregan, cuando menos,
su beldad y un reino en dote,
segunda invidia de Marte,
primera dicha de Adonis.
21. Corona un lascivo enjambre
de Cupidillos menores
la choza, bien como abejas
hueco tronco de alcornoque.
22. ¡Qué de nudos le está dando
a un áspid la Invidia torpe,
contando de las palomas
los arrullos gemidores!
23. ¡Qué bien la destierra Amor,
haciendo la cuerda azote,
porque el caso no se infame
y el lugar no se inficione!
24. Todo es gala el africano:
su vestido espira olores,
el lunado arco suspende,
y el corvo alfanje depone;
25. tórtolas enamoradas
son sus roncos atambores,
y los volantes de Venus
sus bien seguidos pendones.
26. Desnuda el pecho anda ella,
vuela el cabello sin orden;
si lo abrocha, es con claveles,
con jazmines, si lo coge;

his delights. 19. The hands, then, whose fingers were gods of this life, restore to Medoro new health, redoubled strength, 20. and they give him, as a minimum, her beauty and a kingdom for a dowry, Mars' second envy, Adonis' first delight. 21. A wanton swarm of little Cupids encircle the hut, just as bees do the hollow trunk of the cork-oak. 22. What a lot of knots clumsy Envy is tying on an asp, as she counts the moaning coos of the doves! 23. How well Love chases her away, making a whip of the cord, so that the affair won't become a scandal and the locale be poisoned! 24. The African is all decked out: his clothing breathes fragrances, he hangs up his moon-

27. el pie calza en lazos de oro,
porque la nieve se goce,
y no se vaya por pies
la hermosura del orbe.
28. Todo sirve a los amantes:
plumas les baten, veloces,
airecillos lisonjeros,
si no son murmuradores.
29. Los campos les dan alfombras,
los árboles pabellones,
la apacible fuente sueño,
música los ruiseñores.
30. Los troncos les dan cortezas
en que se guarden sus nombres
mejor que en tablas de mármol
o que en láminas de bronce.
31. No hay verde fresno sin letra,
ni blanco chopo sin mote;
si un valle «Angélica» suena,
otro «Angélica» responde.
32. Cuevas do el silencio apenas
deja que sombras las moren,
profanan con sus abrazos,
a pesar de sus horrores.
33. Choza, pues, tálamo y lecho,
cortesanos labradores,
aires, campos, fuentes, vegas
cuevas, troncos, aves, flores,

shaped bow and lays down his curved cutlass; 25. loving turtledoves are his hoarse drums, and Venus' frills are banners that he follows. 26. She goes around with her breast uncovered, her hair blows disordered; if she buttons it up, it's with carnations, with jasmines if she ties it back. 27. On her feet she ties golden laces, so that their snow may be appreciated, and so that the world's beauty may not run away. 28. Everything is in the lovers' service: swift feathers beat for them breezes that flatter, if they don't murmur [gossip]. 29. The fields give them carpets, the trees pavilions, the quiet spring a sleepy sound, music the nightingales. 30. The tree trunks give them bark on which to record their names better than on marble tablets or on brass plates. 31. No green ash is without its letter, nor white poplar without its emblem; if one valley resounds with "Angelica," another replies "Angelica." 32. Caves in which the silence hardly permits shadows to dwell, they profane with their embraces, despite the caves' gloom. 33. Hut, then, and wedding bed, courtly farmers, breezes, fields, springs, meadows, caves, tree trunks,

34. fresnos, chopos, montes, valles,
contestes de estos amores:
¡el cielo os guarde, si puede,
de las locuras del Conde!
[1602]

ROMANCE XXXII

(amoroso)

1. Servía en Orán al Rey
un español con dos lanzas,
y con el alma y la vida
a una gallarda africana,
2. tan noble como hermosa,
tan amante como amada,
con quien estaba una noche,
cuando tocaron al arma.
3. Trescientos cenetes eran
de este rebato la causa,
que los rayos de la luna
descubrieron sus adargas;
4. las adargas avisaron
a las mudas atalayas,
las atalayas los fuegos,
los fuegos a las campanas;
5. y ellas al enamorado,
que en los brazos de su dama
oyó el militar estruendo
de las trompas y las cajas.

birds, flowers, 34. ash trees, poplars, mountains, valleys, fellow-witnesses of their love: may heaven protect you, if it can, from the mad deeds of the Count [Orlando, Angelica's Christian lover]!

BALLAD XXXII (LOVE): 1. In Oran a Spaniard was serving the king with two lances, and with his soul and life an attractive African girl, 2. as noble as she was beautiful, as loving as she was beloved, with whom he was one night when they sounded the call to arms. 3. Three hundred tribesmen were the cause of this alarm, for the rays of the moon had discovered their shields; 4. the shields notified the mute watchtowers, the towers the flames, and the flames the bells; 5. and these notified the lover, who in the arms of his lady heard the military uproar of the trumpets and drums. 6. The spurs of

6. Espuelas de honor le pican
y freno de amor le para;
no salir es cobardía,
ingratitud es dejalla.
7. Del cuello pendiente ella,
viéndole tomar la espada,
con lágrimas y suspiros
le dice aquestas palabras:
8. «Salid al campo, señor,
bañen mis ojos la cama;
que ella me será también,
sin vos, campo de batalla.
9. Vestíos y salid apriesa,
que el General os aguarda;
yo os hago a vos mucha sobra
y vos a él mucha falta.
10. Bien podéis salir desnudo,
pues mi llanto no os ablanda;
que tenéis de acero el pecho
y no habéis menester armas.»
11. Viendo el español brioso
cuánto le detiene y habla,
le dice así: «Mi señora,
tan dulce como enojada,
12. porque con honra y amor
yo me quede, cumpla y vaya,
vaya a los moros el cuerpo,

honor prick him, and the reins of love restrain him; not to leave is cowardice, it is ingratitude to leave her. 7. She, hanging from his neck, seeing him take his sword, with tears and sighs speaks to him these words: 8. "Go out on the field, sir, and let my eyes bathe the bed; for it too will be for me, without you, a battlefield. 9. Get dressed and go out quickly, for the general is waiting; I'm quite superfluous to you, and you are quite necessary to him. 10. You can easily go out naked, for my tears do not soften you; for you have a breast of steel and you don't need armor." 11. The lively Spaniard, seeing how she holds him back and talks, speaks to her as follows: "My lady, as sweet as you are angry, 12. in order for me with honor and with love to stay, to do my duty, and to go, let my body go to the Moors and let

y quede con vos el alma.
13. Concededme, dueño mío,
licencia para que salga
al rebato en vuestro nombre,
y en vuestro nombre combata».
[1587]

ROMANCILLO XLIX

(amoroso)

La más bella niña
de nuestro lugar,
hoy viuda y sola,
y ayer por casar,
viendo que sus ojos
a la guerra van,
a su madre dice,
que escucha su mal:
Dejadme llorar
orillas del mar.

Pues me distes, madre,
en tan tierna edad
tan corto el placer,
tan largo el pesar,
y me cautivastes
de quien hoy se va
y lleva las llaves
de mi libertad:
dejadme llorar
orillas del mar.

my soul stay with you. 13. Grant me, my mistress, leave to go out to the attack in your name, and in your name to combat."

BALLAD XLIX (LOVE): The most beautiful girl in our village, today a widow and alone, and yesterday not yet married, seeing that her beloved is going off to war, says to her mother, who listens to her plaint: *Let me weep beside the sea.* Since you gave me, mother, at so tender an age so brief a pleasure, so long a suffering, and you enslaved me to him who today is going away and taking with him the keys to my freedom: *let me weep beside the sea.* From today on let my eyes change to weeping their pleasant task of sweetly

En llorar conviertan
mis ojos, de hoy más,
el sabroso oficio
del dulce mirar,
pues que no se pueden
mejor ocupar,
yéndose a la guerra
quien era mi paz:
dejadme llorar
orillas del mar.

No me pongáis freno
ni queráis culpar;
que lo uno es justo,
lo otro por demás.
Si me queréis bien,
no me hagáis mal;
harto peor fuera
morir y callar:
dejadme llorar
orillas del mar.

Dulce madre mía,
¿quién no llorará,
aunque tenga el pecho
como un pedernal,
y no dará voces
viendo marchitar
los más verdes años
de mi mocedad?
Dejadme llorar
orillas del mar.

glancing, since they can't be used for anything better, with him who was my peace going off to war: *let me weep beside the sea.* Don't restrain me or try to blame me; the former would be just, the latter excessive. If you love me well, don't do me harm; it would be much worse to keep quiet and die: *let me weep beside the sea.* Sweet mother of mine, tell me who will not weep, even if he has a heart as hard as flint, and who will not cry out when he sees withering away the greenest years of my youth? *Let me weep beside*

Váyanse las noches,
pues ido se han
los ojos que hacían
los míos velar;
váyanse y no vean
tanta soledad,
después que en mi lecho
sobra la mitad.
Dejadme llorar
orillas del mar.

[1580]

Lope de Vega

(1562–1635)

ROMANCES PRIMEROS

A Filis

[XII]

Hortelano era Belardo
de las huertas de Valencia,
que los trabajos obligan
a lo que el hombre no piensa.
Pasado el hebrero loco,
flores para mayo siembra,

the sea. Let the nights go away, for the eyes have gone away which used to keep mine awake; let them go away and not see so much solitude, now that half of my bed is superfluous. *Let me weep beside the sea.*

EARLY BALLADS, *To Phyllis,* [*XII*]*:* Belardo [Lope] was a farmer on the farms of Valencia, for troubles oblige a man to do things that he hasn't planned on. After February's bad weather, he plants flowers for May, for

que quiere que su esperanza
dé fruto a la primavera.
El trébol para las niñas
pone al lado de la huerta,
por que la fruta de amor
de las tres hojas aprenda.
Albahacas amarillas,
a partes verdes y secas,
trasplanta para casadas
que pasan ya de los treinta;
y para las viudas pone
muchos lirios y verbena,
porque lo verde del alma
encubre la saya negra.
Torongil para muchachas
de aquellas que ya comienzan
a deletrear mentiras,
que hay poca verdad en ellas.
El apio a las opiladas
y a las preñadas almendras;
para melindrosas cardos
y ortigas para las viejas.
Lechugas para briosas
que cuando llueve se queman,
mastuerzo para las frías
y ajenjos para las feas.
De los vestidos que un tiempo
trujo en la Corte, de seda,

he wants his hope to bear fruit in the spring. Clover for young girls he puts in at the edge of the garden, so that love's offspring may learn from the three leaves. Yellow basil, partly fresh and partly dry, he transplants for married women who are over thirty; and for widows he puts in many lilies and verbena, because their souls' youthfulness is concealed by their black dresses. Lemon balm for young ladies who are already learning to tell lies, for there is little truth in them. Celery for the sallow sick, and almonds for the pregnant; for the prudish, nettles, and thistles for the old. Lettuce for the lively who warm up when it rains, peppergrass for the frigid, and wormwood for the ugly. Out of the silk clothes that he had once worn at Court

ha hecho para las aves
un espantajo de higuera:
las lechuguillazas grandes,
almidonadas y tiesas,
y el sombrero boleado,
que adornan cuello y cabeza,
y sobre un jubón de raso
la más guarnecida cuera,
sin olvidarse las calzas
españolas y tudescas.
Andando regando un día,
vióle en medio de la higuera,
y riéndose de velle,
le dice desta manera:
—¡O ricos despojos
de mi edad primera,
y trofeos vivos
de esperanzas muertas!
¡Qué bien parecéis
de dentro y de fuera,
sobre que habéis dado
fin a mi tragedia!
¡Galas y penachos
de mi soldadesca,
un tiempo colores
y agora tristeza!
Un día de Pascua
os llevé a mi aldea
por galas costosas,
invenciones nuevas.
Desde su balcón

[in Madrid] he made for the birds a figtree scarecrow: the big ruffed collar, starched and stiff, and the round hat, that adorn one's neck and head, and upon a satin blouse the fanciest leather jacket, without forgetting his tights, both Spanish-style and German. One day as he was watering, he saw it in the middle of the figtree, and laughing at the sight, he speaks to it as follows: "Oh rich spoils of my youth, and living trophies of hopes that are dead! How well you look inside and out, after having brought my tragedy to an end! Pomps and plumes of my soldierly career, once bright colors and now mere sadness! One holiday I wore you to my village as a display of wealth and the latest fashion. From her balcony a maiden ["Belisa," Isabel

me vió una doncella
con el pecho blanco
y la ceja negra.
Dejóse burlar;
caséme con ella,
que es bien que se paguen
tan honrosas deudas.
Supo mi delito
aquella morena
que reinaba en Troya
cuando fué mi reina.
Hizo de mis cosas
una grande hoguera,
tomando venganzas
en plumas y letras.

A Belisa

[II]

—Mira, Zaide, que te aviso
que no pases por mi calle
ni hables con mis mujeres,
ni con mis cautivos trates,
ni preguntes en qué entiendo
ni quién viene a visitarme,
qué fiestas me dan contento
o qué colores me aplacen;
basta que son por tu causa
las que en el rostro me salen,
corrida de haber mirado

de Urbina] saw me, with her white breast and black eyebrows. She let me seduce her; I married her, for it is well to pay such debts of honor. My crime reached the ears of that brunette who reigned in Troy when she was my queen ["Filis," Helen, Elena Osorio]. She made a great bonfire out of my things, avenging herself with pen and ink [law suit, leading to exile in Valencia]." *To Belisa* [*II*]: "Look, Zaide [Lope's Moorish pseudonym], I'm warning you not to go down my street or to talk to my women, or to have anything to do with my slaves, or to ask what I'm up to or who comes to visit me, what entertainments give me pleasure or what colors I like; it's enough for you to have caused the blushing colors of my face, angry to have

moro que tan poco sabe.
Confieso que eres valiente,
que hiendes, rajas y partes,
y que has muerto más cristianos
que tienes gotas de sangre;
que eres gallardo ginete,
que danzas, cantas y tañes,
gentil hombre, bien criado
cuanto puede imaginarse;
blanco, rubio por extremo,
señalado por linaje,
el gallo de las bravatas,
la nata de los donaires;
y pierdo mucho en perderte
y gano mucho en amarte,
y que si nacieras mudo,
fuera posible adorarte;
y por este inconveniente
determino de dejarte,
que eres pródigo de lengua
y amargan tus libertades;
y habrá menester ponerte
quien quisiere sustentarte
un alcázar en el pecho
y en los labios un alcaide.
Mucho pueden con las damas
los galanes de tus partes,
porque los quieren briosos,
que rompan y que desgarren;
mas tras esto, Zaide amigo,

looked at such an ignorant Moor. I admit that you're brave, that you rend and slash and tear, and that you've killed more Christians than you have drops of blood; that you're a handsome horseman, that you dance and sing and play, a gentleman as well-bred as can be imagined; fair, extremely blond, of noble lineage, the cock of the strutting walk, the perfection of charm; and I lose a lot in losing you, and I gain a lot in loving you, and if you had been born dumb, it would be possible to adore you; it's just because of this defect that I'm deciding to leave you, that you're prodigal with words, and your liberties cause trouble; and anyone who wants to put up with you will have to build a prison around your heart and put a jailer in charge of your lips. The ladies are much taken with gifted young men like you, for they like them lively, aggressive and destructive; but after this, friend Zaide, if they

si algún convite te hacen
al plato de sus favores,
quieren que comas y calles.
Costoso fué el que te hice;
venturoso fueras, Zaide,
si conservarme supieras
como supiste obligarme.
Apenas fuiste salido
de los jardines de Tarfe
cuando hiciste de la tuya
y de mi desdicha alarde.
A un morito mal nacido
me dicen que le enseñaste
la trenza de los cabellos
que te puse en el turbante;
no quiero que me la vuelvas
ni quiero que me la guardes,
mas quiero que entiendas, moro,
que en mi desgracia la traes.
También me certificaron
cómo le desafiaste
por las verdades que dijo,
que nunca fueran verdades.
De mala gana me río:
¡qué donoso disparate!
No guardas tú tu secreto
¿y quieres que otro le guarde?
No quiero admitir disculpa;
otra vez vuelvo a avisarte
que ésta será la postrera

invite you to dine on their favors, they want you to eat and shut up. My invitation to you was expensive; you would be lucky, Zaide, if you knew as well how to keep me as to win me. You had hardly left the Tarfe gardens when you boasted of your luck and mine. They tell me you showed, to a baseborn little Moor, the tresses I put on your turban; I don't want them back, nor do I want you to keep them for me, but I want you to realize, Moor, that it's my misfortune that you have them. They also bore witness as to how you challenged him because of the true words he spoke, which I wish had been false. I'm laughing, but not happily: what ridiculous idiocy! You don't keep your own secrets, and you expect other people to keep them? I won't accept any excuses; once more I warn you that this will be the last time we

que me hables y te hable.—
Dijo la discreta Zaida
a un altivo bencerraje,
y al despedirle repite:
«Quien tal hace, que tal pague».

CANCIONES POPULARES

Canción de velador

Velador que el castillo velas,
vélale bien y mira por tí,
que velando en él me perdí.

Mira las campañas llenas
de tanto enemigo armado.
Ya estoy, amor, desvelado
de velar en las almenas.
Ya que las campanas suenas,
toma ejemplo y mira en mí,
que velando en él me perdí.

Cantar de siega

Blanca me era yo
cuando entré en la siega;
dióme el sol y ya soy morena.
Blanca solía yo ser
antes que a segar viniese
mas no quiso el sol que fuese
blanco el fuego en mi poder.

talk to one another." So spoke bright Zaida [Elena Osorio's Moorish pseudonym] to a haughty Moorish warrior, and as she dismisses him, she repeats: "One bad turn deserves another."

FOLK SONGS, *Watchman's Song:* Watchman watching the castle, watch it well and look out for yourself, for, while watching there, I was destroyed. Look at the countryside, filled with armed enemies. I'm worn out, love, from watching in the turrets. Since the bells are ringing, follow my example and look at me, for, while watching here, I was destroyed. *Reapers' Song:* I was fair when I joined the reapers; the sun struck me, and now I am dark. I used to be fair before I came to reap, but the sun didn't want the fire in my power to be white. In my early youth I was a gleaming lily; the sun

Mi edad al almanecer
era lustrosa azucena;
dióme el sol y ya soy morena.

Serranas

I

—Reverencia os hago,
linda vizcaína,
que no hay en Vitoria
doncella más linda.
Lleváisla del alma
que esos ojos mira,
y esas blancas tocas
son prisiones ricas.
Más preciara haceros
mi querida amiga
que vencer los moros
que a Navarra lidian.
—Id con Dios, el conde;
mirad que soy niña,
y he miedo a los hombres
que andan en la villa.
Si me ve mi madre,
a fe que me riña.
Yo no trato en almas,
sino en almohadillas.
—Dadme vuestra mano;
vámonos, mi vida,
a la mar, que tengo
cuatro naves mías.
—¡Ay Dios, que me fuerzan!
¡Ay Dios, que me obligan!—

struck me, and now I am dark. *Pastorales, I:* "I pay you my respects, pretty Basque girl, for in all Vitoria there's no prettier maiden. You win the respect of my soul, looking at those eyes of yours, and your white headdress is a wonderful imprisonment. I would rather make you my beloved mistress than conquer the Moors fighting in Navarre." "Goodby, sir count; I'm just a little girl, you see, and I'm afraid of the men who go around in this village. If my mother sees me, I'm sure she'll scold me. I don't deal in souls, but in cushions." "Give me your hand; let's go, my love, to the sea, where I have four ships of my own." "Alas, I'm being forced! Alas, they're making me

Tómala en los brazos
y a la mar camina.

II

A caza va el caballero
por los montes de París,
la rienda en la mano izquierda
y en la derecha el neblí.
Pensando va en su señora
que no la ha visto al partir,
porque como era casada,
estaba su esposo allí.
Como va pensando en ella,
olvidado se ha de sí;
los perros siguen las sendas
entre hayas y peñas mil.
El caballo va a su gusto,
que no le quiere regir.
Cuando vuelve el caballero,
hallóse de un monte al fin;
volvió la cabeza al valle
y vió una dama venir,
en el vestido serrana
y en el rostro serafín.

—Por el montecico sola
¿cómo iré?
¡Ay Dios, si me perderé!
¿Cómo iré triste, cuitada,
de aquel ingrato dejada?
Sola, triste, enamorada,
¿dónde iré?

go!" He takes her in his arms and heads for the sea. *II:* The knight goes a-hunting in the woods of Paris, in his left hand the reins and in his right the falcon. He is thinking of his lady whom he didn't see when he left, for since she was married, her husband was there. As he thinks of her, he forgets himself; his dogs follow trails among many trees and rocks. His horse goes where it wants to, for he doesn't try to guide it. When the knight stopped dreaming, he found himself at the top of a hill; he turned his face toward the valley and saw a lady coming, dressed in country clothing and with an angelic face. "Through the hills all alone, how shall I go? Alas, if I should lose my way! How shall I go, sad and suffering, abandoned by that

¡Ay Dios, si me perderé!

—¿Dónde vais, serrana bella,
por este verde pinar?
Si soy hombre y voy perdido,
mayor peligro lleváis.
—Aquí cerca, caballero,
me ha dejado mi galán
por ir a matar un oso
que ese valle abajo está.
—¡Oh, mal haya el caballero
en el monte al lubricán,
que a solas deja su dama
por matar un animal!
Si os place, señora mía,
volved conmigo al lugar,
y porque llueve, podréis
cubriros con mi gabán.—
Perdido se han en el monte
con la mucha obscuridad;
al pie de una parda peña
el alba aguardando están;
la ocasión y la ventura
siempre quieren soledad.

Maya

I

En las mañanicas
del mes de mayo

ungrateful man? All alone, sad and in love, where shall I go? Alas, if I should lose my way!" "Where are you going, beautiful country lass, in this green grove of pines? If I as a man am lost, you're in greater danger." "Near here, sir knight, my sweetheart left me to go kill a bear down in that valley." "Oh, curst be the knight in the mountains at twilight who leaves his lady all alone to kill an animal! If you wish, my lady, return to the village with me, and since it's raining, you may cover yourself with my cloak." They got lost in the woods, with all that darkness; at the foot of a black cliff they are waiting for dawn; opportunity and good fortune always call for solitude. *May Song I:* In the early mornings of the month of May, the

cantan los ruiseñores,
retumba el campo.

En las mañanicas,
como son frescas,
cubren ruiseñores
las alamedas.
Ríense las fuentes
tirando perlas
a las florecillas
que están más cerca.
Vístense las plantas
de varias sedas,
que sacar colores
poco les cuesta.
Los campos alegran
tapetes varios,
cantan los ruiseñores,
retumba el campo.

Sale el mayo hermoso
con los frescos vientos,
que le ha dado marzo,
de céfiros bellos.
Las lluvias de abril
flores le trujeron:
púsose guirnaldas
en rojos cabellos.
Los que eran amantes
amaron de nuevo
y los que no amaban
a buscarlo fueron.
Y luego que vieron

nightingales sing and the countryside echoes. In the early mornings, since they are cool, nightingales fill the poplar groves. The springs laugh as they throw pearls at the little flowers that are closest. The plants dress up in different silks, for it doesn't bother them to blush with colors. The fields are bright with different carpets, the nightingales sing and the countryside echoes. May begins lovely with the cool breezes, contributed by March, of pleasant zephyrs. The rains of April have brought on the flowers. May has put garlands on her red hair. Those who were lovers have loved anew, and those who didn't know love have gone to look for it. And as soon as

mañanas de mayo,
cantan los ruiseñores,
retumba el campo.

Letras Varias

V

Claros aires de Valencia
que dais a la mar embates,
a sus verdes plantas flores
y a sus naranjos azâres;
huéspedes frescos de abril,
instrumentos de sus aves,
campanitas del amor
que despertáis los amantes:
llevad mis suspiros,
aires suaves,
al azâr de unas manos
que en ellas nacen.

VII

No ser, Luscinda, tus bellas
niñas formalmente estrellas
bien puede ser;
pero que en su claridad
no tengan cierta deidad,
no puede ser.

Que su boca celestial
no sea el mismo coral,
bien puede ser;
mas que no exceda la rosa
en ser roja y olorosa,

they saw the mornings of May, the nightingales sing and the countryside echoes. *Various Songs, V:* Bright breezes of Valencia raising breakers on the sea, putting flowers on the green plants and blossoms on the orange trees; cool April visitors, musical instruments of its birds, little bells of love awakening the lovers: take my sighs, gentle breezes, to the orange-blossom hands that gave them birth. *VII:* That the lovely pupils of your eyes, Luscinda, are not, strictly speaking, stars, it may well be; but that in their brightness there dwell not a certain divinity, it cannot be. That her heavenly mouth is not real coral, may well be; but that it not be redder and more

no puede ser.

Que no sea el blanco pecho
de nieve o cristales hecho
bien puede ser;
mas que no exceda en blancura
cristales y nieve pura,
no puede ser.

Que no sea sol ni Apolo,
ángel puro y fénix solo
bien puede ser;
pero que de ángel no tenga
lo que con ángel convenga,
no puede ser.

Que no sean lirios sus venas
ni sus manos azucenas,
bien puede ser,
mas que en ellas no se vean
cuantas gracias se desean,
no puede ser.

IX

Si os partiéredes al alba,
quedito, pasito, amor,
no espantéis al ruiseñor.

Si os levantáis de mañana
de los brazos que os desean,
porque en los brazos no os vean
de alguna envidia liviana,
pisad con planta de lana,
quedito, pasito, amor,
no espantéis al ruiseñor.

fragrant than the rose, cannot be. That her white breast is not made of snow or crystal, may well be; but that it not be whiter than crystal and pure snow, cannot be. That she is not the sun or Apollo, a genuine angel and unique phoenix, may well be; but that she not have those angelic qualities which befit an angel, cannot be. That her veins are not irises nor her hands lilies, may well be; but that in them be not found all desirable graces, cannot be. *IX:* If you leave at dawn, be quiet, step softly, my love; don't scare the nightingale. If in the morning you arise from the arms that desire you, so as not to be discovered in the arms of some casual envy, tread with woolen sole, be quiet, step softly, my love; don't scare the nightingale.

Letrillas jocosas

Mariquita me llaman
los carreteros,
Mariquita me llaman...
voime con ellos.

Lavaréme en el Tajo
muerta de risa,
que el arena en los dedos
me hace cosquillas.

Que no quiero bonetes,
que soy muy boba,
y en andando con picos
me pico toda.

Si te echares al agua,
bien de mis ojos,
llévame en tus brazos,
nademos todos.

Cuantas veces me brindan
tus ojos bellos,
como son de pimienta,
bebo con ellos.

Mi forzado me dice
que no le sigo;
daré viento a las velas
con mis suspiros.

Humorous Songs: Little Mary the cart-men call me, little Mary they call me . . . I'm going away with them. I shall bathe in the Tagus dying with laughter, for the sand between my toes tickles me. I don't want *bonetes* [pointed academic cap], for I am very dumb, and if I wear points, I get piqued all over. If you jump in the water, love of my eyes, take me in your arms and let's both swim together. Whenever your lovely eyes toast me, since they are as piquant as pepper, I drink to them. My galley slave tells me I'm not to go with him; I'll put wind in his sails with my sighs. *Song of Saint John's Eve. II:* The little girl was going off, on St. John's Eve, to find the cool sea

Canción de San Juan

II

Ibase la niña,
noche de San Juan,
a coger los aires
al fresco del mar.
Miraba los remos
que remando van
cubiertos de flores,
flores de azahar.
Salió un caballero
por el arenal,
dijérale amores
cortés y galán.
Respondió la esquiva,
quísola abrazar;
con temor que tiene
huyendo se va.
Salióle al camino
otro por burlar,
las hermosas manos
le quiere tomar.
Entre estos desvíos
perdido se han
sus ricos zarcillos;
vanlos a buscar.
«¡Dejadme llorar
orillas del mar!»
«¡Por aquí, por allí los ví,
por aquí deben de estar!»

breezes. She looked at the oars rowing all covered with flowers, orange blossoms. A gentleman came up along the beach and to her spoke gallant, courtly words of love. She answered evasively, he tried to embrace her; she is so frightened she goes running away. Another one, to tease, stepped out in front of her and tried to take her by her lovely hands. With all this dodging she has lost her costly earrings; they try to find them. "Let me weep beside the sea!" "Over here, over there I saw them, over here they

Lloraba la niña,
no los puede hallar;
danse para ellos,
quiérenla engañar.
«¡Dejadme llorar
orillas del mar!»
«¡Por aquí, por allí los vi,
por aquí deben de estar!»
«Tomad, niña, el oro
y no lloréis más,
que todas las niñas
nacen en tomar,
que las que no toman
después llorarán
el no haber tomado
en su verde edad.»

Seguidillas de la noche
de San Juan

I

Salen de Valencia
noche de San Juan
mil coches de damas
al fresco del mar.
¡Cómo retumban los remos,
madre, en el agua,
con el fresco viento
de la mañana!
Despertad, señora mía,
despertad,

must be!" The little girl was weeping, she can't find them; they offer to hunt for them and try to fool her. "Let me weep beside the sea!" "Over here, over there I saw them, over here they must be!" "Take, little girl, the gold and don't weep any more, for all little girls are born of taking; those who don't take, afterwards weep for not having taken when they were young."

Songs of Saint John's Eve, I: Out of Valencia come on St. John's Eve a thousand ladies' coaches for the cool sea air. How the oars thump, mother, in the water, with the cool morning breeze! Wake up, my lady, wake up,

porque viene el alba
del señor San Juan.

II

Vamos a la playa
noche de San Juan,
que alegra la tierra
y retumba el mar.
En la playa hagamos
fiestas de mil modos,
coronados todos
de verbena y ramos.
A su arena vamos,
noche de San Juan,
que alegra la tierra
y retumba el mar.

SONETOS

Rimas Humanas [1602]

I

Versos de amor, conceptos esparcidos
engendrados del alma en mis cuidados,
partos de mis sentidos abrasados,
con más dolor que libertad nacidos;
expósitos al mundo en que perdidos,
tan rotos anduvistes y trocados
que sólo donde fuistes engendrados
fuérades por la sangre conocidos:
pues que le hurtáis el laberinto a Creta,
a Dédalo los altos pensamientos,
la furia al mar, las llamas al abismo,

for the dawn is coming of St. John's Day. *II:* Let's go to the beach on St. John's Eve, for the earth is gay and the sea echoes. On the beach let's celebrate a thousand ways, all in crowns of verbena and twigs. Let's go to the sand on St. John's Eve, for the earth is gay and the sea echoes.

SONNETS, *Human Rhymes, I:* Poetry of love, random thoughts begotten by my soul upon my worries, offspring of my heated senses, born with more pain than freedom; abandoned to the world, where you were so lost, battered and changed that only where you were begotten would you be recognized as relatives: since you steal Crete's labyrinth, Dedalus's soaring thoughts, the sea's fury and the flames of depths, if that lovely asp does not

si aquel áspid hermoso no os aceta,
dejad la tierra, entretened los vientos,
descansaréis en vuestro centro mismo.

XIV

Vierte racimos la gloriosa palma
y sin amor se pone estéril luto;
Dafne se queja en su laurel sin fruto,
Narciso en blancas hojas se desalma.
Está la tierra sin la lluvia en calma,
viles hierbas produce el campo enjuto;
porque nunca pagó al amor tributo,
gime en su piedra de Anaxarte el alma.
Oro engendra el amor de agua y de arenas;
porque las conchas aman el rocío,
quedan de perlas orientales llenas.
No desprecies, Lucinda hermosa, el mío,
que al trasponer del sol, las azucenas
pierden el lustre y nuestra edad el brío.

LXI

Ir y quedarse y con quedar partirse,
partir sin alma y ir con alma ajena;
oír la dulce voz de una sirena
y no poder del árbol desasirse;
arder como la vela y consumirse
haciendo torres sobre tierna arena;
caer de un cielo y ser demonio en pena
y de serlo jamás arrepentirse;
hablar entre las mudas soledades,

accept you, leave the earth, play with the winds, and you will be resting in your proper element. *XIV:* The glorious palm tree sheds its branches and, without love, clothes itself in sterile mourning; Daphne in her laurel tree fruitlessly complains, Narcissus in white petals sheds his soul. The earth without rain is becalmed, the dry field produces foul weeds; because she refused to pay tribute to love, Anaxarete's soul moans within its stone. The love affair of water and sand begets gold; because oyster shells love the dew, they become pregnant with oriental pearls. Don't scorn my love, beautiful Lucinda, for when the sun sets, the lilies lose their luster and our life its liveliness. *LXI:* To go and yet to stay and staying to go away, to leave without one's soul and to go with another's; to listen to a siren's sweet voice, being unable to free oneself from the mast; to burn like a candle and be consumed, forming castles upon the soft sand; to fall from a heaven and be a devil tormented, and never to repent; to talk in mute solitude, to bor-

pedir prestada sobre fé paciencia
y lo que es temporal llamar eterno;
creer sospechas y negar verdades
es lo que llaman en el mundo ausencia:
fuego en el alma y en la vida infierno.

LXXI

De Europa y Júpiter

Pasando el mar el engañoso toro,
volviendo la cerviz, el pie besaba
de la llorosa ninfa que miraba
perdido de las ropas el decoro.
Entre las aguas y las hebras de oro
ondas el fresco viento levantaba
a quien con los suspiros ayudaba
del mal guardado virginal tesoro.
Cayéronsele a Europa de las faldas
las rosas al decirle el toro amores,
y ella, con el dolor de sus guirnaldas,
dicen que lleno el rostro de colores,
en perlas convirtió sus esmeraldas
y dijo:—¡Ay triste, yo perdí las flores!

LXXVIII

Al triunfo de Judit

Cuelga sangriento de la cama al suelo
el hombro diestro del feroz tirano
que opuesto al muro de Betulia en vano

row patience loaned on faith, and to call what is temporal eternal; to believe suspicions and to deny truths is what in this world is known as absence: fire in one's soul and hell during one's life. *LXXI, On Europa and Jupiter:* Crossing the sea, the deceptive bull, turning his head, was kissing the foot of the weeping nymph as she regarded the lost decorum of her clothes. Among her watery tears and golden hair the fresh wind raised waves, helping her to sigh for the loss of her virginal treasure. Roses had fallen from Europa's skirts when the bull spoke loving words, and she, grieving for her garlands, they say, with blushing face, changed her emeralds [green eyes] into pearls [tears] and said, "Alas, I have lost my flowers!" *LXXVIII, To Judith's Triumph:* Bloodily hangs from the bed to the ground the right shoulder of the ferocious tyrant [Holophernes] who, opposing Bethulia's

despidió contra sí rayos al cielo.
  Revuelto con el ansia el rojo velo
del pabellón a la siniestra mano,
descubre el espectáculo inhumano
del tronco horrible convertido en hielo.
  Vertido Baco el fuerte arnés afea,
los vasos y la mesa derribada;
duermen las guardas que tan mal emplea;
  y sobre la muralla coronada
del pueblo de Israel, la casta hebrea
con la cabeza resplandece armada.

CXXXVII

A la noche

  Noche, fabricadora de embelecos,
loca, imaginativa, quimerista,
que muestras al que en ti su bien conquista
los montes llanos y los mares secos;
  habitadora de celebros huecos,
mecánica, filósofa, alquimista,
encubridora vil, lince sin vista,
espantadiza de tus mismos ecos:
  la sombra, el miedo, el mal se te atribuya,
solícita, poeta, enferma, fría,
manos del bravo y pies del fugitivo.
  Que vele o duerma, media vida es tuya:
si velo, te lo pago con el día,
y si duermo no siento lo que vivo.

wall in vain, to his own hurt threw thunderbolts against heaven. Twisted up in his agony, the red veil of the pavilion reveals, to the left, the cruel spectacle of his horrid trunk now ice-cold. Spilled Bacchus [wine] stains his armor, the glasses and the upset table; the guards sleep whom he so uselessly employs; and upon the serrated wall of the people of Israel the chaste Hebrew woman is resplendently armed with his head. *CXXXVII, To the Night:* Oh night, fabricator of deceptions, mad, fantastic, chimeric, causing him who delights in you to see the mountains as flat and the seas as dry; dweller in empty brains, low engineer, natural philosopher, alchemist, foul accomplice, sightless lynx, scared of your own echoes: may you be considered responsible for darkness, fear and evil, you solicitor, poetess, sick and frigid woman, with ruffian's hands and fugitive's feet. Whether awake or asleep, half my life belongs to you: if I stay awake, I repay you the following day, and if I sleep, I'm not aware that I am alive. *CLXXXVIII:* Free my gentle

CLXXXVIII

Suelta mi manso, mayoral extraño,
pues otro tienes de tu igual decoro;
deja la prenda que en el alma adoro,
perdida por tu bien y por mi daño.
Ponle su esquila de labrado estaño
y no le engañen tus collares de oro;
toma en albricias este blanco toro
que a las primeras yerbas cumple un año.
Si pides señas, tiene el vellocino
pardo, encrespado, y los ojuelos tiene
como durmiendo en regalado sueño.
Si piensas que nó soy su dueño, Alcino,
suelta y verásle si a mi choza viene,
que aun tienen sal las manos de su dueño.

CLXXXIX

Querido manso mío que venistes
por sal mil veces junto aquella roca
y en mi grosera mano vuestra boca
y vuestra lengua de clavel pusistes,
¿por qué montañas ásperas subistes
que tal selvatiquez el alma os toca?
¿Qué furia os hizo condición tan loca
que la memoria y la razón perdistes?
Paced la anacardina por que os vuelva
de ese crüel y interesable sueño,
y no bebáis del agua del olvido.

sheep, you alien shepherd, for you have another one of your own kind; let go the creature which my soul adores, whose loss is your gain and my disaster. Put on her the bell of wrought tin, and don't fool her with your golden necklaces; accept in exchange this white bull which is a year old this spring. If you demand identification, she has dark curly fleece and little eyes that look pleasantly sleepy. If you think I am not her owner, Alcino, free her and you'll see if she comes to my hut, for her owner's hands still have salt on them. *CLXXXIX:* Dear tame sheep of mine who came for salt many times near that rock, putting into my coarse hand your mouth and carnation tongue, what steep mountains have you climbed to make your soul so wild? What rage has driven you so mad as to lose your memory and reason? Graze on the memory plant [cashew?] to bring you out of that cruel, mercenary slumber, and don't drink of the water of oblivion. This is your

Aquí está vuestra vega, monte y selva;
yo soy vuestro pastor y vos mi dueño,
vos mi ganado y yo vuestro perdido.

CXCI

Es la mujer del hombre lo más bueno,
y locura decir que lo más malo;
su vida suele ser y su regalo,
su muerte suele ser y su veneno.
Cielo a los ojos cándido y sereno,
que muchas veces al infierno igualo,
por raro al mundo su valor señalo;
por falso al hombre su rigor condeno.
Ella nos da su sangre, ella nos cría;
no ha hecho el cielo cosa más ingrata;
es un ángel y a veces una harpía;
quiere, aborrece, trata bien, maltrata,
y es la mujer, al fin, como sangría,
que a veces da salud y a veces mata.

Rimas Sacras [1614]

I

Cuando me paro a contemplar mi estado
y a ver los pasos por donde he venido,
me espanto de que un hombre tan perdido
a conocer su error haya llegado.
Cuando miro los años que he pasado

meadow, hill and woods; I am your shepherd and you my owner, you my flock and I your lost one. *CXCI:* Woman is the best of man, and it's madness to say the worst; she is his life and his delight, she is his death and poison. For one's eyes a heaven candid and serene, which I often equate with hell, I point to her worth as something rare in this world; I condemn as false her cruelty to man. She gives us her blood, she nurses us; heaven has created nothing more unpleasant; she's an angel and at times a harpy; she loves, hates, treats well, mistreats, and, in sum, woman is like a bleeding, which sometimes cures and sometimes kills. *Sacred Rhymes, I:* When I pause to consider my state and to look at the road along which I have come, I am amazed that so misguided a man has reached the point of recognizing his error. When I see the years I've spent ignoring divine reason, I recognize

la divina razón puesta en olvido,
conozco que piedad del cielo ha sido
no haberme en tanto mal precipitado.
Entré por laberinto tan extraño
fiando al débil hilo de la vida
el tarde conocido desengaño,
mas, de tu luz mi escuridad vencida,
el monstruo muerto de mi ciego engaño,
vuelve a la patria la razón perdida.

XIV

Pastor que con tus siblos amorosos
me despertaste del profundo sueño;
tú que hiciste cayado de ese leño
en que tiendes los brazos poderosos:
vuelve los ojos a mi fe piadosos,
pues te confieso por mi amor y dueño
y la palabra de seguirte empeño
tus dulces silbos y tus pies hermosos.
Oye, pastor, pues por amores mueres,
no te espante el rigor de mis pecados,
pues tan amigo de rendidos eres.
Espera, pues, y escucha mis cuidados...
Pero ¿cómo te digo que me esperes
si estás para esperar los pies clavados?

that it has been by the grace of heaven that I have not plunged headlong down the cliffs of evil. I entered this strange labyrinth trusting the weak thread of my life to lead me to the undeception which I finally realize, but, my darkness having been vanquished by your light, and slaughtered the monster of my blind deception, lost reason returns to its heavenly home. *XIV:* Shepherd who with your fond whistling calls have awakened me from deep sleep; you who have made a crook out of that piece of wood upon which you stretch out your powerful arms: turn your kind eyes upon my faith, for I confess you as my lord and love and pledge you my word to follow your sweet whistling calls and your beautiful feet. Listen, shepherd, since you die for love, don't be frightened at the evil of my sins, for you are such a friend of the helpless. Wait, then, and hear my troubles . . . But why should I tell you to wait for me if you are constrained to wait by the nails through your

XVIII

¿Qué tengo yo que mi amistad procuras?
¿Qué interés se te sigue, Jesús mío,
que a mi puerta, cubierto de rocío,
pasas las noches del invierno escuras?
¡Oh, cuánto fueron mis entrañas duras,
pues no te abrí! ¡Qué estraño desvarío
si de mi ingratitud el yelo frío
secó las llagas de tus plantas puras!
¡Cuántas veces el ángel me decía:
Alma, asómate agora a la ventana,
verás con cuánto amor llamar porfía!
¡Y cuántas, hermosura soberana:
Mañana le abriremos—respondía—,
para lo mismo responder mañana!

XLVI

No sabe qué es amor quien no te ama,
celestial hermosura, esposo bello;
tu cabeza es de oro, y tu cabello
como el cogollo que la palma enrama;
tu boca como lirio, que derrama
licor al alba; de marfil tu cuello;
tu mano el torno, y en su palma el sello,
que el alma por disfraz jacintos llama.
¡Ay Dios! ¿en qué pensé cuando, dejando
tanta belleza y las mortales viendo,

feet? *XVIII:* What do I have that you seek my friendship? What profit is there in it for you, my Jesus, that at my door, covered with dew, you should spend the dark winter nights? Oh, how hard my heart was, for me not to open to you! What a strange madness if the cold ice of my ingratitude froze the wounds of your pure feet! How often my angel said to me, "Soul, come now to the window and you will see how lovingly he persists in knocking!" And how often, oh sovereign beauty, I would reply, "I will open to him tomorrow," only to make the same reply again the following day! *XLVI:* He doesn't know what love is who doesn't love you, celestial beauty, handsome bridegroom; your head is of gold, and your hair like the crown of the palm tree, covered with branches; your mouth like a lily, overflowing with nectar at dawn; your neck is ivory; your hand is the potter's wheel, and on its palm the seal, which the soul deceptively calls hyacinths. Alas, what did I think of when, abandoning such beauty and looking at mortal

perdí lo que pudiera estar gozando?
Mas si del tiempo que perdí me ofendo,
tal prisa me daré, que un hora amando
venza los años que pasé fingiendo.

La Circe [1624]

XXXII

De la abrasada eclíptica que ignora
intrépido corrió las líneas de oro
mozo infeliz, a quien el verde coro
vió sol, rayo tembló, difunto llora.
Centellas, perlas no, vertió el aurora,
llamas el pez austral, bombas el toro,
etnas la nieve del Atlante moro,
la mar incendios y cenizas Flora.
Así me levanté, y a la presencia
llegué de un sol; así también me asombra
cayendo en noche eterna de su ausencia.
Así a los dos el Po Faetontes nombra,
pero muertos con esta diferencia,
que él quiso ser el sol y yo la sombra.

beauties, I lost what I could have been enjoying? But although I am angry at the time I've lost, I shall make such haste that one hour of loving will outweigh the years I've spent pretending. *Circe, XXXII:* The golden lines of the blazing ecliptic, unfamiliar to him, are followed in intrepid haste by the unhappy youth [Phaeton], whom the green chorus [his sisters] beheld as the sun, trembled at as a thunderbolt, and weeps over when dead. Sparks, not pearls, were shed by the dawn, flames by Piscis Australis, bombs by Taurus, volcanos by the snows of African Atlas, conflagrations by the sea, and ashes by Flora. Thus I soared and reached the presence of a sun; thus also am I overshadowed as I plunge into the eternal night of its absence. Thus the Po names us both Phaetons, but we died with this difference, that he wanted to be the sun and I the shade. *Divine Triumphs,*

Triunfos Divinos
Temores en el favor

Cuando en mis manos, rey eterno, os miro,
y la cándida víctima levanto,
de mi atrevida indignidad me espanto
y la piedad de vuestro pecho admiro.
Tal vez el alma con temor retiro,
tal vez la doy al amoroso llanto,
que arrepentido de ofenderos tanto
con ansias temo y con dolor suspiro.
Volved los ojos a mirarme humanos
que por las sendas de mi error siniestras
me despeñaron pensamientos vanos;
no sean tantas las miserias nuestras
que a quien os tuvo en sus indignas manos
vos le dejéis de las divinas vuestras.
[1625]

El Laurel de Apolo

—Boscán, tarde llegamos. ¿Hay posada?
—Llamad desde la posta, Garcilaso.
—¿Quién es? —Dos caballeros del Parnaso.
—No hay donde nocturnar palestra armada.
—No entiendo lo que dice la criada.
Madona, ¿qué decís? —Que afecten paso,
que obstenta limbos el mentido ocaso
y el sol depinge la porción rosada.

Fear of grace: When in my hands, Eternal King, I look at you and elevate the gleaming Host, I am aghast at my daring and unworthiness, and I admire the mercy of your heart. Sometimes I fearfully withdraw my soul, sometimes I surrender it to tears of love, because, repenting of having offended you so often, I anxiously fear and painfully sigh. Turn your kind eyes and look upon me, for down the sinister path of my error I was hurled by vain thoughts; don't let my wretchedness be so great that he who has held you in his unworthy hands should be abandoned by the hands of God. *Apollo's Laurels:* "Boscán, we've come too late. Is there a vacant room?" "Call from the stable, Garcilaso." "Who is it?" "Two gentlemen from Parnassus." "There is no lectern erected whereon to nocturnate." "I don't understand what the servant says. My lady, what did you say?" "That you should ambulate for nimbuses are displayed by the deceptive sunset and the sun is

—¿Estás en ti, mujer? —Negóse al tino
el ambulante huésped—. ¡Que en tan poco
tiempo tal lengua entre cristianos haya!
Boscán, perdido habemos el camino;
preguntad por Castilla, que estoy loco
o no habemos salido de Vizcaya.

[1630]

La Dorotea

Canta pájaro amante en la enramada
selva a su amor, que por el verde suelo
no ha visto el cazador que con desvelo
le está escuchando, la ballesta armada.
Tírale, yerra, vuela y la turbada
voz en el pico transformada en yelo,
vuelve y de ramo en ramo acorta el vuelo
por no alejarse de la prenda amada.
Desta suerte el amor canta en el nido;
mas luego que los celos que recela
le tiran flechas de temor de olvido,
huye, teme, sospecha, inquiere, cela
y hasta que ve que el cazador es ido,
de pensamiento en pensamiento vuela.

[1632]

broidering the pink portion." "Are you in your right mind, woman?" "The wayfaring stranger is the one who is off the track." "How short a time it's taken for such a language to develop in our own country! Boscán, we've lost our way; ask the way to Castile, for either I'm crazy or we haven't yet left the Basque country." *La Dorotea:* A lovebird sings in the leafy woods to his love, for he doesn't see on the green ground the hunter who alertly listens to him with crossbow cocked. He shoots and misses; the bird flies off, with upset voice frozen in his beak, returns, and takes short flights from branch to branch so as not to leave behind his dearest love. Thus love sings in its nest; but then when suspicious jealousy shoots at him arrows of the fear of being forgotten, he flies away, fears, suspects, inquires, spies, and until he sees that the hunter has gone, flits from thought to thought. *Unex-*

Soneto de repente

Un soneto me manda hacer Violante,
que en mi vida me he visto en tanto aprieto;
catorce versos dicen que es soneto:
burla burlando van los tres delante.
Yo pensé que no hallara consonante
y estoy a la mitad de otro cuarteto,
mas si me veo en el primer terceto,
no hay cosa en los cuartetos que me espante.
Por el primer terceto voy entrando,
y parece que entré con pie derecho,
pues fin con este verso le voy dando.
Ya estoy en el segundo, y aun sospecho
que voy los trece versos acabando;
contad si son catorce, y está hecho.

LA ARCADIA

Canción III

¡Oh libertad preciosa,
no comparada al oro
ni al bien mayor de la espaciosa tierra;
más rica y más gozosa
que el precioso tesoro
que el mar del sur entre su nácar cierra!
Con armas, sangre y guerra,
con las vidas y famas
conquistada en el mundo;

pected Sonnet: Violante orders me to write a sonnet, and I've never been in such a tight spot; they say a sonnet is fourteen lines: just fooling around, three precede this one. I thought I wouldn't find a rhyme and I'm in the middle of another quatrain, but if I reach the first tercet, there's nothing in the quatrains that can frighten me. I'm beginning the first tercet, and it seems that I started on the right foot, for with this line I'm bringing it to an end. Now I'm in the second, and I even suspect that I'm finishing thirteen lines; count to see if there are fourteen, and it's done.

ARCADIA, *Song III:* Oh precious liberty, not to be compared with gold or the greatest possession of the spacious earth; more valuable and enjoyable than the precious treasure which the southern sea encloses within its mother-of-pearl! By arms, blood and war, by lives and reputations won in this world;

paz dulce, amor profundo,
que el mal apartas y a tu bien nos llamas:
en ti sola se anida
oro, tesoro, paz, bien, gloria y vida.
Cuando de las humanas
tinieblas, vi del cielo
la luz, principio de mis dulces días,
aquellas tres hermanas
que nuestro humano velo
tejiendo llevan por inciertas vías,
las duras penas mías
trocaron en la gloria
que en libertad poseo,
con siempre igual deseo;
donde verá por mi dichosa historia,
quien más leyere en ella,
que es dulce libertad lo menos della.
Yo, pues, señor exento
desta montaña y prado,
gozo la gloria y libertad que tengo;
soberbio pensamiento
jamás ha derribado
la vida humilde y pobre que entretengo.
Cuando a las manos vengo
con el muchacho ciego,
haciendo rostro embisto,
venzo, triunfo y resisto
la flecha, el arco, la ponzoña, el fuego,
y con libre albedrío
lloro el ajeno mal y canto el mío.

sweet peace, deep love, keeping away evil and calling us to your joy: in you alone are nestled gold, treasure, peace, joy, glory and life. When emerging from human shadows I saw the light of heaven, the beginning of my pleasant life, those three sisters [the Fates] who by spinning take our human veil along uncertain roads, exchanged my painful suffering for the glory which I possess in liberty, with desires always balanced; wherein he who reads further in my happy story will see that sweet liberty is the least of it. I, then, as exempt lord of this mountain and meadow, enjoy the glory and liberty that I have; a haughty thought has never turned upside down the humble, simple life I lead. When I come to blows with the blind lad [Cupid, love], I face him and charge, I conquer, triumph and prevail over his arrow, bow, poison, fire, and with my free will I weep for others' misfortune and celebrate

Cuando el aurora baña
con helado rocío
de aljófar celestial el monte y prado,
salgo de mi cabaña,
riberas deste río,
a dar el nuevo pasto a mi ganado;
y cuando el sol dorado
muestra sus fuerzas graves,
al sueño el pecho inclino
debajo un sauce o pino,
oyendo el son de las parleras aves,
o ya gozando el aura,
donde el perdido aliento se restaura.

Cuando la noche fría
con su estrellado manto
el claro día en su tiniebla encierra,
y suena en la espesura
el tenebroso canto
de los nocturnos hijos de la tierra,
al pie de aquesta sierra
con rústicas palabras
mi ganadillo cuento,
y el corazón, contento
del gobierno de ovejas y de cabras,
la temerosa cuenta
del cuidadoso rey me representa.

Aquí la verde pera
con la manzana hermosa,
de gualda y roja sangre matizada,
y de color de cera

my own. When dawn bathes in icy dew of heavenly pearls the mountain and meadow, I come out of my cabin beside this river to let my cattle graze on the new grass; and when the golden sun displays his harshest powers, I incline my breast in sleep beneath a willow or pine, hearing the sound of the chattering birds, or else enjoying the breeze, which restores the breath I've lost. When cold night with her starry mantle encloses bright day in her shadows, and there resounds in the thicket the shadowy song of the nocturnal offspring of earth, at the foot of this mountain range with rustic words I count my cattle, and my heart, satisfied with the management of sheep and goats, brings to mind the fearful accounting of the care-worn king. Here the green pear with the lovely apple, shaded with yellow and red blood, and the

la cermeña olorosa
tengo, y la endrina de color morada;
aquí de la enramada
parra que al olmo enlaza
melosas uvas cojo,
y en cantidad recojo,
al tiempo que las ramas desenlaza
el caluroso estío,
membrillos que coronan este río.
No me da descontento
el hábito costoso
que de lascivo el pecho noble infama;
es mi dulce sustento
del campo generoso
estas silvestres frutas que derrama;
mi regalada cama
de blandas pieles y hojas,
que algún rey la envidiara,
y de ti, fuente clara,
que bullendo el arena y agua arrojas,
estos cristales puros,
sustentos pobres, pero bien seguros.
Estése el cortesano
procurando a su gusto
la blanda cama y el mejor sustento;
bese la ingrata mano
del poderoso injusto,
formando torres de esperanza al viento;
viva y muera sediento
por el honroso oficio:
y goce yo del suelo,

wax-colored fragrant little pear I have, and the purple-colored sloe; here from the branching vine which entwines the elm I pick honeyed grapes, and in quantity I collect, when hot summer loosens the branches, quinces that encircle this river. I am not made unhappy by the costly clothing which defames as lascivious the noble breast; my sweet sustenance is these wild fruits poured out by the abundant countryside; my comfortable bed of soft skins and leaves, the envy of some king, and from you, clear spring, which bubbles up sand and water, these pure crystals [drops] [are my] sustenance simple, but quite secure. Let the courtier stay there, looking for a soft bed and the best sustenance to suit his taste; let him kiss the ungrateful hand of the unjust man of power, building hopeful castles in the wind; let him live and die thirsting for the honorary appointment: and let me enjoy the soil,

al aire, al sol y al hielo
ocupado en mi rústico ejercicio,
que más vale pobreza
en paz que en guerra mísera riqueza.
 Ni temo al poderoso
ni al rico lisonjeo,
ni soy camaleón del que gobierna;
ni me tiene envidioso
la ambición y deseo
de ajena gloria ni de fama eterna.
Carne sabrosa y tierna,
vino aromatizado,
pan blanco de aquel día,
en prado, en fuente fría,
halla un pastor con hambre fatigado;
que el grande y el pequeño
somos iguales lo que dura el sueño.

[1598]

LOS PASTORES DE BELÉN
[1612]
Romance VIII

 La niña a quien dijo el ángel
que estaba de gracia llena,
cuando de ser de Dios madre
le trujo tan altas nuevas,
ya le mira en un pesebre
llorando lágrimas tiernas,
que obligándose a ser hombre,
también se obliga a sus penas.

busy in the breeze, sun, and ice with my rustic tasks, for poverty is better in peace than in war wretched wealth. I neither fear the powerful nor flatter the rich, nor am I the governor's chameleon; I am not made envious by ambition and desire for other people's glory or for eternal fame. Tender, tasty meat, fragrant wine, fresh-baked white bread, in meadow and cold spring a shepherd finds when beset with hunger; for we are equal, the great and the small, for as long as we stay asleep.

THE SHEPHERDS OF BETHLEHEM, *Ballad VIII:* The girl who was told by the angel that she was full of grace, when he brought her the great news of being God's mother, is now looking at Him in a manger, weeping tender tears, for assuming the obligation to become man. He also assumes his sufferings.

« ¿Qué tenéis, dulce Jesús?—
le dice la niña bella;—
¿tan presto sentís, mis ojos,
el dolor de mi pobreza?
Yo no tengo otros palacios
en que recibiros pueda,
sino mis brazos y pechos
que os regalan y sustentan.
No puedo más, amor mío,
porque si yo más pudiera,
vos sabéis que vuestros cielos
envidiaran mi riqueza.»
El niño recién nacido
no mueve la pura lengua,
aunque es la sabiduría
de su eterno Padre inmensa,
mas revelándole al alma
de la Virgen la respuesta,
cubrió de sueño en sus brazos
blandamente sus estrellas.
Ella entonces, desatando
la voz regalada y tierna,
así tuvo a su armonía
la de los cielos suspensa:

Pues andáis en las palmas,
ángeles santos,
que se duerme mi niño,

"What's the matter, sweet Jesus?", the pretty girl says to him; "do you regret so soon, my love, the misery of my poverty? I have no other palace in which I can receive you, except my arms and breasts which fondle and sustain you. It's all I can do, my love, for if I could do more, you know that your heavens would envy me my wealth." The newborn baby doesn't move His pure tongue, although He is the immense wisdom of His eternal Father, but revealing to the Virgin's soul His reply, in her arms He softly covered with sleep His stars [eyes]. Then she, letting flow her sweet tender voice, suspended the harmony of heaven with her own, as follows: Since you're moving in the palm trees, holy angels, and my child is going to sleep, restrain

tened los ramos.

Palmas de Belén
que mueven airados
los furiosos vientos
que suenan tanto:
no le hagáis ruido,
corred más paso;
que se duerme mi niño,
tened los ramos.

El niño divino,
que está cansado
de llorar en la tierra,
por su descanso
sosegar quiere un poco
del tierno llanto.
Que se duerme mi niño,
tened los ramos.

Rigurosos yelos
le están cercando;
ya veis que no tengo
con qué guardarlo.
Angeles divinos
que vais volando,
que se duerme mi niño,
tened los ramos.

the branches. Palms of Bethlehem moved angrily by the mad winds that sound so loud: don't make noise for him, move more quietly; since my child is going to sleep, restrain the branches. The divine child, who is tired of weeping on earth, in order to rest wants a little respite from his tender tears. Since my child is going to sleep, restrain the branches. Harsh frosts are closing in upon him; you see that I have nothing with which to protect him. Divine angels flying, since my child is going to sleep, restrain the branches.

LA DOROTEA

[1632]

I

A mis soledades voy,
de mis soledades vengo,
porque para andar conmigo
me bastan mis pensamientos.
No sé qué tiene el aldea
donde vivo y donde muero,
que con venir de mí mismo
no puedo venir más lejos.
Ni estoy bien ni mal conmigo,
mas dice mi entendimiento
que un hombre que todo es alma
está cautivo en su cuerpo.
Entiendo lo que me basta
y solamente no entiendo
cómo se sufre a sí mismo
un ignorante soberbio.
De cuantas cosas me cansan
fácilmente me defiendo,
pero no puedo guardarme
de los peligros de un necio.
El dirá que yo lo soy,
pero con falso argumento,
que humildad y necedad
no caben en un sujeto.
La diferencia conozco
porque en él y en mí contemplo
su locura en su arrogancia,

LA DOROTEA, *I:* To my solitude I go, from my solitude I come, for to go along by myself my own thoughts suffice me. I don't know what's peculiar about the village where I live and die, but when I come away from myself, I can't come any further. I'm neither happy nor unhappy with myself, but my intellect says that a man who is all soul is imprisoned in his body. I understand enough for myself and only don't understand how a proud ignoramus can stand himself. From everything that wearies me I easily defend myself, but I cannot protect myself from the dangers of a fool. He'll say that I'm one, but by a false argument, for humility and stupidity can't coexist in one person. I know the difference because in him and in myself I see his madness

mi humildad en mi desprecio.
O sabe naturaleza
más que supo en este tiempo,
o tantos que nacen sabios
es porque lo dicen ellos.
«Sólo sé que no sé nada»,
dijo un filósofo, haciendo
la cuenta con su humildad,
adonde lo más es menos.
No me precio de entendido,
de desdichado me precio,
que los que no son dichosos
¿cómo pueden ser discretos?
No puede durar el mundo,
porque dicen, y lo creo,
que suena a vidrio quebrado
y que ha de romperse presto.
Señales son del juïcio
ver que todos le perdemos,
unos por carta de más,
otros por carta de menos.
Dijeron que antiguamente
se fué la verdad al cielo;
tal la pusieron los hombres
que desde entonces no ha vuelto.
En dos edades vivimos
los proprios y los ajenos;
la de plata los extraños
y la de cobre los nuestros.
¿A quién no dará cuidado,
si es español verdadero,

in his arrogance, my humility in my scorn. Either nature knows more now than it did know, or everyone born wise is so on the strength of his own words. "I only know that I know nothing," said a philosopher, balancing his accounts with his humility, in which the most is least. I don't pride myself on intelligence, I pride myself on misfortune, for those who are not fortunate, how can they be intelligent? The world can't last, because they say, and I believe it, that it sounds like cracked glass and has to break up soon. Signs of the judgment are that we all lose our own, some by excess and others by deficit. They have said that long ago the truth went away to heaven; men treated it so badly that since then it hasn't come back. We live in two different ages, as Spaniards and as aliens: foreigners in the age of silver and our people in that of copper. Who isn't concerned, if he's a true Spaniard, to see old

ver los hombres a lo antiguo
y el valor a lo moderno?
Todos andan bien vestidos,
y quéjanse de los precios,
de medio arriba, romanos,
de medio abajo, romeros.
Dijo Dios que comería
su pan el hombre primero
en el sudor de su cara
por quebrar su mandamiento;
y algunos, inobedientes
a la vergüenza y al miedo,
con las prendas de su honor
han trocado los efetos.
Virtud y filosofía
peregrinan como ciegos;
el uno se lleva al otro,
llorando van y pidiendo.
Dos polos tiene la tierra,
universal movimiento:
la mejor vida, el favor,
la mejor sangre, el dinero.
Oigo tañer las campanas
y no me espanto, aunque puedo,
que en lugar de tantas cruces
haya tantos hombres muertos.
Mirando estoy los sepulcros,
cuyos mármoles eternos
están diciendo sin lengua
que no lo fueron sus dueños.
¡Oh, bien haya quien los hizo,

style men and modern valor? Everyone's well dressed, and complains of the prices, the upper half being Romans and the lower half being pilgrims. God said that the first man would eat his bread in the sweat of his face for breaking his commandment; and some men, responding neither to shame nor to fear, by pawning their honor have reversed the situation. Virtue and philosophy make pilgrimages as blind men do; one leads the other as they go weeping and begging. The earth has two poles and a single movement: the best life is favoritism, the best blood is money. I hear the bells ringing and I'm not surprised, although I might be, that instead of so many crosses there should be so many dead men. I am looking at the graves, and their eternal marble is saying tongueless that their owners were not so. Oh, good for the

porque solamente en ellos
de los poderosos grandes
se vengaron los pequeños!
Fea pintan a la envidia,
yo confieso que la tengo
de unos hombres que no saben
quién vive pared en medio.
Sin libros y sin papeles,
sin tratos, cuentas ni cuentos
cuando quieren escribir
piden prestado el tintero.
Sin ser pobres ni ser ricos
tienen chimenea y huerto;
no los despiertan cuidados,
ni pretensiones, ni pleitos;
ni murmuraron del grande
ni ofendieron al pequeño;
nunca, como yo, firmaron
parabién ni pascuas dieron.
Con esta envidia que digo
y lo que paso en silencio,
a mis soledades voy,
de mis soledades vengo.

VI

¡Pobre barquilla mía
entre peñascos rota,
sin velas desvelada
y entre las olas sola!
¿Adónde vas perdida,
adónde, di, te engolfas,

man who worked the marble, because only in it have the small people taken vengeance upon the powerful and great! They depict envy as ugly; I confess that I am envious of certain men that do not know who lives in the house next door. Without books and without paperwork, without commerce, accounts or tales, when they wish to write they borrow the inkwell. Without being poor or rich, they have a fireplace and an orchard; they are not awakened by cares or petitions or lawsuits; they have neither gossiped of the great nor offended the small; they have never, as I have, signed congratulations or given gifts. With this envy that I mention, and what I pass over in silence, to my solitude I go, from my solitude I come. *VI:* My poor little boat, broken among the reefs, sleeplessly bereft of sails and alone among the waves! Where are you going so lost? Where, tell me, are you en-

que no hay deseos cuerdos
con esperanzas locas?
Como las altas naves
te apartas animosa
de la vecina tierra
y al fiero mar te arrojas.
Igual en las fortunas,
mayor en las congojas,
pequeña en las defensas,
incitas a las ondas.
Advierte que te llevan
a dar entre las rocas
de la soberbia envidia,
naufragio de las honras.
Cuando por las riberas
andabas costa a costa,
nunca del mar temiste
las iras procelosas:
segura navegabas,
que por la tierra propia
nunca el peligro es mucho
adonde el agua es poca.
(Verdad es que en la patria
no es la virtud dichosa,
ni se estimó la perla
hasta dejar la concha.)
Dirás que muchas barcas
con el favor en popa,
saliendo desdichadas,

gulfing yourself, for there are no sane desires among mad hopes? Like the big ships, you bravely go away from the neighboring shore and hurl yourself into the fierce sea. Stable in the storms, stronger in grief, weak in your defenses, you incite the waves. Look out, they are dashing you against the rocks of haughty envy, the shipwreck of reputations. When along the shore you used to go from coast to coast, you never feared the stormy wrath of the sea: you sailed in safety, for on one's own terrain the danger is never great where there isn't much water. (It is true that in one's own country virtue is not fortunate, nor was the pearl esteemed until it left the shell.) You may say that many boats with a favoring tail wind, setting out in misfortune,

volvieron venturosas.
No mires los ejemplos
de las que van y tornan,
que a muchas ha perdido
la dicha de las otras.
Para los altos mares
no llevas cautelosa
ni velas de mentiras
ni remos de lisonjas.
¿Quién te engañó, barquilla?
Vuelve, vuelve la proa,
que presumir de nave
fortunas ocasiona.
¿Qué jarcias te entretejen?
¿Qué ricas banderolas
azote son del viento
y de las aguas sombra?
¿En qué gavia descubres,
del árbol alta copa,
la tierra en perspectiva,
del mar incultas orlas?
¿En qué celajes fundas
que es bien echar la sonda
cuando, perdido el rumbo,
erraste la derrota?
Si te sepulta arena,
¿qué sirve fama heroica?;
que nunca desdichados
sus pensamientos logran.
¿Qué importa que te ciñan

have returned with great luck. Don't consider the examples of those that go and return, for many have been destroyed by the fortune of others. For [embarking upon] the high seas you do not cunningly bear either lying sails or flattering oars. Who deceived you, little boat? Turn back, turn back your prow, for a ship's presumption gives rise to storms. What rigging is woven over you? What pretty pennants beat the wind and cast shadows on the water? From what topsail, the mast's very top, do you sight the perspective of land, the uncultivated borders of the sea? What pattern in the sky makes you think that it is well to take a sounding when, having lost your bearings, you are off your course? If the sand buries you, what good is a hero's reputation?; for unfortunate people never carry out their intentions. What does it

ramas verdes o rojas,
que en selvas de corales
salado césped brota?
Laureles de la orilla
solamente coronan
navíos de alto borde
que jarcias de oro adornan.
No quieras que yo sea,
por tu soberbia pompa,
Faetonte de barqueros
que los laureles lloran.
Pasaron ya los tiempos
cuando, lamiendo rosas,
el céfiro bullía
y suspiraba aromas.
Ya fieros huracanes
tan arrogantes soplan,
que salpicando estrellas,
del sol la frente mojan.
Ya los valientes rayos
de la vulcana forja,
en vez de torres altas,
abrasan pobres chozas.
Contenta con tus redes,
a la playa arenosa
mojado me sacabas,
pero vivo; ¿qué importa?
Cuando de rojo nácar
se afeitaba la aurora,
más peces te llenaban
que ella lloraba aljófar.

matter whether you're covered by green or red branches?, for in the coral jungles a salty turf sprouts. Laurels of the shore crown only ships of deep draught, adorned with golden rigging. Don't ask me to be, for your proud show, a boatmen's Phaeton, wept for by laurels. The times have passed when, licking roses, Zephyr simmered and sighed aromas. Now fierce storms so arrogantly blow that, splashing the stars, they wet the sun's forehead. Now the brave thunderbolts of Vulcan's forge, instead of high towers, burn down humble shacks. Happy with your nets, you used to bring me back, wet, to the sandy beach, but alive; what does it matter? When the dawn put on makeup of red nacre, you were filled with more fishes than her pearly

Al bello sol que adoro,
enjuta ya la ropa,
nos daba una cabaña
la cama de sus hojas;
esposo me llamaba,
yo la llamaba esposa,
parándose de envidia
la celestial antorcha.
Sin pleito, sin disgusto,
la muerte nos divorcia:
¡ay de la pobre barca
que en lágrimas se ahoga!
Quedad sobre la arena,
inútiles escotas,
que no ha menester velas
quien a su bien no torna.
Si con eternas plantas
las fijas luces doras,
¡oh dueño de mi barca!
y en dulce paz reposas,
merezca que le pidas
al bien que eterno gozas
que adonde estás me lleve,
más pura y más hermosa.
Mi honesto amor te obligue,
que no es digna victoria
para quejas humanas
ser las deidades sordas.
Mas ¡ay, que no me escuchas!...

tears. After my clothes had dried in the lovely sun that I adore, a cabin furnished us with the bed of its leaves; she called me husband, I called her wife, and the torch of heaven stood still with envy. Without disagreement or unpleasantness, death has divorced us: alas for the poor boat drowning in tears! Stay on the sand, useless sheets, for he doesn't need sails who cannot return to his love. If with eternal feet you gild the fixed stars, oh mistress of my boat!, and repose in sweet peace, may I merit your begging the eternal bliss which you enjoy that where you are, Hc will take me, in your greater purity and beauty. May my chaste love oblige you, for it is an unworthy triumph over human complaints for deities to be deaf. But, alas, you don't

Pero la vida es corta:
viviendo, todo falta;
muriendo, todo sobra.

Juan de Arguijo

(1567–1623)

SONETOS

XII

A Narciso

Crece el insano amor, crece el engaño
Del que en las aguas vió su imagen bella;
Y él, sola causa en su mortal querella,
Busca el remedio y acrecienta el daño.
Vuelve a ver en la fuente ¡caso extraño!
Que de ella sale el fuego; mas en ella
Templarlo piensa, y la enemiga estrella
Sus ojos cierra al fácil desengaño.
Fallecieron las fuerzas y el sentido
Al ciego amante amado; que a su suerte
La belleza fatal cayó rendida:
Y ahora, en flor purpúrea convertido,
La agua, que fué principio de su muerte,
Hace que crezca, y prueba a darle vida.

hear me! . . . Yet life is short: as long as I live, I lack everything, and in death, everything is too much.

SONNETS, *XII, To Narcissus:* The mad love and deception grows in him who saw his beautiful image in the water; and he, the sole cause of his own mortal complaint, seeks a cure and aggravates the illness. He looks again in the spring and sees (strange case!) that out of it love's fire comes; but in the same spring he tries to cool the fire, and the stars, his enemies, blind his eyes to simple undeception. His strength and senses failed the beloved lover; his fatal beauty fell victim to his fate: and now, converted into a bright flower, the water, which caused his death, makes him grow and tries

XVI

A una estatua de Niobe,
que labró Praxiteles
(de Ausonio)

Viví, y en dura piedra convertida,
Labrada por la mano artificiosa
De Praxiteles, Niobe hermosa,
Vengo segunda vez a tener vida.
A todo me volvió restituída,
Mas no al sentido, la arte poderosa;
Que no lo tuve yo, cuando furiosa
Los altos dioses ofendí atrevida.
¡Ay triste! cuán en vano me consuelo,
Si ardiente llanto espira el mármol frío,
Sin que mi antigua pena el tiempo cure;
Pues ha querido el riguroso cielo,
Para que sea eterno el dolor mío,
Que faltándome el alma, el llanto dure.

XXIII

A Ariadna, dejada de Teseo

«¿A quién me quejaré del cruel engaño,
Arboles mudos, en mi triste duelo?
¡Sordo mar! ¡Tierra extraña! ¡Nuevo cielo!
¡Fingido amor! ¡Costoso desengaño!
«Huye el pérfido autor de tanto daño,
Y quedo sola en peregrino suelo,
Do no espero a mis lágrimas consuelo;
Que no permite alivio mal tamaño.

to give him life. *XVI, To a statue of Niobe, wrought by Praxiteles* (*From Ausonius*): I lived before, and converted now into hard stone, wrought by the artful hand of Praxiteles, I, beautiful Niobe, come to life a second time. I was restored to everything, except my senses, by his powerful art; those I did not have when madly I offended the lofty gods in my daring. Alas, how vainly I try to console myself, if cold marble breathes out burning tears, and time does not cure my ancient grief; for cruel heaven has willed that, for my pain to be eternal, though lacking a soul, my tears should persist. *XXIII, To Ariadne, abandoned by Theseus:* "To whom shall I complain of the cruel deception, mute trees, in my sad lament? Deaf sea! Alien earth! Strange heaven! Feigned love! Costly undeception! The perfidious author of so much harm flees, and I am left alone on foreign soil, where I don't expect consolation for my tears; for so great an evil permits no respite. Gods,

«Dioses, si entre vosotros hizo alguno
De un desamor ingrato amarga prueba,
Vengadme, os ruego, del traidor Teseo».
Tal se queja Ariadna en importuno
Lamento al cielo; y entretanto lleva
El mar su llanto, el viento su deseo.

XLIII

Si pudo de Anfión el dulce canto
Juntar las piedras del tebano muro;
Si con suave lira osó seguro
Bajar el Tracio al reino del espanto;
Si la voz regalada pudo tanto
Que abrió las puertas de diamante duro,
Y un rato suspendió de aquel oscuro
Lugar la pena y miserable llanto;
Y si del canto la admirable fuerza
Enternece los fieros animales,
Si enfrena la corriente de los ríos:
¿Qué nueva pena en mi dolor se esfuerza,
Pues con lo que descrecen otros males
Se van acrecentando más los míos?

XLIV

La tempestad y la calma

Yo vi del rojo sol la luz serena
Turbarse, y que en un punto desparece
Su alegre faz, y en torno se oscurece

if any among you has had the bitter experience of unloving ingratitude, avenge me, I beg you, upon the traitorous Theseus." Thus Ariadne complains with importunate lament to heaven; and at the same time the sea sweeps away her tears and the wind her desires. *XLIII:* If the sweet song of Amphion was able to join the stones of the Theban wall; if with sweet lyre the Thracian safely dared to descend to the kingdom of fear; if his lovely voice was so powerful that it opened the gates of hard diamond and for a while suspended that dark place's suffering and wretched tears; and if the amazing power of his song tames the fierce animals, if it restrains the rivers' currents: what unusual penalty is imposed upon my suffering, for that which diminishes other griefs makes mine grow more and more? *XLIV, Tempest and Calm:* I saw the serene light of the red sun become turbulent and in a moment his gay face disappear, and all around the sky become dark with

El cielo con tiniebla de horror llena.
  El austro proceloso airado suena,
Crece su furia, y la tormenta crece;
Y en los hombros de Atlante se estremece
El alto Olimpo y con espanto truena.
  Mas luego vi romperse el negro velo
Deshecho en agua, y a su luz primera
Restituírse apriesa el claro día.
  Y de nuevo esplendor ornado el cielo
Miré, y dije: «¿Quién sabe, si le espera
Igual mudanza a la fortuna mía?»

XLV

A Cartago

  Este soberbio monte y levantada
Cumbre, ciudad un tiempo, hoy sepultura
De la grandeza, cuya fama dura
Contra la fuerza de la suerte airada,
  Ejemplo cierto fué en la edad pasada,
Y será fiel testigo a la futura,
Del fin que ha de tener la más segura
Pujanza, vanamente confiada.
  Mas en tanta ruina nueva gloria
No os pudo fallecer, ¡oh celebrados
De la antigua Cartago ilustres muros!,
  Que mucho más creció vuestra memoria,
Porque fuisteis del tiempo derribados,
Que si permaneciérades seguros.

shadows full of terror. The stormy south wind angrily roars, his fury grows, and the storm increases; and on Atlas's shoulders lofty Olympus shudders and thunders in fright. But then I saw the black veil break, melted in water, and bright day quickly restored to its former light. And I looked at the sky, adorned with new splendor, and said: "Who knows whether a similar change awaits my fortune?" *XLV, To Carthage:* This proud mountain and lofty peak, once a city, now the tomb of grandeur, whose fame resists the power of angry fate, was a true example in times gone by, and will be a faithful witness in future times, to the end which awaits the surest ambition, vainly self-confident. But in such ruin a new glory could not fail you, oh famous and illustrious walls of ancient Carthage!, for the memory of you grew even greater, because you were destroyed by time, than if you had remained

XLIX

Júpiter a Ganimedes

No temas, ¡oh bellísimo troyano!,
Viendo que, arrebatado en nuevo vuelo,
Con corvas uñas te levanta al cielo
La feroz ave por el aire vano.
¿Nunca has oído el nombre soberano
Del alto Olimpo, la piedad y el celo
De Júpiter, que da la pluvia al suelo
Y arma con rayos la tonante mano,
A cuyas sacras aras humillado
Gruesos toros ofrece el teucro en Ida,
Implorando remedio a sus querellas?
El mismo soy. No al águila eres dado
En despojo; mi amor te trae: olvida
Tu amada Troya y sube a mis estrellas.

Francisco de Medrano
(1570–1607)

SONETOS

XI

Veré al tiempo tomar de ti, señora,
por mí vengança, hurtando tu 'ermosura;
veré el cabello vuelto en nieve pura,

unharmed. *XLIX, Jupiter to Ganymede:* Fear not, oh most handsome Trojan!, when you see that, snatched away in unusual flight, with curved talons you are raised to heaven by the ferocious bird through the empty air. Have you never heard of the sovereign name of lofty Olympus, of the zealous worship of Jupiter, who gives rain to the earth and arms with bolts the thundering hand, at whose sacred altars the humble Trojan at Ida offers fat bulls, begging for a remedy to his complaints? I am he. You have not been given as a prey to the eagle; you are swept along by my love: forget your beloved Troy and rise to my stars.

SONNETS *XI:* I shall see time take vengeance, my lady, upon you for me, by

que l'arte y juventud encrespa y dora;
y en vez de rosas, con que tiñe ahora
tus mexillas la edad, ay, malsegura,
lilios sucederán en la madura,
que el pesar quiten y la embidia a Flora.
Mas quando a tu belleza el tiempo ciego
los filos embotare, y el aliento
a tu boca hurtare soberana,
bullir verás mi 'erida, arder el fuego:
que ni muere la llama, calmo el viento;
ni la 'erida, embotado el hierro, sana.

XXIX

No sé cómo, ni quándo, ni qué cosa
sentí, que me llenava de dulçura:
sé que llegó a mis braços la 'ermosura,
de gozarse comigo cudiciosa.
Sé que llegó, si bien, con temerosa
vista, resistí apenas su figura:
luego pasmé, como el que en noche escura,
perdido el tino, el pie mover no osa.
Siguió un gran gozo a aqueste pasmo, o sueño
—no sé quándo, ni cómo, ni qué a sido—
que lo sensible todo puso en calma.
Ignorallo es saber; que es bien pequeño
el que puede abarcar solo el sentido,
y éste pudo caber en sola l'alma.

stealing away your beauty; I shall see your hair turned into pure snow, which now your art and youth make curly and golden; and instead of the roses, with which the insecure (alas!) age now dyes your cheeks, lilies will replace them in your maturity, to relieve Flora [the goddess of flowers] of her pain and envy. But when blind time shall dull the edge of your beauty and steal the breath from your sovereign mouth, you will see my wound bubbling, my fire burning: for neither does the flame die down when the wind is calm; nor does the wound, when the weapon is dulled, heal up. *XXIX:* I don't know how, nor where, nor what I felt that filled me with sweetness: I know that beauty came to my arms desirous of taking pleasure with me. I know that it came, even though, with fearful eyes, I could hardly withstand the vision: then I thrilled, like him who in the dark night loses his bearings and dares not move his foot. A great pleasure followed this thrill, or dream (I don't know when, nor how, nor what it was), which calmed down all my senses. To be ignorant is to know; for it is a small joy which the senses are capable of by themselves, and this joy could be con-

XXX

A Don Juan de Arguijo, contra el artificio

Cansa la vista el artificio 'umano,
quanto mayor más presto: la más clara
fuente y jardín compuestos dan en cara
que nuestro ingenio es breve y nuestra mano.
Aquel, aquel descuydo soberano
de la Naturaleza, en nada avara,
con luenga admiración suspende y para
a quien lo advierte con sentido sano.
Ver cómo corre eternamente un río,
cómo el campo se tiende en las llanuras,
y en los montes se añuda y se reduçe,
grandeza es siempre nueva y grata, Argío;
tal, pero, es el autor que las produçe:
¡oh Dios, immenso en todas sus criaturas!

XXXIX

Las almas son eternas, son iguales,
son libres, son espíritus, María:
si en ellas ay amor, con la porfía
de los estorvos creçe, y de los males.
Nacimos en fortuna desiguales,
no en gustos; la violencia nos desvía;
el tiempo corre lento, y deja el día
de sí 'asta en los mármoles señales.
Mas tú ni a tiempo alguno ni a violencia,
ni a aquello desigual de la fortuna,

tained only by the soul. *XXX, To Don Juan de Arguijo, against artificiality:* Human art wearies the sight, and the greater it is, the more quickly: the brightest fountain and formal garden make it obvious that our ingenuity and skill are limited. But that sovereign carelessness of Nature, stingy with nothing, suspends in prolonged amazement and detains him who observes it with uncorrupted sense. To see how a river runs eternally, how the countryside stretches out over the plains, and is knotted up and reduced by the mountains, is a grandeur ever new and delightful, Argio; but such is the author that produces them: oh God, immense in all His creatures! *XXXIX:* Souls are eternal, are equal, are free, are spirits, Maria: if there is love in them, it increases with the struggle against obstacles and evils. We were born different in fortune, but not in tastes; violence separates us; time runs slowly, and the day leaves even in marble traces of itself. But you are not to fear any time or violence, or that inequality of fortune, or the most pro-

ni temas a la más prolixa ausencia;
que si nuestras dos almas son a una,
¿en quién, si ya no en Dios, 'avrá potencia
que las gaste o las fuerçe o las desuna?

Rodrigo Caro

(1573–1647)

CANCIÓN A LAS RUINAS DE ITÁLICA

1. Estos, Fabio, ¡ay dolor! que ves ahora
campos de soledad, mustio collado
fueron un tiempo Itálica famosa.
Aquí de Cipión la vencedora
colonia fué: por tierra derribado
yace el temido honor de la espantosa
muralla, y lastimosa
reliquia es solamente.
De su invencible gente
sólo quedan memorias funerales,
donde erraron ya sombras de alto ejemplo.
Este llano fué plaza, allí fué templo:
de todo apenas quedan las señales.
Del gimnasio y las termas regaladas
leves vuelan cenizas desdichadas.
Las torres que desprecio al aire fueron
a su gran pesadumbre se rindieron.
2. Este despedazado anfiteatro,

longed absence; for if our two souls are united, who, except for God, can have the power to wear them away or violate them or disunite them?

ODE TO THE RUINS OF ITALICA: 1. These, that you now see, alas, Fabio, solitary fields, sad hill, were once famous Italica. Here was the conquering colony of Scipio: razed to the ground lies the fearful honor of the awesome wall, and it is only a pitiful remnant. Of its unconquerable people there remain only funereal memories where once there wandered shades of lofty example. This plain was a forum, over there was a temple: of everything there hardly remain traces. Over the gymnasium and luxurious heated

impío honor de los dioses, cuya afrenta
publica el amarillo jaramago,
ya reducido a trágico teatro,
¡oh fábula del tiempo! representa
cuánta fué su grandeza, y es su estrago.
¿Cómo en el cerco vago
de su desierta arena
el gran pueblo no suena?
¿Dónde, pues fieras hay, está el desnudo
luchador, dónde está el atleta fuerte?
Todo despareció: cambió la suerte
voces alegres en silencio mudo:
mas aun el tiempo da en estos despojos
espectáculos fieros a los ojos:
y miran tan confusos lo presente,
que voces de dolor el alma siente.
3. Aquí nació aquel rayo de la guerra,
gran padre de la patria, honor de España,
pío, felice, triunfador Trajano,
ante quien muda se prostró la tierra
que ve del sol la cuna, y la que baña
el mar también vencido gaditano.
Aquí de Elio Adriano,
de Teodosio divino,
de Silio peregrino
rodaron de marfil y oro las cunas.
Aquí ya de laurel, ya de jazmines

baths lightly float the ashes of misfortune. The towers which scorned the winds have succumbed to their own weight. 2. This fragmented amphitheatre, an impious honor to the gods, whose disgrace is made public by the yellow mustard weed, reduced now to a tragic theatre, oh time's fable!, enacts its former grandeur and its present ruin. Why, in the vague arena of its deserted sand, does the great populace not resound? Where, since there are wild animals, is the naked wrestler? Where is the strong athlete? Everything has disappeared: fate has changed gay voices into mute silence; but time still presents, in this destruction, fierce spectacles to one's eyes, which look in such confusion upon what's present that the soul hears cries of grief. 3. Here was born that thunderbolt of war, the great father of his fatherland, Spain's honor, the pious, happy, triumphant Trajan, before whom the land mutely prostrated itself which sees the sun's cradle and that which is bathed by the sea, also conquered, of Cádiz. Here Aelius Hadrian's, divine Theodosius's, and ingenious Silius's cradles of ivory and gold were rocked. Here they were seen crowned sometimes with laurel, sometimes

coronados los vieron los jardines
que ahora son zarzales y lagunas.
La casa para el César fabricada
¡ay! yace de lagartos vil morada.
Casas, jardines, césares murieron,
y aun las piedras que de ellos se escribieron.
4. Fabio, si tú no lloras, pon atenta
la vista en luengas calles destruídas,
mira mármoles y arcos destrozados,
mira estatuas soberbias, que violenta
Némesis derribó, yacer tendidas;
y ya en alto silencio sepultados
sus dueños celebrados.
Así a Troya figuro,
así a su antiguo muro.
Y a ti, Roma, a quien queda el nombre apenas,
oh patria de los dioses y los reyes:
y a ti, a quien no valieron justas leyes,
fábrica de Minerva, sabia Atenas.
Emulación ayer de las edades,
hoy cenizas, hoy vastas soledades;
que no os respetó el hado, no la muerte
¡ay! ni por sabia a ti, ni a ti por fuerte.
5. Mas ¿para qué la mente se derrama
en buscar al dolor nuevo argumento?
Basta ejemplo menor, basta el presente.
Que aun se ve el humo aquí, aun se ve la llama,

with jasmines in the gardens which now are brambles and swamps. The house built for Caesar, alas, lies as the foul haunt of lizards. Houses, gardens, Caesars have died, and even the stones engraved concerning them. 4. Fabio, if you're not weeping, set your eyes attentively upon the long streets destroyed, look at the wrecked marbles and arches, look at the proud statues, struck down by violent Nemesis, lying prone, and buried now in deep silence their famous owners. So I imagine Troy, so its ancient wall. And you, Rome, whose very name you hardly retain, oh fatherland of the gods and kings; and you, whose just laws did not help you, built by Minerva, wise Athens. Yesterday the competitor of the ages, today ashes, today vast solitudes; for you were not spared by fate or death, alas, neither for being wise [Athens] nor for being strong [Rome]. 5. But to what purpose does my mind pour out itself in search of new reasons for grief? A lesser example suffices, the present one. For here one still sees the smoke, one still sees

aun se oyen llantos hoy, hoy ronco acento.
Tal genio, o religión fuerza la mente
de la vecina gente
que refiere admirada
que en la noche callada
una voz triste se oye que llorando
Cayó Itálica dice: y lastimosa
Eco reclama *Itálica* en la hojosa
selva, que se le opone resonando
Itálica: y el caro nombre oído
de *Itálica* renuevan el gemido
mil sombras nobles en su gran ruina.
Tanto, aun la plebe a sentimiento inclina!
  6. Esta corta piedad, que agradecido
huésped a tus sagrados manes debo,
les dó y consagro, Itálica famosa.
Tú, (si lloroso don han admitido
las ingratas cenizas de que llevo
dulce noticia asaz si lastimosa)
permíteme piadosa
usura a tierno llanto
que vea el cuerpo santo
de Geroncio, tu mártir y prelado.
Muestra de su sepulcro algunas señas,
y cavaré con lágrimas las peñas
que ocultan su sarcófago sagrado.

the flame, one still hears the lamentations today, today the hoarse voices. Some spirit or cult moves the minds of the neighboring folk so that they tell in amazement that in the quiet night a sad voice is heard which weeping says, *Here fell Italica;* and piteous Echo shouts again *Italica* in the leafy forest, which answers back resounding *Italica;* and hearing the dear name of *Italica*, a thousand noble shades renew their moans in the midst of their great destruction. So even the common folk are inclined to mourn! 6. This brief tribute, which as a grateful guest I owe to your sacred shades, I give and consecrate to them. You (if the tearful offering has been accepted by the ungrateful ashes of which I bear tidings quite sweet, though sad) please allow me as a kind return upon my tender tears to see the holy body of Gerontius, your martyr and priest. Show me some traces of his tomb, and with my tears I will dig away the rocks that hide his sacred coffin. But I do

Pero mal pido el único consuelo
de todo el bien que airado quitó el cielo.
Goza en las tuyas sus reliquias bellas,
para invidia del mundo y las estrellas.

Andrés Fernández de Andrada

(fl. ca. 1610)

EPÍSTOLA MORAL A FABIO

1. Fabio, las esperanzas cortesanas
prisiones son do el ambicioso muere
y donde al más activo nacen canas.
2. El que no las limare o las rompiere,
ni el nombre de varón ha merecido,
ni subir al honor que pretendiere.
3. El ánimo plebeyo y abatido
procura, en sus intentos temeroso,
antes estar suspenso que caído;
4. que el corazón entero y generoso
al caso adverso inclinará la frente
antes que la rodilla al poderoso.
5. Más coronas, más triunfos dió al prudente
que supo retirarse, la fortuna,
que al que esperó obstinada y locamente.

wrong to ask for the only consolation for all the happiness that angry heaven has taken away. Enjoy among relics of yourself his fair relics, to the envy of the world and the stars.

MORAL EPISTLE TO FABIO: 1. Fabio, the hopes of courtiers are shackles in which the ambitious man dies and even the most active candidate grows gray hairs. 2. He who doesn't use a file on them or break them does not deserve to be called a man or to rise to the position which he seeks. 3. The cowed plebeian spirit prefers, in its timid enterprises, to be kept in suspense, rather than to fall; 4. but the self-reliant noble heart will bow his head to adverse fortune rather than his knee to the powerful. 5. More crowns and triumphs have been given to the prudent man, who knew how to withdraw, by fortune, than to the man who persisted in mad obstinacy. 6. This

6. Esta invasión terrible e importuna
de contrarios sucesos nos espera
desde el primer sollozo de la cuna.
7. Dejémosla pasar como a la fiera
corriente del gran Betis, cuando airado
dilata hasta los montes la ribera.
8. Aquel entre los héroes es cantado
que el premio mereció, no quien le alcanza
por vanas consecuencias del estado.
9. Peculio proprio es ya de la privanza
cuanto de Astrea fué, cuanto regía
con su temida espada y su balanza.
10. El oro, la maldad, la tiranía
del inicuo, precede y pasa al bueno.
¿Qué espera la virtud o qué confía?
11. Vente, y reposa en el materno seno
de la antigua Romúlea, cuyo clima
te será más humano y más sereno.
12. Adonde, por lo menos, cuando oprima
nuestro cuerpo la tierra, dirá alguno:
"Blanda le sea," al derramarla encima;
13. donde no dejarás la mesa ayuno
cuando en ella te falte el pece raro
o cuando su pavón nos niegue Juno.
14. Busca, pues, el sosiego dulce y caro,
como en la oscura noche del Egeo
busca el piloto el eminente faro;

terrifying and importunate onslaught of conflicting events awaits us from our first sob in the cradle. 7. Let us allow it to go by like the fierce current of the great Betis [Guadalquivir River], when it angrily extends its banks up to the mountains. 8. He is counted among the heroes who has earned the prize, not he who gets it for vain reasons of state. 9. Now private property of the king's favorite is everything which belonged to Astraea [Goddess of Justice], everything which she controlled with her fearful sword and her scales. 10. Gold, evil, the iniquitous man's tyranny precede and bypass the good man. What does virtue hope for or trust in? 11. Come away and rest in the maternal bosom of ancient Romulea, whose climate you'll find to be kinder and more serene; 12. where at least, when the earth shall cover our bodies, someone will say, "May it lie softly upon him" as he scatters it over us; 13. where you won't leave the table hungry when there's no unusual fish to eat or when Juno denies us her peacock. 14. Seek, then, sweet beloved quietness, as in the dark Aegean night the pilot seeks the lofty lighthouse; 15.

15. que si acortas y ciñes tu deseo
dirás: "Lo que desprecio he conseguido;
que la opinión vulgar es devaneo."
16. Más quiere el ruiseñor su pobre nido
de pluma y leves pajas, más sus quejas
en el monte repuesto y escondido,
17. que agradar lisonjero las orejas
de algún príncipe insigne, aprisionado
en el metal de las doradas rejas.
18. Triste de aquel que vive destinado
a esa antigua colonia de los vicios,
augur de los semblantes del privado.
19. Cese el ansia y la sed de los oficios;
que acepta el don y burla del intento
el ídolo, a quien haces sacrificios.
20. Iguala con la vida el pensamiento,
y no le pasarás de hoy a mañana,
ni aun quizá de un momento a otro momento.
21. Apenas tienes ni una sombra vana
de nuestra antigua Itálica, y ¿esperas?
¡Oh error perpetuo de la vida humana!
22. Las enseñas grecianas, las banderas
del senado y romana monarquía
murieron, y pasaron sus carreras.
23. ¿Qué es nuestra vida más que un breve día,
do apenas sale el sol, cuando se pierde
en las tinieblas de la noche fría?

for if you trim and restrain your desires, you will say: "What I despise I have achieved; for the common view is foolishness." 16. The nightingale loves more his poor nest of feathers and light straw, his complaints in the withdrawn and hidden woods he loves more 17. than to please with flattery the ears of some distinguished prince, while imprisoned by the metal of golden bars. 18. Sad is he who lives fated for that ancient colony of vices, as a soothsayer reading the face of the king's favorite. 19. Let the anxiety cease and the thirst for positions; for the gift is accepted and your intention frustrated by the idol to whom you make sacrifices. 20. Balance your life and your thoughts, and you won't be concerned from one day to the next or even, perhaps, from one moment to the next. 21. You hardly have left even an empty shadow of our ancient Italica, and yet you have hopes? Oh perpetual error of humankind! 22. The insignia of Greece, the flags of the senate and monarchy of Rome have died, and their careers are over. 23. What more is our life than a brief day in which the sun hardly comes up before it's lost in the shadows of cold night? 24. What is it more than hay,

24. ¿Qué más que el heno, a la mañana verde,
seco a la tarde? ¡Oh ciego desvarío!
¿Será que de este sueño se recuerde?
25. ¿Será que pueda ser que me desvío
de la vida viviendo, y que esté unida
la cauta muerte al simple vivir mío?
26. Como los ríos, que en veloz corrida
se llevan a la mar, tal soy llevado
al último suspiro de mi vida.
27. De la pasada edad ¿qué me ha quedado?
O ¿qué tengo yo a dicha, en la que espero,
sino alguna noticia de mi hado?
28. ¡Oh si acabase, viendo cómo muero,
de aprender a morir, antes que llegue
aquel forzoso término postrero;
29. antes que aquesta mies inútil siegue
de la severa muerte dura mano,
y a la común materia se la entregue!
30. Pasáronse las flores del verano,
el otoño pasó con sus racimos,
pasó el invierno con sus nieves cano;
31. las hojas que en las altas selvas vimos
cayeron, ¡y nosotros a porfía
en nuestro engaño inmóviles vivimos!
32. Temamos al Señor que nos envía
las espigas del año y la hartura,
y la temprana pluvia y la tardía.
33. No imitemos la tierra siempre dura

green in the morning and dry in the afternoon? Oh blind madness! Is it possible to awaken from this dream? 25. Is it remotely possible for me to realize that I depart from life by living and that stealthy death is merged with my simple process of living? 26. Like the rivers, which swiftly running are borne to the sea, thus am I borne to the final sigh of my life. 27. What have I left of the past? Or what can I consider happy in the hoped-for future, except a notice of my fate? 28. Oh, if I could only, seeing how I die, finish learning to die, before that necessary, final terminus arrives; 29. before this useless grain is reaped by the harsh hand of cruel death and is consigned to common matter! 30. The summer flowers have passed, the autumn has passed with its grape clusters, the winter has passed, white with its snows; 31. the leaves which we saw in the deep forests have fallen, and yet we persist in living, unshaken in our deception! 32. Let us fear the Lord who sends us the annual harvest and superabundance, the early rain and the late. 33. Let us not imitate the earth which always resists the waters of

a las aguas del cielo y al arado,
ni la vid cuyo fruto no madura.
34. ¿Piensas acaso tú que fué criado
el varón para el rayo de la guerra,
para sulcar el piélago salado,
35. para medir el orbe de la tierra
o el cerco por dó el sol siempre camina?
¡Oh, quien así lo piensa, cuánto yerra!
36. Esta nuestra porción, alta y divina,
a mayores acciones es llamada
y en más nobles objetos se termina.
37. Así aquella, que al hombre solo es dada,
sacra razón y pura me despierta,
de esplendor y de rayos coronada,
38. y en la fría región, dura y desierta,
de aqueste pecho enciende nueva llama,
y la luz vuelve a arder que estaba muerta.
39. Quiero, Fabio, seguir a quien me llama,
y callado pasar entre la gente,
que no afecto los nombres ni la fama.
40. El soberbio tirano del Oriente,
que maciza las torres de cien codos
de cándido metal puro y luciente,
41. apenas puede ya comprar los modos
del pecar; la virtud es más barata,
ella consigo misma ruega a todos.
42. Mísero aquel que corre y se dilata
por cuantos son los climas y los mares,
perseguidor del oro y de la plata!

heaven and the plow, or the vine whose fruit does not ripen. 34. Do you perchance think that man was created for war's thunderbolt, to plow the salty sea, 35. to measure the earth's globe or the orbit ever followed by the sun? Oh, how wrong he is, whoever thinks so! 36. These our higher, divine faculties are called to greater actions and destined for more noble objects. 37. Thus that sacred pure reason, granted to man alone, awakens me, with its crown of splendor and light, 38. and in the cold, hard desert region of my breast it kindles a new flame, and the light burns again which was dead. 39. I want, Fabio, to follow Him who calls me and to pass in silence among people, for I do not pretend to name or fame. 40. The proud tyrant of the Orient, who solidly packs 100 cubit towers with pure white, shining metal, 41. can hardly afford any longer the means of sinning; virtue is cheaper, and she urges everyone to accept her for herself. 42. Wretched is he who runs far and wide over all the climates and seas in pursuit of gold and silver! 43.

43. Un ángulo me basta entre mis lares,
un libro y un amigo, un sueño breve,
que no perturben deudas ni pesares.
44. Esto tan solamente es cuanto debe
naturaleza al parco y al discreto,
y algún manjar común, honesto y leve.
45. No, porque así te escribo, hagas conceto
que pongo la virtud en ejercicio:
que aun esto fué difícil a Epicteto.
46. Basta, al que empieza, aborrecer el vicio,
y el ánimo enseñar a ser modesto;
después le será el cielo más propicio.
47. Despreciar el deleite no es supuesto
de sólida virtud; que aun el vicioso
en sí proprio le nota de molesto.
48. Mas no podrás negarme cuán forzoso
este camino sea al alto asiento,
morada de la paz y del reposo.
49. No sazona la fruta en un momento
aquella inteligencia que mensura
la duración de todo a su talento.
50. Flor la vimos ayer hermosa y pura,
luego materia acerba y desabrida,
y sabrosa después, dulce y madura.
51. Tal la humana prudencia es bien que mida
y compase y dispense las acciones
que han de ser compañeras de la vida.

For me a corner is enough, among my household gods, and a book and a friend, a short sleep undisturbed by debts and griefs. 44. This alone is all that nature owes to the thrifty and the discreet man, and some common food, temperate and light. 45. Don't imagine, because I'm writing to you in this way, that I put virtue into practice, for this was difficult even for Epictetus. 46. It is enough for the beginner to hate vice and to teach his spirit to be modest; afterwards heaven will be more propitious to him. 47. To despise pleasure is not enough for solid virtue, for even the man of vices in himself notices that pleasure is annoying. 48. But you cannot deny that this is a most necessary route toward the high seat and abode of peace and rest. 49. Fruit does not ripen immediately for that intelligence which measures the duration of everything according to its own ability. 50. We saw it [the fruit] yesterday as a flower lovely and pure, then as bitter, sour matter, and later tasty, sweet, and ripe. 51. Thus it is fitting for human prudence to measure and set the pace and distribute the actions which are to be life's

52. No quiera Dios que siga los varones
que moran nuestras plazas macilentos,
de la virtud infames histriones;
53. estos inmundos trágicos, atentos
al aplauso común, cuyas entrañas
son oscuros e infaustos monumentos.
54. ¡Cuán callada que pasa las montañas
el aura, respirando mansamente!
¡Qué gárrula y sonora por las cañas!
55. ¡Qué muda la virtud por el prudente!
¡Qué redundante y llena de ruido
por el vano, ambicioso y aparente!
56. Quiero imitar al pueblo en el vestido,
en las costumbres sólo a los mejores,
sin presumir de roto y mal ceñido.
57. No resplandezca el oro y las colores
en nuestro traje, ni tampoco sea
igual al de los dóricos cantores.
58. Una mediana vida yo posea,
un estilo común y moderado,
que no le note nadie que le vea.
59. En el plebeyo barro mal tostado
hubo ya quien bebió tan ambicioso
como en el vaso Múrino preciado;
60. y alguno tan ilustre y generoso
que usó, como si fuera vil gaveta,
del cristal transparente y luminoso.

companions. 52. God forbid that one should imitate the men who wanly inhabit our public squares, infamous fakers of virtue: 53. those filthy actors, intent upon popular praise, whose hearts are dark, ill-fated tombs. 54. How silently the breeze goes over the mountains, breathing gently! How chattering and noisily [it goes] through the cane brake! 55. How silent virtue is in the prudent man! How repetitive and full of noise in the vain, ambitious and deceptive! 56. I wish to imitate the common man in my clothing, the better men only in my customs, not presuming to be ragged and poorly dressed. 57. Let not gold and colors shine in our clothing, nor yet let it be like that of the Doric singers: 58. let me lead a moderate life, a common, middling style, which will not attract the attention of anyone who sees it. 59. From poorly glazed plebeian clay one has been known to drink as ambitiously as from a precious murrhine vessel; 60. and another has been so refined and noble that he used, as if it were a common cup, bright transparent crystal.

61. Sin la templanza ¿viste tú perfeta
alguna cosa? ¡Oh muerte! Ven callada,
como sueles venir en la saeta;
62. no en la tonante máquina preñada
de fuego y de rumor; que no es mi puerta
de doblados metales fabricada.
63. Así, Fabio, me enseña descubierta
su esencia la verdad, y mi albedrío
con ella se compone y se concierta.
64. No te burles de ver cuánto confío,
ni al arte de decir, vana y pomposa,
el ardor atribuyas de este brío.
65. ¿Es por ventura menos poderosa
que el vicio la verdad? ¿O menos fuerte?
No la arguyas de flaca y temerosa.
66. La codicia en las manos de la suerte
se arroja al mar, la ira a las espadas,
y la ambición se ríe de la muerte.
67. Y ¿no serán siquiera tan osadas
las opuestas acciones, si las miro
de más nobles objetos ayudadas?
68. Ya, dulce amigo, huyo y me retiro
de cuanto simple amé: rompí los lazos:
ven y sabrás al grande fin que aspiro,
antes que el tiempo muera en nuestros brazos.

61. Without temperance, have you ever seen anything perfect? Oh death, come silently, as you usually come in the arrow; 62. not in the thundering engine pregnant with fire and noise; for my door is not constructed of welded metal. 63. Thus, Fabio, truth shows me her essence, fully revealed, and my will adjusts itself and harmonizes with her. 64. Don't make fun of my great faith, nor attribute to the vain and pompous art of rhetoric my enthusiasm. 65. Is the truth perchance less powerful than evil, or less strong? Don't accuse it of being weak and timid. 66. In the hands of fate, greed hurls itself into the sea, anger into swords, and ambition laughs at death. 67. And can't the opposite activities be at least that daring, when I see them aided by more noble aims? 68. At last, sweet friend, I flee and withdraw from everything which in my simplicity I love; I have broken the bonds: come and you will see the great purpose to which I aspire, before time dies away in our arms.

Pedro Espinosa

(1578–1650)

SONETOS

A la Asunción de la Virgen María

En turquesadas nubes y celajes
Están en los alcázares empirios,
Con blancas hachas y con blancos cirios,
Del sacro Dios los soberanos pajes;
Humean de mil suertes y linajes,
Entre amaranto y plateados lirios,
Enciensos indios y pebetes sirios,
Sobre alfombras de lazos y follajes.
Por manto el sol, la luna por chapines,
Llegó la Virgen a la empírea sala,
Visita que esperaba el Cielo tanto.
Echáronse a sus pies los serafines,
Cantáronle los ángeles la gala,
Y sentóla a su lado el Verbo santo.

A la santísima Virgen María
Soneto en alejandrinos

Como el triste piloto que por el mar incierto
Se ve, con turbios ojos, sujeto de la pena

SONNETS, ***On the Assumption of the Virgin Mary:*** In turquoise clouds and skyscapes are in the empyrian fortress, holding white torches and white candles, the sovereign pages of sacred God; smoke rises of many sorts and types, among amaranth and silver lilies, from Indian incenses and Syrian joss-sticks, over carpets of ribbons and foliage. With the sun as her mantle, the moon as her slippers, the Virgin reached the empyrian hall, a visit long awaited by heaven. The seraphim threw themselves at her feet, the angels sang of her array, and the holy Word seated her at His side. ***To the most holy Virgin Mary (sonnet in alexandrines):*** Like the sad pilot who on the uncertain sea beholds himself, with clouded eyes, tormented upon the

Sobre las corvas olas, que, vomitando arena,
Lo tienen de la espuma salpicado y cubierto,
   Cuando, sin esperanza, de espanto medio muerto,
Ve el fuego de Santelmo lucir sobre la antena,
Y, adorando su lumbre, de gozo el alma llena,
Halla su nao cascada surgida en dulce puerto:
   Así yo el mar sulcaba de penas y de enojos,
Y, con tormenta fiera, ya de las aguas hondas
Medio cubierto estaba, la fuerza y luz perdida,
   Cuando miré la lumbre ¡oh Virgen! de tus ojos,
Con cuyos resplandores, quietándose las ondas,
Llegué al dichoso puerto donde escapé la vida.

Francisco de Quevedo

(1580–1645)

POEMAS METAFÍSICOS

2

Represéntase la brevedad de lo que se vive y cuán nada parece lo que se vivió

   «¡Ah de la vida!» ... ¿Nadie me responde?
¡Aquí de los antaños que he vivido!
La Fortuna mis tiempos ha mordido;

curved waves which, vomiting sand, have splashed him and covered him with foam, when, hopeless and half-dead with fright, he sees St. Elmo's fire gleaming upon the rigging and, worshipping its light, his soul full of joy, he finds his battered ship afloat in a welcome harbor: so I plowed the sea of suffering and unhappiness and, in a fierce storm, was already half-covered by the deep waters, my strength and light exhausted, when I looked at the light, oh Virgin, of your eyes, and with their brilliance, the waves being quieted, I reached the happy harbor where I saved my life.

METAPHYSICAL POEMS, *2, Dramatizes the brevity of life in progress and the apparent nothingness of past life:* "Life, ahoy!" No one answers me? Come back, past years that I have lived! Fortune has chewed away my time; my

las Horas mi locura las esconde.
¡Que sin poder saber cómo ni adónde,
la salud y la edad se hayan huído!
Falta la vida, asiste lo vivido,
y no hay calamidad que no me ronde.
Ayer se fue; mañana no ha llegado;
hoy se está yendo sin parar un punto;
soy un fue, y un será, y un es cansado.
En el hoy y mañana y ayer, junto
pañales y mortaja, y he quedado
presentes sucesiones de difunto.

3

Significase la propria brevedad de la vida,
sin pensar y con padecer,
salteada de la muerte

¡Fue sueño ayer; mañana será tierra!
¡Poco antes, nada; y poco después, humo!
¡Y destino ambiciones, y presumo
apenas punto al cerco que me cierra!
Breve combate de importuna guerra,
en mi defensa soy peligro sumo;
y mientras con mis armas me consumo,
menos me hospeda el cuerpo, que me entierra.
Ya no es ayer; mañana no ha llegado;
hoy pasa, y es, y fue, con movimiento

madness hides the hours. That without being able to know how or whither, my health and lifetime have flown away! Life is absent, my having lived is present, and there is no calamity which does not beset me. Yesterday has gone; tomorrow hasn't arrived; today is going away without stopping for one moment; I am a "was" and a "will be" and an "is" tired. In my today and tomorrow and yesterday, I link together diapers and shroud, and I am merely a present sequence of a dead man. *3, Indicates life's intrinsic brevity, without anticipation and with suffering, under death's assault.* Yesterday was a dream; tomorrow will be earth! A little while ago, nothing; and a little later, smoke! And I plot ambitions, and my presumption is hardly a point on the circular siege which closes me in! A brief skirmish in a pressing war, in my own defense I am a great danger; and as I destroy myself with my own weapons, my body is less my host than my burial. It is no longer yesterday; tomorrow hasn't arrived; today passes, and is, and was,

que a la muerte me lleva despeñado.
Azadas son la hora y el momento,
que, a jornal de mi pena y mi cuidado,
cavan en mi vivir mi monumento.

6

Arrepentimiento y lágrimas debidas al engaño de la vida

Huye sin percibirse, lento, el día,
y la hora secreta y recatada
con silencio se acerca, y, despreciada,
lleva tras sí la edad lozana mía.
La vida nueva, que en niñez ardía,
la juventud robusta y engañada,
en el postrer invierno sepultada,
yace entre negra sombra y nieve fría.
No sentí resbalar mudos los años;
hoy los lloro pasados, y los veo
rïendo de mis lágrimas y daños.
Mi penitencia deba a mi deseo,
pues me deben la vida mis engaños,
y espero el mal que paso, y no le creo.

8

Conoce la diligencia con que se acerca la muerte, y procura conocer también la conveniencia de su venida, y aprovecharse de ese conocimiento

Ya formidable y espantoso suena

with a movement which sweeps me down the cliff to death. The hour and the moment are spades which, for wages paid by my grief and worry, excavate in my life my tomb. *6, Repentance and tears due to life's deception:* The day slowly slips away without being perceived, and the secret, stealthy hour approaches silently and, though scorned, takes away with it my lush youth. My new life, which blazed in childhood, my robust and deceived youth, buried in final winter, lies among black shadows and cold snow. I didn't perceive the mute years slip by; today I weep for their being past, and I see them laughing at my tears and destruction. Let my penance be due to my desire, for my deception owes me life, and I await the evil which I undergo, and don't believe it. *8, Recognizes the speed with which death is approaching and tries also to recognize the appropriateness of its arrival,*

dentro del corazón el postrer día;
y la última hora, negra y fría,
se acerca. de temor y sombras llena.
Si agradable descanso, paz serena
la muerte en traje de dolor envía,
señas da su desdén de cortesía:
más tiene de caricia que de pena.
¿Qué pretende el temor desacordado
de la que a rescatar piadosa viene
espíritu en miserias anudado?
Llegue rogada, pues mi bien previene;
hálleme agradecido, no asustado;
mi vida acabe, y mi vivir ordene.

11

Descuido del divertido vivir a quien la muerte llega impensada

Vivir es caminar breve jornada,
y muerte viva es, Lico, nuestra vida,
ayer al frágil cuerpo amanecida,
cada instante en el cuerpo sepultada:
nada, que, siendo, es poco, y será nada
en poco tiempo, que ambiciosa olvida,
pues, de la vanidad mal persuadida,
anhela duración, tierra animada.
Llevada de engañoso pensamiento
y de esperanza burladora y ciega,

and to take advantage of this recognition: Now formidably and frightfully resounds within my heart the final day; and the last hour, black and cold, approaches, full of fear and shadows. If death sends pleasant rest and serene peace in the guise of pain, her harshness is a sign of courtesy: she is more caressing than punishing. What purpose is there to the discordant fear of her who kindly comes to rescue a soul bound in misery? Let her come sought-for, since she prepares my own good; let her find me grateful, not frightened; let her end my life and bring order to my living. *11, The carelessness of the entertaining life to which death comes unanticipated:* To live is to travel for a short day, and our life, Lico, is a living death, which dawned yesterday upon a fragile body and is buried each instant in the body: a nothing which, by being, is a little, and will be nothing in a little while, ambitiously forgetful, for, falsely convinced by vanity, animated earth, it longs to last. Swept along by deceptive thoughts and by hope which sneers and is

tropezará en el mismo monumento,
  como el que, divertido, el mar navega,
y, sin moverse, vuela con el viento,
y antes que piense en acercarse, llega.

Heráclito Cristiano

28

Salmo XVI

  Ven ya, miedo de fuertes y de sabios:
irá la alma indignada con gemido
debajo de las sombras, y el olvido
beberán por demás mis secos labios.
  Por tal manera Curios, Decios, Fabios
fueron; por tal ha de ir cuanto ha nacido;
si quieres ser a alguno bien venido,
trae con mi vida fin a mis agravios.
  Esta lágrima ardiente con que miro
el negro cerco que rodea a mis ojos
naturaleza es, no sentimiento.
  Con el aire primero este suspiro
empecé, y hoy le acaban mis enojos,
porque me deba todo al monumento.

[1613]

29

Salmo XVII

  Miré los muros de la patria mía,
si un tiempo fuertes, ya desmoronados,

blind, it will stumble upon the same tomb, like him who, entertained, sails the sea and, without moving, flies with the wind, and before he thinks of being near, arrives. *28, The Christian Heraclitus, Psalm XVI:* Come now, terror of the strong and the wise: my indignant soul will go with a moan under the shadows, and my dry lips will drink, unnecessarily, forgetfulness [Lethe]. Thus the Curiuses, the Deciuses, the Fabiuses went; thus will go everything that has been born; if you wish to be welcomed by someone, put an end, not only to my life, but to my suffering. This burning tear with which I look at the black ring which surrounds my eyes is [the reaction of] nature, not regret. With my first breath I began this sigh, and today my worries end it, so that I may belong wholly to the tomb. *29 Psalm XVII:* I looked at the walls of my native land, if once strong, now dilapidated, tired by the

de la carrera de la edad cansados,
por quien caduca ya su valentía.
Salíme al campo; vi que el sol bebía
los arroyos del yelo desatados,
y del monte quejosos los ganados,
que con sombras hurtó su luz al día.
Entré en mi casa; vi que, amancillada,
de anciana habitación era despojos;
mi báculo, más corvo y menos fuerte.
Vencida de la edad sentí mi espada,
y no hallé cosa en que poner los ojos
que no fuese recuerdo de la muerte.

30

Salmo XVIII

Todo tras sí lo lleva el año breve
de la vida mortal, burlando el brío
al acero valiente, al mármol frío,
que contra el Tiempo su dureza atreve.
Antes que sepa andar el pie, se mueve
camino de la muerte, donde envío
mi vida oscura: pobre y turbio río
que negro mar con altas ondas bebe.
Todo corto momento es paso largo
que doy, a mi pesar, en tal jornada,
pues, parado y durmiendo, siempre aguijo.
Breve suspiro, y último, y amargo,
es la muerte, forzosa y heredada:
mas si es ley, y no pena, ¿qué me aflijo?

racing of time, which now causes their bravery to fail. I went out into the fields; I saw that the sun was drinking the brooks freed from ice, and the cattle were complaining of the mountain which with shadows was stealing the light of day. I entered my house; I saw that, all stained, it was the remnants of an ancient habitation; my cane, more bent and less strong. I felt my sword to be conquered by age, and I found nothing on which to set my eyes that wasn't a reminder of death. *30, Psalm XVIII:* All is swept along with it by the brief year of mortal life, outwitting the vigor of brave steel, of cold marble, which pits its hardness against time. Before the foot knows how to walk, it moves along toward death, where I send my obscure life: a poor, turbid river which a black sea with high waves drinks. Every short moment is a long step which I take, despite myself, on this journey, for, even standing still and sleeping, I always spur ahead. A brief sigh, a final bitter one, is death, our inevitable heritage: but if it's the law, and not a

31

Salmo XIX

¡Cómo de entre mis manos te resbalas!
¡Oh, cómo te deslizas, edad mía!
¡Qué mudos pasos traes, oh muerte fría,
pues con callado pie todo lo igualas!
Feroz, de tierra el débil muro escalas,
en quien lozana juventud se fía;
mas ya mi corazón del postrer día
atiende el vuelo, sin mirar las alas.
¡Oh condición mortal! ¡Oh dura suerte!
¡Que no puedo querer vivir mañana
sin la pensión de procurar mi muerte!
Cualquier instante de la vida humana
es nueva ejecución, con que me advierte
cuán frágil es, cuán mísera, cuán vana...

POEMAS MORALES

52

A la violenta y injusta prosperidad

Ya llena de sí solo la litera
Matón, que apenas anteayer hacía
(flaco y magro malsín) sombra, y cabía,
sobrando sitio, en una ratonera.
Hoy, mal introducida con la esfera
su casa, al sol los pasos le desvía,
y es tropezón de estrellas; y algún día,

penalty, why do I complain? *31, Psalm XIX:* How you slide from between my hands! Oh, how you slip away, my life! What mute steps you take, cold death, for with silent foot you make all things equal! Ferociously you scale the weak earthen wall upon which lusty youth relies; but now my heart awaits the last day's flight, without looking at its wings. Oh mortal condition! Oh harsh fate! That I can't desire to live tomorrow without [paying] the price of seeking my own death! Any instant in human life is a new execution whereby it reminds me how fragile it is, how wretched, how vain . . .

MORAL POEMS, *52, To violent, unjust prosperity:* A ruffian [or Matho] now fills the sedan chair all by himself, who hardly the day before yesterday cast a shadow (the lean and skinny stool pigeon!) and could fit with plenty of space into a mousetrap. Today, his house, mistakenly raised to heaven, causes the sun to change its route and is the stumbling block of stars; and

si fuera más capaz, pocilga fuera.
   Cuando a todos pidió, le conocimos;
no nos conoce cuando a todos toma;
y hoy dejamos de ser lo que ayer dimos.
   Sóbrale tanto cuanto falta a Roma;
y no nos puede ver, porque le vimos:
lo que fue esconde; lo que usurpa asoma.

131

Desde la Torre

   Retirado en la paz de estos desiertos,
con pocos, pero doctos libros juntos,
vivo en conversación con los difuntos
y escucho con mis ojos a los muertos.
   Si no siempre entendidos, siempre abiertos,
o enmiendan, o fecundan mis asuntos;
y en músicos callados contrapuntos
al sueño de la vida hablan despiertos.
   Las grandes almas que la muerte ausenta,
de injurias de los años, vengadora,
libra, ¡oh gran don Iosef!, docta la emprenta.
   En fuga irrevocable huye la hora;
pero aquélla el mejor cálculo cuenta
que en la lección y estudios nos mejora.

132

Muestra lo que se indigna Dios de las peticiones execrables de los hombres,

someday, if it were more capacious, it would be a pigpen. When he begged from all, we got to know him; he doesn't know us now that he takes from all; and today we cease being what we gave yesterday. He has a surplus of everything that Rome lacks; and he can't stand the sight of us because we saw him; what he was, he conceals; what he usurps, he shows. *131, From the Tower* [*Quevedo's estate*]: Withdrawn into the peace of this desert, having gathered together some books, few but learned, I live in conversation with the deceased and I listen with my eyes to the dead. If not always understood, yet always open, they [the books] either correct or fertilize my actions; and in silent musical counterpoint they, awake, speak to the dream [sleep] of life. The great souls which death takes away are freed from the damage of the years, oh great Sir Joseph, by an avenger, the learned printing press. In irrevocable flight the hour flees; but that hour scores the highest which improves us by reading and study. *132, He shows how indignant God gets at the unspeakable requests of men, and that their offerings*

y que sus oblaciones para alcanzarlas
son graves ofensas

Con mudo incienso y grande ofrenda, ¡oh, Licas!,
cogiendo a Dios a solas, entre dientes,
los ruegos, que recatas de las gentes,
sin voz a sus orejas comunicas.
Las horas pides prósperas y ricas,
y que para heredar a tus parientes,
fiebres reparta el cielo pestilentes,
y de ruinas fraternas te fabricas.
¡Oh grande horror! Pues cuando de ejemplares
rayos a Dios armó la culpa, el vicio,
víctimas le templaron los pesares;
y hoy le ofenden ansí, no ya propicio,
que, vueltos sacrilegios los altares,
arma su diestra el mesmo sacrificio.

146

Epístola satírica y censoria contra las costumbres presentes de los castellanos, escrita a don Gaspar de Guzmán, conde de Olivares, en su valimiento

No he de callar, por más que con el dedo,
ya tocando la boca, o ya la frente,
silencio avises, o amenaces miedo.

¿No ha de haber un espíritu valiente?
¿Siempre se ha de sentir lo que se dice?
¿Nunca se ha de decir lo que se siente?

to *achieve them are serious offenses:* With mute incense and a great offering, oh Licas!, catching God alone, between your teeth, you voicelessly communicate to his ears the prayers which you conceal from people. You ask for prosperous, rich hours and, in order to inherit from your relatives, for heaven to distribute pestilential fevers, and you build yourself upon your brothers' ruins. Oh how terrible! For when sin and vice armed God with exemplary thunderbolts, sacrificial victims tempered his wrath; and today, no longer propitious, he is so offended that, the altars having been turned sacrilegious, the sacrifice itself arms his right hand. *146, A satirical epistle, critical of the present customs of Castilians, written to Don Gaspar de Guzmán, the Count of Olivares, in support of him:* I will not keep quiet, no matter how, with your finger touching now your mouth, now your forehead, you may urge silence or threaten fear. Is there not to be one valiant soul? Must one always regret what one says? Must one never say what one

Hoy, sin miedo que libre escandalice,
puede hablar el ingenio, asegurado
de que mayor poder le atemorice.

En otros siglos pudo ser pecado
severo estudio y la verdad desnuda,
y romper el silencio el bien hablado.

Pues sepa quien lo niega, y quien lo duda,
que es lengua la verdad de Dios severo,
y la lengua de Dios nunca fue muda.

Son la verdad y Dios, Dios verdadero;
ni eternidad divina los separa,
ni de los dos alguno fue primero.

Si Dios a la verdad se adelantara,
siendo verdad, implicación hubiera
en ser, y en que verdad de ser dejara.

La justicia de Dios es verdadera,
y la misericordia, y todo cuanto
es Dios, todo ha de ser verdad entera.

Señor Excelentísimo, mi llanto
ya no consiente márgenes ni orillas:
inundación será la de mi canto.

Ya sumergirse miro mis mejillas,
la vista por dos urnas derramada
sobre las aras de las dos Castillas.

feels? Today, without fear of its freedom causing scandal, intelligence can speak, assured of not being intimidated by superior power. In other centuries, rigorous study could be a sin, and [so could] the naked truth, and the well-spoken man's breaking the silence. So let him that denies it and him that doubts it know that the truth is the tongue of a severe God, and the tongue of God was never mute. The truth and God are the true God; neither does divine eternity separate them, nor did either of the two come first. If God came before truth, being Himself truth, there would be a contradiction in His being and truth's ceasing to be. God's justice is true, and His mercy, and everything that is God must all be wholly true. Most excellent lord, my tears will no longer tolerate edges or shores: an inundation will be that of my song. I already see my cheeks being submerged, my vision poured out through two urns upon the altars of the two Castiles. That

Yace aquella virtud desaliñada,
que fue, si rica menos, más temida,
en vanidad y en sueño sepultada,

y aquella libertad esclarecida,
que en donde supo hallar honrada muerte,
nunca quiso tener más larga vida.

Y pródiga de l'alma, nación fuerte,
contaba por afrentas de los años,
envejecer en brazos de la suerte.

Del tiempo el ocio torpe, y los engaños
del paso de las horas y del día,
reputaban los nuestros por extraños.

Nadie contaba cuánta edad vivía,
sino de qué manera: ni aun un'hora
lograba sin afán su valentía.

La robusta virtud era señora,
y sola dominaba al pueblo rudo;
edad, si mal hablada, vencedora.

El temor de la mano daba escudo
al corazón, que, en ella confiado,
todas las armas despreció desnudo.

Multiplicó en escuadras un soldado
su honor precioso, su ánimo valiente,
de sola honesta obligación armado.

unadorned virtue, which was, if less rich, more feared, lies buried in vanity and in sleep, and also that distinguished liberty which, where it discovered how to die an honorable death, chose never to prolong its life. And, prodigally magnanimous, our mighty nation considered it an insult of the years to grow old in destiny's arms. The lazy waste of time and the deceptive ways of passing hours and days were considered strange by our people. No one counted how long he lived, but in what way: his valor did not complete even a single hour without making some effort. Robust virtue ruled and all alone dominated the crude populace: a period, if rough-spoken, victorious. The fear of one's hand shielded one's heart, which, trusting the hand, nakedly scorned all armor. One soldier multiplied into squadrons his precious honor, his brave spirit, armed only with his honest sense of duty. And beneath the

Y debajo del cielo aquella gente,
si no a más descansado, a más honroso
sueño entregó los ojos, no la mente.

Hilaba la mujer para su esposo
la mortaja, primero que el vestido;
menos le vio galán, que peligroso.

Acompañaba el lado del marido
más veces en la hueste, que en la cama;
sano le aventuró, vengóle herido.

Todas matronas, y ninguna dama:
que nombres del halago cortesano
no admitió lo severo de su fama.

Derramado y sonoro el Oceano
era divorcio de las rubias minas
que usurparon la paz del pecho humano.

Ni les trujo costumbres peregrinas
el áspero dinero, ni el Oriente
compró la honestidad con piedras finas.

Joya fue la virtud pura y ardiente;
gala el merecimiento y alabanza;
sólo se codiciaba lo decente.

No de la pluma dependió la lanza,
ni el cántabro con cajas y tinteros
hizo el campo heredad, sino matanza.

sky that race yielded its eyes, but not its mind, to a more honorable, if not more restful sleep. Woman spun for her husband his shroud before [spinning] his clothes; she saw him less frequently a dandy than in danger. She was beside her husband more often in the army than in bed; when he was healthy, she risked, and when wounded, avenged him. They were all matrons, and none a lady: names given by the flattering courtier were not permitted by the severity of their reputation. The far-flung, sounding Ocean was a barrier to the bright mines which stole peace from the human heart. The rough new coin did not bring them foreign customs, nor did the Orient buy chastity with precious stones. Their jewel was virtue, pure and ardent; their finery was merit and praise; one coveted only what was appropriate. The lance was not dependent on the pen, nor did the Cantabrian with papers and inkwells convert fields into his heritage, but with bloody battle. And

Y España, con legítimos dineros,
no mendigando el crédito a Liguria,
más quiso los turbantes que los ceros.

Menos fuera la pérdida y la injuria,
si se volvieran Muzas los asientos;
que esta usura es peor que aquella furia.

Caducaban las aves en los vientos,
y espiraba decrépito el venado:
grande vejez duró en los elementos;

que el vientre entonces bien disciplinado
buscó satisfación, y no hartura,
y estaba la garganta sin pecado.

Del mayor infanzón de aquella pura
república de grandes hombres, era
una vaca sustento y armadura.

No había venido al gusto lisonjera
la pimienta arrugada, ni del clavo
la adulación fragrante forastera.

Carnero y vaca fue principio y cabo,
y con rojos pimientos, y ajos duros,
tan bien como el señor comió el esclavo.

Bebió la sed los arroyuelos puros:
después mostraron del carchesio a Baco
el camino los brindis mal seguros.

Spain, with sound currency, not begging credit from Liguria [the Genoese bankers], sought after turbans more than zeroes. There would be less loss and injury if the loans became Moorish captains, for the present usury is worse than that militant fury. Birds grew old in the wind, and deer died decrepit: great old age endured under the elements; for the belly then, well disciplined, sought satisfaction, and not excess, and the throat was sinless. For the greatest nobleman of that pure republic of great men, one cow was sustenance and armor. One's taste had not been flattered by wrinkled black pepper, nor the fragrant, foreign adulation of the clove. Mutton and beef were the first course and last, and with red pimentos and hard garlic, the slave ate as well as his master. Thirst drank up the pure little brooks: afterwards staggering toasts showed to Bacchus the way to the cup. The thin face,

El rostro macilento, el cuerpo flaco
eran recuerdo del trabajo honroso,
y honra y provecho andaban en un saco.

Pudo sin miedo un español velloso
llamar a los tudescos bacchanales,
y al holandés hereje y alevoso.

Pudo acusar los celos desiguales
a la Italia; pero hoy, de muchos modos,
somos copias, si son originales.

Las descendencias gastan muchos godos,
todos blasonan, nadie los imita;
y no son sucesores, sino apodos.

Vino el betún precioso que vomita
la ballena, o la espuma de las olas,
que el vicio, no el olor, nos acredita;

y quedaron las huestes españolas
bien perfumadas, pero mal regidas,
y alhajas las que fueron pieles solas.

Estaban las hazañas mal vestidas,
y aún no se hartaba de buriel y lana
la vanidad de fembras presumidas.

A la seda pomposa siciliana,
que manchó ardiente múrice, el romano
y el oro hicieron áspera y tirana.

the lean body were a reminder of honest work, and honors and profit wore a plain simple suit. A hairy Spaniard could fearlessly call the Germans drunkards and the Hollander a heretic and rebel. He could accuse Italy of vacillating zeal; but today, in many ways, we are copies, if they are originals. Genealogies display many Gothic ancestors, everyone boasts of them, but no one imitates them; and they are not successors, but surnames. There came the expensive ambergris, vomited by the whale or the waves' foam, which accredits our addictions, not our fragrance; and the Spanish forces were left well perfumed, but badly managed, and jewels replaced simple skins. Great deeds were poorly dressed, and even the vanity of presumptuous females did not get tired of natural homespun and wool. The fancy Sicilian silk, stained by glowing purple, was made harsh and tyrannical by the Roman and by gold. The worm had never been able to persuade the tough

Nunca al duro español supo el gusano
persuadir que vistiese su mortaja,
intercediendo el can por el verano.

Hoy desprecia el honor al que trabaja,
y entonces fue el trabajo ejecutoria,
y el vicio gradüó la gente baja.

Pretende el alentado joven gloria,
por dejar la vacada sin marido,
y de Ceres ofende la memoria;

un animal a la labor nacido,
y símbolo celoso a los mortales,
que a Jove fue disfraz, y fue vestido;

que un tiempo endureció manos reales,
y detrás de él los cónsules gimieron,
y rumia luz en campos celestiales:

¿por cuál enemistad se persuadieron
a que su apocamiento fuese hazaña,
y a las mieses tan grande ofensa hicieron?

¡Qué cosa es ver un infanzón de España,
abreviado en la silla a la gineta,
y gastar un caballo en una caña!

Que la niñez al gallo le acometa
con semejante munición apruebo,
mas no la edad madura y la perfeta.

Spaniard to wear his shroud [i.e., of the silkworm], even at the intercession of the dog-days in the summer. Now honor despises him who works, and then work was one's pedigree, and luxury graded the lower folk. The spirited youth seeks glory by depriving the herd of cows of its mate [the bull], and he offends the memory of Ceres [agriculture]; an animal born to work and a symbol of zealousness to mortals, who served Jove as disguise and clothing; who once hardened royal hands, and consuls groaned behind him, and he ruminates light on the fields of heaven [Taurus]: because of what enmity did they persuade themselves that to destroy him was a great deed, and thus committed so great an offense against the wheat fields? How ridiculous it is to see a nobleman of Spain cramped into a short-stirruped saddle and wearing out a horse with a cane lance! I approve of childhood attacking a rooster with such a weapon, but not full-grown maturity. Let the youth test his strength in squadron fronts; not his holly spear on the forehead of the useful animal. The diligent trumpet calls him, giving the force of law

Ejercite sus fuerzas el mancebo
en frentes de escuadrones, no en la frente
del útil bruto l'asta del acebo.

El trompeta le llama diligente,
dando fuerza de ley al viento vano,
y al son esté el ejército obediente.

¡Con cuánta majestad llena la mano
la pica, y el mosquete carga el hombro,
del que se atreve a ser buen castellano!

Con asco entre las otras gentes nombro
al que de su persona, sin decoro,
más quiere nota dar, que dar asombro.

Gineta y cañas son contagio moro;
restitúyanse justas y torneos,
y hagan paces las capas con el toro.

Pasadnos vos de juegos a trofeos,
que sólo grande rey y buen privado
pueden ejecutar estos deseos.

Vos, que hacéis repetir siglo pasado,
con desembarazarnos las personas,
y sacar a los miembros de cuidado,

vos distes libertad con las valonas,
para que sean corteses las cabezas,
desnudando el enfado a las coronas.

Y, pues vos enmendastes las cortezas,
dad a la mejor parte medicina:
vuélvanse los tablados fortalezas.

to the empty wind, and let the army be obedient to the sound. With what majesty the pike fills the hand and the musket weighs down the shoulder of him who dares to be a good Castilian! I mention with disgust him who among other nations prefers, undecorously, attracting their attention with his figure to overwhelming them. Short stirrups and cane lances are a Moorish infection; let jousts and tourneys be restored, and let the capes make peace with the bull. Take us, sir, from games to heroic trophies, for only a great king and a good prime minister can carry out my desires. You, who cause a past century to return by disencumbering our bodies and freeing our limbs from vexations [i.e., of fancy clothing], you gave liberty along with Vandyke collars, freeing our heads [i.e., from ruffs] to be courteous and removing the annoyance from the crowns. And, since you have improved the externals, give treatment also to the better part: let bull rings be turned

Que la cortés estrella, que os inclina
a privar sin intento y sin venganza
(milagro que a la invidia desatina),

tiene por sola bienaventuranza
el reconocimiento temeroso,
no presumida y ciega confianza.

Y si os dio el ascendiente generoso
escudos, de armas y blasones llenos,
y por timbre el martirio gloriöso,

mejores sean por vos los que eran buenos
Guzmanes, y la cumbre desdeñosa
os muestre a su pesar campos serenos.

Lograd, señor, edad tan venturosa;
y cuando nuestras fuerzas examina
persecución unida y belicosa,

la militar valiente disciplina
tenga más platicantes que la plaza;
descansen tela falsa y tela fina.

Suceda a la marlota la coraza,
y si el Corpus con danzas no los pide,
velillos y oropel no hagan baza;

el que en treinta lacayos los divide,
hace suerte en el toro, y con un dedo
la hace en él la vara que los mide.

into fortresses. For the courteous star which inclines you to rule without ulterior motives and vengenace (a miracle which confuses envy) considers its sole blessing fearful recognition [of duty], not presumptuous, blind self-confidence. And if your noble ancestor gave you shields full of arms and blazons, and glorious martyrdom for a crest, let those who were good Guzmáns be all the better because of you, and let the proud peak of power lead you, despite itself, to serene fields. Bring to perfection, my lord, so fortunate an age; and while a united warlike opposition is testing our strength, let brave military discipline have more practitioners than the arena; let cloth targets and fine clothing be laid to rest. Let metal breastplate replace Moorish jerkin, and unless Corpus Christi dances require them, let gauze and tinsel cease prospering; he who distributes them [gauze and tinsel] among thirty lackeys tries his luck on the bull, and with one finger the yardstick which measures them [i.e., government regulations] has a go

Mandadlo ansí, que aseguraros puedo
que habéis de restaurar más que Pelayo;
pues valdrá por ejércitos el miedo,
y os verá el cielo administrar su rayo.

POEMA RELIGIOSO

151

En la muerte de Cristo, contra la dureza del corazón del hombre

Pues hoy derrama noche el sentimiento
por todo el cerco de la lumbre pura,
y amortecido el sol en sombra obscura
da lágrimas al fuego y voz al viento;
pues de la muerte el negro encerramiento
descubre con temblor la sepultura,
y el monte, que embaraza la llanura
del mar cercano, se divide atento:
dc piedra es, hombre duro, de diamante
tu corazón, pues muerte tan severa
no anega con tus ojos tu semblante.
Mas no es de piedra, no; que si lo fuera,
de lástima de ver a Dios amante,
entre las otras piedras se rompiera.

at him. Give orders of this sort, and I can assure you that you will restore more than Pelayo did; for fear will be worth armies, and heaven will see you administering its thunderbolts.

RELIGIOUS POEM, *151, On the death of Christ, against the hardness of man's heart:* Since sadness today sheds night upon the whole sphere of pure light, and the deadened sun in shadowy darkness gives the fire tears and the wind a voice; since the black enclosure of death tremblingly reveals the sepulcher, and the mountain, which makes pregnant the flatness of the nearby sea, splits attentively: your heart, hard man, is of stone, of diamond, since so cruel a death does not drown your face in your eyes. But no, it is not of stone; for if it were, with the pity of seeing God so loving, it would break, along with the other stones.

EPITAFIOS

212

A Roma sepultada en sus ruinas

Buscas en Roma a Roma, ¡oh, peregrino!,
y en Roma misma a Roma no la hallas:
cadáver son las que ostentó murallas,
y tumba de sí proprio el Aventino.
Yace donde reinaba el Palatino;
y limadas del tiempo, las medallas
más se muestran destrozo a las batallas
de las edades que blasón latino.
Sólo el Tibre quedó, cuya corriente,
si ciudad la regó, ya sepoltura
la llora con funesto son doliente.
¡Oh, Roma!, en tu grandeza, en tu hermosura,
huyó lo que era firme, y solamente
lo fugitivo permanece y dura.

222

Memoria inmortal de don Pedro Girón, duque de Osuna, muerto en la prisión

Faltar pudo su patria al grande Osuna,
pero no a su defensa sus hazañas;
diéronle muerte y cárcel las Españas,
de quien él hizo esclava la Fortuna.
Lloraron sus invidias una a una

EPITAPHS, *212, To Rome buried in its ruins:* You search in Rome for Rome, oh pilgrim!, and in Rome itself you don't find Rome: a corpse is the walls which it once displayed, and a tomb for itself the Aventine. The Palatine lies where it used to reign; and the medallions, worn away by time, reveal themselves to be more the victims of the ages' battles than the glory of Latium. Only the Tiber has remained, whose current, if it once watered it as a city, now weeps over it as a tomb with funereal sound. Oh Rome!, in your grandeur, in your beauty, that which was firm has fled, and only what is fugitive remains and endures. *222, To the immortal memory of Don Pedro Girón, Duke of Osuna, who died in prison [1624]:* His country could fail the great Osuna, but his deeds could not fail its defense; he was given death and prison by the same Spain to whom he had enslaved Fortune. Foreign nations, along with his own, wept for their envies one by one; his tomb is

con las proprias naciones las extrañas;
su tumba son de Flandres las campañas,
y su epitafio la sangrienta luna.
En sus exequias encendió al Vesubio
Parténope, y Trinacria al Mongibelo;
el llanto militar creció en diluvio.
Diole el mejor lugar Marte en su cielo;
la Mosa, el Rhin, el Tajo y el Danubio
murmuran con dolor su desconsuelo.

274

A la muerte del Rey de Francia

En tierra sí, no en fama, consumida,
yaces, oh vida, cuando más temblada,
de la púrpura al mármol derribada
por, más que a sangre, a llanto abierta herida:
llorada ya de cuantos fue temida;
del hado no, del mundo respetada;
en quien con vil usar sangrienta espada
tantos quitó a la muerte en una vida.
Cuando poner presume en mil victorias
tintos los campos y los mares rojos,
desnudos centros de invidiosas glorias,
viste el suelo un traidor de sus despojos;
de horror, su lis; de ejemplo, las memorias;
de ocio, las manos; de piedad, los ojos.

the Flemish campaigns, and his epitaph the bloodstained moon [the Mohammedan flag]. At his funeral Naples ignited Vesuvius and Sicily Mongibello; the soldiers' tears grew into a flood. Mars gave him the best place in his heaven; the Meuse, the Rhine, the Tagus and the Danube sadly murmur their disconsolation. *274, On the death of the King of France:* On earth destroyed, but not in fame, you lie, oh life, when most feared, struck down from purple to marble by a wound opened, more than to blood, to tears: wept for now by all who feared him; respected not by fate, but by the world; in whom a bloodstained sword, foully used, saved so many men from death in one life. When he presumes in a thousand victories to stain the fields and turn red the seas, the stripped sites of envy-producing glory, the earth clothes a traitor with his spoils, his *fleur de lys* with horror, his memory with exemplarity, one's hands with idleness, one's eyes with sorrow.

POEMAS AMOROSOS

294

Con ejemplos muestra a Flora
la brevedad de la hermosura
para no malograrla

La mocedad del año, la ambiciosa
vergüenza del jardín, el encarnado
oloroso rubí, Tiro abrevïado,
también del año presunción hermosa;
la ostentación lozana de la rosa,
deidad del campo, estrella del cercado;
el almendro en su propria flor nevado,
que anticiparse a los calores osa,
reprehensiones son, ¡oh Flora!, mudas
de la hermosura y la soberbia humana,
que a las leyes de flor está sujeta.
Tu edad se pasará mientras lo dudas;
de ayer te habrás de arrepentir mañana,
y tarde y con dolor serás discreta.

336

Amante agradecido a las lisonjas
mentirosas de un sueño

¡Ay Floralba! Soñé que te ... ¿Dirélo?
Sí, pues que sueño fue: que te gozaba.
¿Y quién, sino un amante que soñaba,
juntara tanto infierno a tanto cielo?

LOVE POEMS, *294, By example he shows Flora the brevity of beauty, so that she will not waste it:* The year's youth, the garden's ambitious shyness, the red fragrant ruby, a brief Tyre [the city of purple dye], and also the year's lovely presumptuousness; the lush ostentation of the rose, the field's deity and the enclosure's star; the almond tree snow-covered with its own flowers, which dares to anticipate the heat, are silent warnings, oh Flora!, to beauty and human pride, which is subject to the flower's laws. Your time will pass away while you hesitate; for yesterday you will have to repent tomorrow, and too late and painfully you will be wise. *336, A lover grateful for the deceptive flattery of a dream:* Alas, Floralba!, I dreamt that you were . . . Shall I say it? Yes, for it was a dream: that I was making love to you. And who, except a lover who was dreaming, could combine such a hell with

Mis llamas con tu nieve y con tu yelo,
cual suele opuestas flechas de su aljaba,
mezclaba Amor, y honesto las mezclaba,
como mi adoración en su desvelo.
Y dije: «Quiera Amor, quiera mi suerte,
que nunca duerma yo, si estoy despierto,
y que si duermo, que jamás despierte».
Mas desperté del dulce desconcierto;
y vi que estuve vivo con la muerte,
y vi que con la vida estaba muerto.

337

Venganza de la edad
en hermosura presumida

Cuando tuvo, Floralba, tu hermosura,
cuantos ojos te vieron, en cadena,
con presunción, de honestidad ajena,
los despreció soberbia tu locura.
Persuadióte el espejo conjetura
de eternidades en la edad serena,
y que a su plata el oro en tu melena
nunca del tiempo trocaría la usura.
Ves que la que antes eras, sepultada
yaces en la que vives, y quejosa
tarde te acusa vanidad burlada.
Mueres doncella, y no de virtuosa,
sino de presumida y despreciada:
esto eres vieja, esotro fuiste hermosa.

such a heaven? My flames with your snow and ice were being mixed by Love, as he is wont to do with the opposing arrows of his quiver, and he mixed them chastely, as is my adoration in his wakefulness. And I said: "May Love, may my fate will that I never sleep, if I'm awake, and that if I'm asleep, I never wake." But I did awaken from the sweet discord; and I found that I was alive with death, and I found that with life I was dead. *337, The vengeance of age upon presumptuous beauty:* When, Floralba, your beauty held enchained every eye that saw you, with an unchaste presumptuousness your proud madness scorned them. The mirror persuaded you to conjecture eternities of serene age, and that time's usury would never change the gold of your hair into his silver. You see that the woman you once were lies buried in the living one you are now, and plaintively accuses you too late of deceived vanity. You die a virgin, and not because you are virtuous, but presumptuous and despised: the latter you are when you're old, the former you were when you were beautiful. *396, Sleep (silva)*: For

396

El sueño
(silva)

¿Con qué culpa tan grave,
sueño blando y süave,
pude en largo destierro merecerte
que se aparte de mí tu olvido manso,
pues no te busco yo por ser descanso,
sino por muda imagen de la muerte?
Cuidados veladores
hacen inobedientes mis dos ojos
a la ley de las horas;
no han podido vencer a mis dolores
las noches, ni dar paz a mis enojos;
madrugan más en mí que en las auroras
lágrimas a este llano,
que amanece a mi mal siempre temprano;
y tanto, que persuade la tristeza
a mis dos ojos, que nacieron antes
para llorar que para verte, sueño.
De sosiego los tienes ignorantes,
de tal manera, que al morir el día
con luz enferma, vi que permitía
el sol que le mirasen en poniente.
Con pies torpes, al punto, ciega y fría,
cayó de las estrellas blandamente
la noche tras las pardas sombras mudas

what grave offense, soft, sweet sleep, have I deserved of you that in distant exile your gentle oblivion should abandon me, for I do not seek you because you are restful, but because you are the mute image of death? Wakeful worries make my two eyes disobedient to the hours' law; the nights have not been able to overcome my suffering or pacify my sorrows; in me they awaken earlier than this plain's tears [dew] at dawn, for morning always comes early to my troubles; so much so that grief persuades my eyes that they were born to weep rather than to see you, sleep. You keep them so ignorant of rest that, when the day died with a sickly light, I saw the sun allow them to look at him as he set. Immediately, with clumsy feet, dark and cold, night fell softly from the stars behind the dark, mute shadows which

que el sueño persuadieron a la gente.
Escondieron las galas a los prados,
[y quedaron desnudas]
estas laderas, y sus peñas, solas;
duermen ya, entre sus montes recostados,
los mares y las olas.
Si con algún acento
ofenden las orejas,
es que, entre sueños, dan al cielo quejas
del yerto lecho y duro acogimiento,
que blandos hallan en los cerros duros.
Los arroyuelos puros
se adormecen al son del llanto mío,
y, a su modo, también se duerme el río.
Con sosiego agradable
se dejan poseer de ti las flores;
mudos están los males;
no hay cuidado que hable:
faltan lenguas y voz a los dolores,
y en todos los mortales
yace la vida envuelta en alto olvido.
Tan sólo mi gemido
pierde el respeto a tu silencio santo;
yo tu quietud molesto con mi llanto
y te desacredito
el nombre de callado, con mi grito.
Dame, cortés mancebo, algún reposo;
no seas digno del nombre de avariento,
en el más desdichado y firme amante

urged sleep upon people. They hid the meadows' finery, and these slopes were left naked, and their crags in solitude; the seas and waves are now asleep, curled up among their mountains. If they assault the ears with any noise, it is because, half asleep, they complain to the sky of the hard bed and unfriendly reception that their softness found upon the hard hills. The clear brooks are lulled to sleep to the sound of my tears, and in its way the river also goes to sleep. With pleasant relaxation the flowers let themselves be possessed by you; troubles are mute; no worry speaks: griefs lack tongues and voices, and in all mortals life lies wrapped in deep oblivion. Only my moan is disrespectful of your holy silence; I disturb your quietness with my weeping and I discredit your reputation for silence with my cry. Give me, courteous youth [Morpheus], some rest; don't win the reputation of being stingy toward the most unfortunate and steadfast lover, who de-

que lo merece ser por dueño hermoso;
débate alguna pausa mi tormento.
Gózante en las cabañas
y debajo del cielo
los ásperos villanos;
hállate en el rigor de los pantanos
y encuéntrate en las nieves y en el yelo
el soldado valiente,
y yo no puedo hallarte, aunque lo intente,
entre mi pensamiento y mi deseo.
Ya, pues, con dolor creo
que eres más riguroso que la tierra,
más duro que la roca,
pues te alcanza el soldado envuelto en guerra,
y en ella mi alma por jamás te toca.
Mira que es gran rigor. Dame siquiera
lo que de ti desprecia tanto avaro
por el oro en que alegre considera,
hasta que da la vuelta el tiempo claro;
lo que había de dormir en blando lecho,
y da el enamorado a su señora,
y a ti se te debía de derecho.
Dame lo que desprecia de ti agora
por robar el ladrón; lo que desecha
el que invidiosos celos tuvo y llora.
Quede en parte mi queja satisfecha:
tócame con el cuento de tu vara;
oirán siquiera el ruido de tus plumas
mis desventuras sumas;

serves to be so for the sake of a beautiful mistress; let my torment be indebted to you for respite. In their cabins and under the sky crude villagers enjoy you; in the discomfort of the swamps and in snow and ice the brave soldier finds you, and I can't find you, although I try, between my thoughts and my desires. So now painfully I believe that you are harsher than the earth, harder than the rock, for the soldier involved in war achieves you, and my soul at war never touches you. Consider how harsh it is. Give me at least that portion of you which many a miser scorns for the sake of the gold which he gloats over, until fair weather changes; that portion which the lover should have spent sleeping on a soft bed and gives to his lady, and was by rights owed to you. Give me that portion of you which the thief now despises for the sake of robbing; that portion wasted by him who was enviously jealous and weeps. Let my complaint be partially relieved: touch me with the tip of your wand; my extreme misfortune will hear at least the

que yo no quiero verte cara a cara,
ni que hagas más caso
de mí que hasta pasar por mí de paso;
o que a tu sombra negra, por lo menos,
si fueres a otra parte peregrino,
se le haga camino
por estos ojos, de sosiego ajenos.
Quítame, blando sueño, este desvelo,
o de él alguna parte,
y te prometo, mientras viere el cielo,
de desvelarme sólo en celebrarte.

448
Afectos varios de su corazón fluctuando en las ondas de los cabellos de Lisi

En crespa tempestad del oro undoso,
nada golfos de luz ardiente y pura
mi corazón, sediento de hermosura,
si el cabello deslazas generoso.
Leandro, en mar de fuego proceloso,
su amor ostenta, su vivir apura;
Icaro, en senda de oro mal segura,
arde sus alas por morir glorioso.
Con pretensión de fénix, encendidas
sus esperanzas, que difuntas lloro,
intenta que su muerte engendre vidas.
Avaro y rico y pobre, en el tesoro,
el castigo y la hambre imita a Midas,
Tántalo en fugitiva fuente de oro.

sound of your feathers; for I don't want to see you face to face, or for you to give me any more attention than to pass over me once lightly; or for your dark shadow, at least, if you go wandering off elsewhere, to make a path across these eyes, deprived of rest. Take from me, sweet sleep, this wakefulness, or some part of it, and I promise you, as long as I see heaven, to stay awake only to praise you. *448, Various emotions of his heart fluctuating within the waves of Lisi's hair:* In a frothy tempest of wavy gold, across gulfs of pure burning light swims my heart, thirsting for beauty, if you unbind your generous hair. Leander, on a stormy sea of fire, displays his love, refines his life; Icarus, on an unsafe golden path, burns up his wings for a glorious death. With the ambition of a phoenix, setting fire to his hopes, for whose death I weep, he [my heart] tries to make his death engender lives. Miserly and rich and poor in the midst of this treasure, he imitates the punishment and hunger of Midas, a Tantalus in a fleeing fountain of gold.

464

Retrato de Lisi que traía en una sortija

En breve cárcel traigo aprisionado,
con toda su familia de oro ardiente,
el cerco de la luz resplandeciente,
y grande imperio del Amor cerrado.
Traigo el campo que pacen estrellado
las fieras altas de la piel luciente,
y a escondidas del cielo y del Oriente,
día de luz y parto mejorado.
Traigo todas las Indias en mi mano,
perlas que, en un diamante, por rubíes,
pronuncian con desdén sonoro yelo,
y razonan tal vez fuego tirano,
relámpagos de risa carmesíes,
auroras, gala y presunción del cielo.

471

Amor constante más allá de la muerte

Cerrar podrá mis ojos la postrera
sombra que me llevare el blanco día,
y podrá desatar esta alma mía
hora a su afán ansioso lisonjera;
mas no, de esotra parte, en la ribera,
dejará la memoria, en donde ardía:
nadar sabe mi llama la agua fría,

464, A portrait of Lisi which he carried in a ring: In a narrow jail I bear imprisoned, with its whole family of burning gold, the resplendent sphere of light, and Love's great empire enclosed. I bear the starry field which is grazed by the lofty beasts of gleaming skin, and concealed from the heavens and the rising sun, an improved bright sky and new birth. I bear all the Indies on my hand, pearls [teeth] which, set in a diamond [hard, cruel], through rubies [lips], pronounce with scorn tinkling ice, and sometimes they speak forth tyrannical fire, scarlet lightning-flashes of laughter, dawns, the finery and presumption of the heavens. *471, A love constant beyond death:* My eyes may be closed by the final shadow which will take away from me the bright day, and this soul of mine may be freed by an hour indulgent to its anxious longing; but it will not, on the further shore, leave the memory in which it used to burn; my flame is able to swim across the cold

y perder el respeto a ley severa.
  Alma a quien todo un dios prisión ha sido,
venas que humor a tanto fuego han dado,
medulas que han gloriosamente ardido:
  su cuerpo dejará, no su cuidado;
serán ceniza, mas tendrá sentido;
polvo serán, mas polvo enamorado.

474

Amante desesperado del premio y obstinado en amar

  ¡Qué perezosos pies, qué entretenidos
pasos lleva la muerte por mis daños!
El camino me alargan los engaños,
y en mí se escandalizan los perdidos.
  Mis ojos no se dan por entendidos;
y, por descaminar mis desengaños,
me disimulan la verdad los años
y les guardan el sueño a los sentidos.
  Del vientre a la prisión vine en naciendo;
de la prisión iré al sepulcro amando,
y siempre en el sepulcro estaré ardiendo.
  Cuantos plazos la muerte me va dando,
prolijidades son que va creciendo
porque no acabe de morir penando.

water and disobey a harsh law. A soul which has been imprisoned by no less than a god, the veins which have supplied the moisture to so great a fire, the marrow which has gloriously burned: it will leave its body, not its [loving] anguish; they will be ash, but it will have feelings; they will be dust, but dust which is in love. *474, A lover who despairs of the prize and persists in loving:* What lagging feet, what prolonged steps death drags over my injuries! My road is lengthened by deceptions, and at me even the damned are scandalized. My eyes pretend not to understand; and to sidetrack my undeceptions, the years disguise truth for me and keep my senses asleep. From the womb into prison I came when I was born; from the prison I shall go to the tomb in love, and forever in the tomb I shall be burning. All the reprieves that death keeps giving me are procrastinations which death prolongs so that I may not complete the process of dying in pain, *477, He*

477

Exhorta a los que amàren, que no sigan los pasos por donde ha hecho su viaje

Cargado voy de mí: veo delante
muerte que me amenaza la jornada;
ir porfiando por la senda errada,
más de necio será que de constante.
Si por su mal me sigue ciego amante
(que nunca es sola suerte desdichada),
¡ay!, vuelva en sí y atrás: no dé pisada
donde la dio tan ciego caminante.
Ved cuán errado mi camino ha sido,
cuán solo y triste, y cuán desordenado,
que nunca ansí le anduvo pie perdido;
pues, por no desandar lo caminado,
viendo delante y cerca fin temido,
con pasos que otros huyen le he buscado.

POEMAS SATÍRICOS

522

A un hombre de gran nariz

Erase un hombre a una nariz pegado,
érase una nariz superlativa,
érase una alquitara medio viva,
érase un peje espada mal barbado;

exhorts those who love not to follow the footsteps along which he has traveled: I'm loaded down with myself: I see before me death threatening my journey; to insist on following a mistaken route is more the act of a fool than of a faithful man. If to his hurt a blind lover follows me (for misfortune is never single), alas!, let him come to his senses and turn back: let him not take a step where steps were taken by so blind a wayfarer. See how mistaken my way has been, how lonely and sad, and how disorderly, for never has a misguided foot so wandered; because, so as not to retrace my course, seeing a fearful end ahead and close, with steps which others avoid I have sought it.

SATIRICAL POEMS, *522, To a man with a big nose:* There once was a man fastened to a nose, there once was a superlative nose, there was once a half-alive alembic, there once was a badly bearded swordfish; there was a

era un reloj de sol mal encarado,
érase un elefante boca arriba,
érase una nariz sayón y escriba,
un Ovidio Nasón mal narigado.
Erase el espolón de una galera,
érase una pirámide de Egito,
los doce tribus de narices era;
érase un naricísimo infinito,
frisón archinariz, caratulera,
sabañón garrafal, morado y frito.

545

A Apolo siguiendo a Dafne

Bermejazo platero de las cumbres,
a cuya luz se espulga la canalla:
la ninfa Dafne, que se afufa y calla,
si la quieres gozar, paga y no alumbres.
Si quieres ahorrar de pesadumbres,
ojo del cielo, trata de compralla:
en confites gastó Marte la malla,
y la espada en pasteles y en azumbres.
Volvióse en bolsa Júpiter severo;
levantóse las faldas la doncella
por recogerle en lluvia de dinero.
Astucia fue de alguna dueña estrella,
que de estrella sin dueña no lo infiero:
Febo, pues eres sol, sírvete de ella.

lopsided sundial, there once was an elephant face up, there once was a nose for the scribes and executioners, an Ovidius Naso badly nosed. There was once the bowsprit of a galley, there was once a pyramid of Egypt, the twelve tribes of noses it was; there once was an infinite nosiest, a Frisian archnose, a mask-mold, a freak chilblain, all purple and fried. *545, To Apollo, pursuing Daphne:* Redheaded silversmith of the peaks, in whose sunlight the beggars pick their fleas: the nymph Daphne, who scrams and is silent, if you want to possess her, pay her and don't give light. If you want to save yourself trouble, eye of heaven, try to buy her: Mars sold his coat of mail for sweets, and his sword for pastries and jugs. Severe Jupiter turned himself into a purse; the maiden raised her skirt to catch him in a shower of gold. That was the guile of some duenna star, for I can't attribute it to a star without a duenna: Phoebus, since you're the sun, make use

546

A Dafne, huyendo de Apolo

«Tras vos, un alquimista va corriendo,
Dafne, que llaman Sol, ¿y vos tan cruda?
Vos os volvéis murciégalo sin duda,
pues vais del Sol y de la luz huyendo.
»El os quiere gozar, a lo que entiendo,
si os coge en esta selva tosca y ruda:
su aljaba suena, está su bolsa muda;
el perro, pues no ladra, está muriendo.
»Buhonero de signos y planetas,
viene haciendo ademanes y figuras,
cargado de bochornos y cometas.»
Esto la dije; y en cortezas duras
de laurel se ingirió contra sus tretas,
y, en escabeche, el Sol se quedó a escuras.

668

Letrilla satírica

Vuela, pensamiento, y diles
a los ojos que más quiero
que hay dinero.

Del dinero que pidió,
a la que adorando estás
las nuevas la llevarás,
pero los talegos no.
Di que doy en no dar yo,

of her. *546, To Daphne, fleeing from Apollo:* "After you an alchemist is running, Daphne, whom they call the Sun, and you're so rough? You are doubtless turning into a bat, since you flee from the Sun and the light. He wants to possess you, as I understand it, if he catches you in this rough, rude forest: his quiver makes noise, his purse is mute; the dog, since he isn't barking, is dying. A peddler of signs and planets, he's making gestures and cutting figures, laden with hot weather and comets." This I said to her; and she grafted herself into hard laurel bark against his advances, and the Sun, marinated, was left in the dark, *668, Satirical Song: Fly, my thoughts, and tell my most beloved darling that there's money.* Concerning the money she asked for, you will take the news to her whom you adore, but not the money bags. Tell her I've decided not to give, for in order to

pues para hallar el placer,
el ahorrar y el tener
han mudado los carriles.
Vuela, pensamiento, y diles
a los ojos que más quiero
que hay dinero.

A los ojos, que en mirallos
la libertad perderás,
que hay dineros les dirás,
pero no gana de dallos.
Yo sólo pienso cerrallos,
que no son la ley de Dios,
que se ha de encerrar en dos,
sino en talegos cerriles.
Vuela, pensamiento, y diles
a los ojos que más quiero
que hay dinero.

Si con agrado te oyere
esa esponja de la villa,
que hay dinero has de decilla,
y que ¡ay de quien le diere!
Si ajusticiar te quisiere,
está firme como Martos;
no te dejes hacer cuartos
de sus dedos alguaciles.
Vuela, pensamiento, y diles
a los ojos que más quiero
que hay dinero.

find pleasure, keeping and having have changed my track. *Fly, etc.* To those eyes, which when you see them you will lose your freedom, you'll tell them that there's money, but no inclination to give it. I intend merely to lock it up, for it's not God's law, which can be summed up in two, but enclosed in sealable money bags. *Fly, etc.* If she listens to you with pleasure, that village sponge, you're to tell her that there's money and alas for him who gives it! If she tries to punish you, be as firm as Martos [cliff]; don't let yourself be quartered by her constable fingers. *Fly, etc. 669, Satirical*

669

Letrilla satírica

Poderoso caballero
es don Dinero.

Madre, yo al oro me humillo;
él es mi amante y mi amado,
pues, de puro enamorado,
de contino anda amarillo;
que pues, doblón o sencillo,
hace todo cuanto quiero,
poderoso caballero
es don Dinero.

Nace en las Indias honrado,
donde el mundo le acompaña;
viene a morir en España,
y es en Génova enterrado.
Y pues quien le trae al lado
es hermoso, aunque sea fiero,
poderoso caballero
es don Dinero.

Es galán y es como un oro,
tiene quebrado el color,
persona de gran valor,
tan cristiano como moro.
Pues que da y quita el decoro
y quebranta cualquier fuero,
poderoso caballero
es don Dinero.

Song: A powerful knight is Sir Money. Mother, I humble myself before gold; he is my lover and beloved, for he's so much in love that his complexion is always pale; and since, whether doubloon or of less value, he always does everything I wish, *a powerful knight is Sir Money.* He's honorably born in the Indies, where the whole world attends him; he comes to die in Spain and is buried in [the banks of] Genoa. And since he who has him at his side is handsome, even though he be fierce, *a powerful knight is Sir Money.* He's gallant and bright as a penny, he's off-color, a person of great value, whether Christian or Moorish. Since he gives and takes away appearances and breaks any law whatsoever, *a powerful knight is Sir Money.*

Son sus padres principales,
y es de nobles descendiente,
porque en las venas de Oriente
todas las sangres son reales;
y pues es quien hace iguales
al duque y al ganadero,
poderoso caballero
es don Dinero.

Mas ¿a quién no maravilla
ver en su gloria sin tasa
que es lo menos de su casa
doña Blanca de Castilla?
Pero, pues da al bajo silla
y al cobarde hace guerrero,
poderoso caballero
es don Dinero.

Sus escudos de armas nobles
son siempre tan principales,
que sin sus escudos reales
no hay escudos de armas dobles;
y pues a los mismos robles
da codicia su minero,
poderoso caballero
es don Dinero.

Por importar en los tratos
y dar tan buenos consejos,
en las casas de los viejos
gatos le guardan de gatos.
Y pues él rompe recatos
y ablanda al juez más severo,

His parents are well-to-do people, and he's a descendent of nobles, for in Oriental veins all blood is royal; and since it is he who makes equal the duke and the cattleman, *a powerful gentleman is Sir Money*. But who isn't amazed to discover that in his limitless glory, the least member of his house is Lady Penny of Castile? But, since he gives the lowly a seat and makes the coward a warrior, *a powerful knight is Sir Money*. His coats of noble arms are always so well-to-do that without his royal shields there are no doubloon coat of arms; and since even oak trees are made covetous by his name, *a*

poderoso caballero
es don Dinero.

Y es tanta su majestad
(aunque son sus duelos hartos),
que con haberle hecho cuartos,
no pierde su autoridad;
pero, pues da calidad
al noble y al pordiosero,
poderoso caballero
es don Dinero.

Nunca vi damas ingratas
a su gusto y afición,
que a las caras de un doblón
hacen sus caras baratas;
y pues las hace bravatas
desde una bolsa de cuero,
poderoso caballero
es don Dinero.

Más valen en cualquier tierra
(¡mirad si es harto sagaz!)
sus escudos en la paz
que rodelas en la guerra.
Y pues al pobre le entierra
y hace proprio al forastero,
poderoso caballero
es don Dinero.

powerful knight is Sir Money. Because he's important in dealings and gives such good advice, in the old folks' houses sacks guard him from thieves. And since he breaks down inhibitions and softens the severest judge, *a powerful knight is Sir Money.* And his majesty is so great (although his griefs are extreme) that, even when quartered, he doesn't lose his authority; but, since he gives quality to nobleman and to beggar, *a powerful knight is Sir Money.* I've never seen ladies be hostile to his pleasure and inclination, for in the face of a doubloon they make their dear faces cheap; and since he threatens them from a leather purse, *a powerful knight is Sir Money.* In any land (consider how wise he is!) his coats of arms are worth more in peace than round shields are in war. And since he buries the poor man and naturalizes the foreigner, *a powerful knight is Sir Money. 679, Satirical Song*

679

Letrilla satírica
[*Bueno. Malo.*]

Que le preste el ginovés
al casado su hacienda;
que al dar su mujer por prenda,
preste él paciencia después;
que la cabeza y los pies
le vista el dinero ajeno,
bueno.

Mas que venga a suceder
que sus reales y ducados
se los vuelvan en cornados
los cuartos de su mujer;
que se venga rico a ver
con semejante regalo,
malo.

Que el mancebo principal
aplique por la pobreza
a ser ladrón su nobleza,
por ser arte liberal;
que sea podenco del real
más escondido en el seno,
bueno.

Mas que en tales desatinos
venga el pobre desdichado,
de puro descaminado,

[*Okay. Bad.*]*:* That the Genoese banker should lend the married man his property; that, when he puts up his wife as security, he should be lent patience later; that he should be dressed head and foot in someone else's money, *is okay.* But that it should eventually happen that his pence and pounds be changed into horn-coins [cuckolds] by his wife's quarters; that he should consider himself to be rich with such a gift, *is bad.* That the young gentleman, because of poverty, should apply his nobility to being a thief, as a liberal art; that he should hound the penny best hidden in one's bosom, *is okay.* But that in such wild errors the poor wretch should so lose his way

a parar por los caminos;
que conozca los teatinos
por intercesión de un palo,
malo.

Que el hidalgo, por grandeza,
muestre, cuando riñe a solas,
en la multitud de olas
tormentas en la cabeza;
que disfrace su pobreza
con rostro grave y sereno,
bueno.

Mas que haciendo tanta estima
de sus deudos principales,
coma las ollas nabales,
como batalla marina;
que la haga cristalina
a su capa el pelo ralo,
malo.

779

Pavura de los condes de Carrión [*romance*]

Medio día era por filo,
que rapar podía la barba,
cuando, después de mascar,
el Cid sosiega la panza:
la gorra sobre los ojos
y floja la martingala,
boquiabierto y cabizbajo,

that he ends up [quartered] at the crossroad; that he should get to know the confessor-priests by the intercession of a gallows, *is bad*. That the aristocrat, for grandeur, should reveal, when he scolds himself, in the midst of waves, tempests in his head; that he should disguise his poverty with a calm, solemn face, *is okay*. But that, holding so high an opinion of his well-born relatives, he should eat navy beans [literally, turnip stews], as a form of sea battle; that its thinning nap should make his cape transparent, *is bad*. ***779, The Fright of the Counts of Carrion*** [*ballad*]: It was noon sharp, which could shave a beard, when, after chewing, the Cid was calming his belly: his cap over his eyes and his breeches loosened, mouth opened and

roncando como una vaca.
Guárdale el sueño Bermudo,
y sus dos yernos le guardan,
apartándole las moscas
del pescuezo y de la cara,
cuando unas voces salidas
por fuerza de la garganta,
no dichas de voluntad,
sino de miedo pujadas,
se oyeron en el palacio,
se escucharon en la cuadra,
diciendo: «¡Guardá: el león!»,
y en esto entró por la sala.
Apenas Diego y Fernando
le vieron tender la zarpa,
cuando hicieron sabidoras
de su temor a sus bragas.
El mal olor de los dos
al pobre león engaña,
y por cuerpos muertos deja
los que tal perfume lanzan.
A venir acatarrado
el león, a los dos mata;
pues de miedo del perfume
no les siguió las espaldas.
El menor, Fernán González,
detrás de un escaño a gatas,
por esconderse, abrumó
sus costillas con las tablas.
Diego, más determinado,

head low, snoring like a cow. Bermudo is watching his sleep, and his two sons-in-law are watching him, shooing the flies from his neck and face, when a couple of shouts, forced out of the throat, not spoken willingly, but pushed by fear, were heard in the palace, were listened to in the stable, saying, "Look out, the lion!" and at this point it entered the hall. Hardly had Diego and Fernando seen him stretch out his claw when they made their pants aware of their fright. The bad odor of the two of them fools the poor lion, and he leaves as dead bodies things that give out such a perfume. If the lion had had a cold, he would have killed them both; because, for fear of the perfume, he didn't pursue their backs. The younger, Fernán González, behind a chair on hands and knees, to hide himself, bruised his ribs against the boards. Diego, more determined, to hide, threads himself

por un boquerón se ensarta
a esconderse, donde van
de retorno las viandas.
 Bermudo, que vio el león,
revuelta al brazo la capa
y sacando un asador
que tiene humos de espada,
 en la defensa se puso.
Despertó al Cid la borrasca;
y abriendo entrambos los ojos
empedrados de lagañas,
 tal grito le dio al león,
que le aturde y le acobarda:
que hay leones enemigos
de voces y de palabras.
 Envióle a su leonera
sin que le diese fianzas;
por sus yernos preguntó,
receloso de desgracia.
 Allí respondió Bermudo:
«Señor, no receléis nada,
pues se guardan vuesos yernos
en Castilla como Pascua.»
 Y remeciendo el escaño,
a Fernán González hallan
devanado en su bohemio,
hecho ovillo en la botarga.
 Las narices del buen Cid
a saberlo se adelantan,
que le trujeron las nuevas

through a hole where food goes on the way back. Bermudo, who saw the lion, wrapping his cape about his arm and taking out a spit which has swordlike pretentions, put himself on guard. The racket woke the Cid; and opening both eyes, paved with granular sand, he gave the lion such a yell that he upsets and cows him: for there are lions who don't like shouts and words. He sent him to his lion cage without asking him for security; he asked for his sons-in-law, fearful of a mishap. At that point Bermudo replied: "Sir, have no fear, for your sons-in-law are keeping themselves as Christmas is kept in Castile." And shaking the chair, they find Fernán González unraveled in his cape, all wound up in his pants. The good Cid's nose goes ahead to find out, for the news was brought to him by the steam

los vapores de sus calzas.
Salió cubierto de tierra
y lleno de telarañas;
corrióse el Cid de mirarlo,
y en esta guisa le fabla:
«Agachado estabais, Conde,
y tenéis mucha más traza
de home que aguardó jeringa,
que del que espera batalla.
»Connusco habedes yantado:
¡oh, que mala pro vos faga,
pues tan presto bajó el miedo
los yantares a las ancas!
»Sacárades a Tizona,
que ella vos asegurara,
pues en vos no es rabiseca,
según la humedad que anda.»
Gil Díaz, el escudero
que al Cid contino acompaña,
con la mano en las narices,
todo sepultado en bascas,
trayendo detrás de sí
a Diego, el yerno que falta,
con una mano le enseña,
mientras con otra se tapa:
«Vedes aquí, señor mío,
un fijo de vuesa casa,
el Conde de Carrïón,
que esconde mal su crianza.

from his trousers. He came out all covered with dirt and full of cobwebs; the Cid got angry when he saw him, and speaks to him in this wise: "You were all crouched down, Count, and you resemble far more a man who waited for an enema than one who waits for battle. You have dined with us: may it not be to your good health, for fear so quickly lowered the dinner to your rump! You should have drawn the sword Tizona, and it would have kept you safe, for on you it isn't dry-tailed, with all that humidity around." Gil Díaz, the squire who always accompanies the Cid, with his hand on his nose, all buried in retches, leading behind him Diego, the missing son-in-law, points at him with one hand while covering himself with the other: "Here you see, my lord, a son of your household, the Count of Carrion, who can't

»De dónde yo le he sacado,
sus vestidos vos lo parlan,
y a voces sus palominos
chillan, señor, lo que pasa.
»Más cedo podréis tomar
a Valencia y sus murallas,
que de ningún cabo al conde,
por no haber de do le asgan.
»Si no merece de yerno
el nombre por esta causa,
tenga el de servidor vueso,
pues tanta parte le alcanza.»
Sañudo le mira el Cid;
con mal talante le encara:
«De esta vez, amigos condes,
descubierto habéis la caca.
»¿Pavor de un león hobistes,
estando con vuesas armas,
fincando en compaña mía,
que para seguro basta?
» Por San Millán, que me corro,
mirándovos de esa traza,
y que, de lástima y asco,
me revolvéis las entrañas.
»El que de infanzón se precia,
face en el pavor y el ansia
de las tripas corazón:
así el refrán vos lo canta.
»Mas, vos, en esta presura,

conceal his breeding. Where I pulled him out of, his clothing tells you, and his squabs [feces] are yelling out loud, sir, what is going on. You can more easily take Valencia and its walls, than take hold of the count from any angle, for there is nowhere to grab him. If for this reason he doesn't deserve the name of son-in-law, let him have that of your servant [*cf. servicios—toilet*], for he has so large a share." The Cid looks at him angrily; he faces him with a scowl: "This time, friend counts, you've uncovered the dung. You were afraid of a lion when wearing your arms and while in my company, which is sufficient security? By St. Millan, I am angry, looking at you in that condition, and you make me so sorry and sick that my stomach is unsettled. He who is proud to be a nobleman, when in fear and anxiety, makes a stout heart out of his guts: that's how the saying goes. But you, in this

sin acatar vuesa casta,
facéis del corazón tripas,
que el puro temor vos vacia.
»Ya que Colada no os fizo
valiente aquesta vegada,
fágavos colada limpio:
echaos, buen conde, en colada.»
«Calledes, el Cid, calledes
—dijo, con la voz muy baja—,
y la cosa que es secreta,
tan pública no se faga.
»Si non fice valentía,
fice cosa necesaria;
y si probáis lo que fice,
lo tendredes por fazaña.
»Más ánimo es menester
para echarse en la privada,
que para vencer a Búcar,
ni a mil leones que salgan.
»Animo sobrado tuve»;
mas en esto el Cid le ataja,
porque, sin un incensario,
ninguno a escuchar le aguarda.
«Id, infante, a doña Sol,
vuesa esposa desdichada,
y decidla que vos limpie,
mientras yo vos busco un ama.
»Y non fabléis ende más,
y obedeced, si os agrada,
aquel refrán que aconseja:
la caca, conde, callarla.»

predicament, ignoring your caste, make guts out of your heart and empty them out of pure fear. Since the sword Colada didn't make you brave this time, let the washtub make you clean: throw yourself, good count, into the wash." "Keep quiet, Cid, keep quiet," he said in a very low voice, "and what is privy don't make so public. If I didn't do something brave, I did do something necessary; and if you check what I did, you'll consider it quite a feat. More bravery is needed to throw oneself in the privy than to defeat Bucar [the Moorish king] or a thousand loose lions. I was more than brave enough." But at this point the Cid cut him short, for, without a censer, no one can stand listening to him. "Go, prince, to Doña Sol, your unfortunate wife, and tell her to clean you up, while I find you a nursemaid. And say no more about it, and obey, if you please, that saying which advises:

797

Pinta a un doctor en medicina que se quería casar [*romance satírico*]

Pues me hacéis casamentero,
Angela de Mondragón,
escuchad de vuestro esposo
las grandezas y el valor.
El es un médico honrado,
por la gracia del Señor,
que tiene muy buenas letras
en el cambio y el bolsón.
Quien os lo pintó cobarde
no lo conoce, y mintió,
que ha muerto más hombres vivos
que mató el Cid Campeador.
En entrando en una casa,
tiene tal reputación
que luego dicen los niños:
«Dios perdone al que murió.»
Y con ser todos mortales
los médicos, pienso yo
que son todos venïales,
comparados al dotor.
Al caminante en los pueblos
se le pide información,
temiéndole más que a peste,
de si le conoce o no.
De médicos semejantes
hace el rey, nuestro señor,

the dung, count, keep it quiet." *797, Depicts a doctor of medicine who wants to get married* [*satirical ballad*]: Since you want me to be a marriage broker, Angela de Mondragon, listen to the great deeds and valor of your fiancé. He's an honorable doctor, by the grace of the Lord, for he has very sound drafts on the exchange and in his purse. He who depicted him to you as a coward doesn't know him, and lied, for he's killed more living men than were killed by the Warrior Cid. When he enters a house, he has such a reputation that the children say at once: "May God have mercy on the dead man's soul." And although all medics are mortal, I think that they are all venial compared to this doctor. The wayfarer in the villages is asked for a formal declaration, he being feared more than the plague, as to whether he's met him or not. Out of such doctors our lord the king makes

bombardas a sus castillos,
mosquetes a su escuadrón.
Si a alguno cura y no muere,
piensa que resucitó,
y por milagro le ofrece
la mortaja y el cordón.
Si acaso, estando en su casa,
oye dar algún clamor,
tomando papel y tinta,
escribe: «Ante mí pasó.»
No se le ha muerto ninguno
de los que cura hasta hoy,
porque antes [de] que se mueran,
los mata sin confesión.
De envidia de los verdugos
maldice al corregidor,
que sobre los ahorcados
no le quiere dar pensión.
Piensan que es la Muerte algunos;
otros, viendo su rigor,
le llaman el día del Juicio,
pues es total perdición.
No come por engordar
ni por el dulce sabor,
sino por matar la hambre,
que es matar su inclinación.
Por matar, mata las luces,
y si no le alumbra el sol,
como murciégalo vive
a la sombra de un rincón.
Su mula, aunque no está muerta,

cannons for his castles, muskets for his troops. If he treats anyone who doesn't die, he thinks he was resurrected, and for the miracle he offers him a free shroud and vow-cord. If by chance, while at home, he hears some noise, taking paper and ink he writes: "In my presence there died." He hasn't had anyone die of all those he's treated till now, for before they can die, he kills them with no time for confession. For envy of the executioners he curses the warden, who for the hanged men refuses to give him a fee. Some think that he is Death; others, seeing his harshness, call him Judgment Day, for he is total perdition. He doesn't eat to get fat or for the sweet taste, but in order to kill hunger, for killing is his hobby. In order to kill, he kills [blows out] the lights, and if the sun doesn't furnish him illumination, like a bat he lives in a corner's shadow. His mule, although she

no penséis que se escapó;
que está matada de suerte
que le viene a ser peor.
El, que se ve tan famoso
y en tan buena estimación,
atento a vuestra belleza,
se ha enamorado de vos.
No pide le deis más dote,
de ver que matáis de amor;
que, en matando de algún modo,
para en uno sois los dos.
Casaos con él, y jamás
vïuda tendréis pasión,
que nunca la misma Muerte
se oyó decir que murió.
Si lo hacéis, a Dios le ruego
que os gocéis con bendición;
pero si no, que nos libre
de conocer al dotor.

850

Contra el mesmo [*Góngora*]

¿Qué captas, noturnal, en tus canciones,
Góngora bobo, con crepusculallas,
si cuando anhelas más garcivolallas,
las reptilizas más y subterpones?
Microcósmote Dios de inquiridiones,
y quieres te investiguen por medallas
como priscos estigmas o antiguallas,
por desitinerar vates tirones.

isn't dead, don't think that she has escaped: she is so badly killed [galled] that she's really worse off. He, finding himself so famous and held in so great esteem, with his eyes on your beauty, has fallen in love with you. He doesn't ask you for any further dowry, seeing that you cause men to die for your love; for, if in any way you cause death, you two are a very good wedding match. Marry him, and you'll never have a widow's grief, for it was never heard tell that Death itself died. If you do so, I pray God that you live together in blessed happiness; but if not, may God deliver us from meeting that doctor. *850, Against the same* [*Góngora*]*:* What do you captivate, nocturnally, in your songs, stupid Góngora, by crepusculating them, if the more you yearn to heron-fly them, the more you reptilize and subterpose them? I microcosmate you God of classical manuals, and you want to be

Tu forasteridad es tan eximia,
que te ha de detractar el que te rumia,
pues ructas viscerable cacoquimia,
farmacofolorando como numia,
si estomacabundancia das tan nimia,
metamorfoseando el arcadumia.

Francisco de Rioja

(ca. 1583–1659)

SONETOS

VIII

Lánguida flor de Venus, que escondida
yaces, y en triste sombra y tenebrosa
ver te impiden la faz al sol hermosa
hojas y espinas de que estás ceñida;
Y ellas, el puro lustre y la vistosa
púrpura en que apuntar te vi teñída
te arrebatan, y a par la dulce vida,
del verdor que descubre ardiente rosa.
Igual es, mustia flor, tu mal al mío;
que si nieve tu frente descolora
por no sentir el vivo rayo ardiente,
A mí en profunda oscuridad y frío

searched for medals like ancient stigmata or relics, in order to confuse the novice poets. Your foreignity is so noteworthy that he who ruminates you must denigrate you, for you eructate intestinable dungistry, pharmacologizing like a Numian (?), if you yield so little stomach-abundance, metamorphosizing the aqueductry.

SONNETS, *VIII:* Languid flower of Venus, lying hidden and in sad, dark shadows unable to see the sun's beautiful face because of the leaves and thorns which surround you; and they strip you of the pure gleam and showy purple which I saw beginning to stain you, and at the same time take away the sweet life of the verdure revealing an ardent rose: your grief, faded flower, is the same as mine; for if snow takes the color from your forehead because you don't feel the living, burning rays, I too, in deep darkness and

hielo también de muerte me colora
la ausencia de mi luz resplandeciente.

XII

Cuando entre luz y púrpura aparece
la alba, y despierto ¡ay triste! y miro el día,
y no hallo la blanca Filis mía,
alba y púrpura y luz se me oscurece.
Lloro y crece mi llanto cuanto crece
más la lumbre, y la sombra se desvía;
y un torpe hielo así me ata y refría
que aun la voz para alivio me fallece.
Y a un punto apura amor con alto fuego
en este ancho desierto el pecho mío,
donde el pensar lo aviva más y enciende:
Lloro, pues, y ardo así y el mal se extiende
tanto, que a luz, y a sombra y a rocío
muero en llamas, y en lágrimas me anego.

SILVAS

X

Al Jazmín

¡Oh en pura nieve púrpura bañado,
Jazmín, gloria y honor del cano estío!
¿Cuál habrá tan ilustre entre las flores,
hermosa flor, que competir presuma
con tu fragante espíritu y colores?

cold ice, am given death's color by the absence of my shining light. *XII:* When between light and redness the dawn appears, and I awake, alas!, and look at the day and don't find my white Phyllis: dawn and redness and light turn dark for me. I weep, and my tears grow as the illumination grows and shadows disappear; and a torpid ice so ties and chills me that even my voice to call for help fails me. And love with great fire in this broad desert presses my heart precisely where thoughts make it most sensitive and ignite it: so I weep and burn thus, and my illness spreads so far that with light and shadows and dew I die in flames, and in tears I drown.

SILVAS, *X, To the Jasmine:* Oh bathed in pure snow and purple, Jasmine, the honor and glory of hoary summer! What can there be so illustrious among the flowers, lovely flower, as to presume to compete with your

Tuyo es el principado
entre el copioso número que pinta
con su pincel y con su varia tinta
el florido Verano.
Naciste entre la espuma
de las ondas sonantes
que blandas rompe y tiende el Ponto en Chío,
y quizá te formó suprema mano,
como a Venus, también de su rocío:
o si no es rumor vano,
la misma blanca diosa de Cithera,
cuando del mar salió la vez primera,
por do la espuma el blando pie estampaba
de la plaza arenosa,
albos jazmines daba;
y de la tersa nieve y de la rosa
que el tierno pie ocupaba,
fiel copia apareció en tan breves hojas.
La dulce flor de su divino aliento
liberal escondió en tu cerco alado:
hizo inmortal en el verdor tu planta,
el soplo la respeta más violento
que impele envuelto en nieve el cierzo cano,
y la luz más flamante
que Apolo esparce altivo y arrogante.
Si de suave olor despoja ardiente
la blanca flor divina,
y amenaza a su cuello y a su frente
cierta y veloz ruina,

fragrant breath and colors? Yours is the primacy among the bounteous number which flowery Summer paints with her brush and varied hue. You were born in the foam of the sounding waves which the Pontus softly breaks and spreads out on Chios, and perhaps a supreme hand shaped you also, like Venus, in its dew; or if it isn't a vain rumor, that same white goddess of Cythera, when she came out of the sea for the first time, wherever on the sandy square her soft foot stamped foam, she produced white jasmines; and of the polished snow and the rose which covered her tender foot, a faithful copy appeared on the tiny petals. She liberally hid within your winged circle the sweet flower of her divine breath. She made immortal your plant's greenness: it is spared by the most violent blast that the hoary Northwind impels enveloped in snow, and by the most flaming light shed by haughty, arrogant Apollo. If blazingly he despoils of delicate fragrance the white flower divine, and threatens its neck and brow with swift and cer-

nunca tan licencioso se adelanta
que al incansable suceder se opone
de la nevada copia,
que siempre al mayor sol igual florece,
e igual al mayor hielo resplandece.
¡Oh jazmín glorioso!
tu solo eres cuidado deleitoso
de la sin par hermosa Citherea,
y tú también su imagen peregrina.
Tu cándida pureza
es más de mí estimada
por nueva emulación de la belleza
de la altiva luz mía,
que por obra sagrada
de la rosada planta de Dione:
a tu excelsa blancura
admiración se debe
por imitar de su color la nieve,
y a tus perfiles rojos
por emular los cercos de sus ojos.
Cuando renace el día
fogoso en Oriente,
y con color medroso en Occidente
de la espantable sombra se desvía,
y el dulce olor te vuelve
que apaga el frío y que el calor resuelve
al espíritu tuyo,
ninguno habrá que iguale

tain destruction, he never so licentiously advances as to stop the tireless succession of the snowy supply, which always blooms the same in the hottest sun and shines the same in the coldest frost. Oh glorious jasmine!, you alone are the delightful concern of the matchlessly beautiful Cytherian [Venus], and you are also her unusual image. Your candid purity is more appreciated by me because of the recent competition with the beauty of my proud light [love], than because of the sacred effect of the rosy foot of Dione [Venus's mother]: your supreme whiteness deserves admiration because it imitates the snow of her color, and your red profiles deserve it for emulating the rims of her eyes. When fiery day is reborn in the east, and with timid color in the west it avoids the fearful darkness, and the sweet fragrance returns to you, which the cold extinguishes and the heat destroys, there will be no

porque entonces imitas
al puro olor que de sus labios sale.
¡Oh, corona mis sienes,
flor, que al olvido de mi luz previenes!

XI

A la Rosa

Pura, encendida rosa,
émula de la llama
que sale con el día,
¿cómo naces tan llena de alegría
si sabes que la edad que te da el cielo
es apenas un breve y veloz vuelo?
Y ni valdrán las puntas de tu rama,
ni púrpura hermosa
a detener un punto
la ejecución del hado presurosa.
El mismo cerco alado
que estoy viendo riente,
ya temo amortiguado,
presto despojo de la llama ardiente.
Para las hojas de tu crespo seno
te dió Amor de sus alas blandas plumas,
y oro de su cabello dió a tu frente.
¡Oh fiel imagen suya peregrina!
Bañóte en su color sangre divina
de la deidad que dieron las espumas.

breath to equal yours, for then you imitate the pure fragrance which comes from her lips. Oh crown my temples, flower, preventing my light's oblivion!

XI, To the Rose: Pure, blazing rose, competitor of the flame that rises with the day, how can you be born so full of gaiety if you know that the time allotted to you by heaven is hardly a short swift flight? And not even the thorns of your twigs nor your beautiful purple will be able to detain for one moment the hasty execution of fate. The same winged ringlet which I see laughing, I'm already afraid to see deadened, the rapid spoils of ardent flame. For the petals of your curly bosom Love gave you soft feathers from his wings and gold from his hair to your brow. Oh faithful image of him, striking! You were bathed in the color of the divine blood of the deity produced by foam. And couldn't this, purple flower, make less violent the sharp

¿Y esto, purpúrea flor, esto no pudo
hacer menos violento el rayo agudo?
Róbate en una hora,
róbate licencioso su ardimiento
el color y el aliento:
tiendes aún no las alas abrasadas
y ya vuelan al suelo desmayadas:
tan cerca, tan unida
está al morir tu vida,
que dudo si en sus lágrimas la aurora
mustia, tu nacimiento o muerte llora.

Esteban Manuel de Villegas

(ca. 1589–1669)

CANTILENAS

VII

De un pajarillo

Yo vi sobre un tomillo
quejarse un pajarillo,
viendo su nido amado,
de quien era caudillo,
de un labrador robado.
Vile tan congojado
por tal atrevimiento
dar mil quejas al viento,
para que al cielo santo
lleve su tierno llanto,

thunderbolt? In one hour, in one hour his licentious daring robs you of color and breath: you haven't yet spread your burnt wings, and already they flutter fainting to the ground: so close, so joined to death is your life that I wonder whether the sad dawn with her tears is weeping for your birth or death.

SONGS, *VII, On a Little Bird:* I saw upon a thyme shrub a little bird complain, seeing that his beloved nest, of which he was the head, had been robbed by a farmer. I saw him, quite distressed by such daring, throw many complaints to the wind, so that it might carry to holy heaven his tender tears,

lleve su triste acento.
Ya con triste armonía,
esforzando el intento,
mil quejas repitía;
ya cansado callaba,
y al nuevo sentimiento
ya sonoro volvía;
ya circular volaba,
ya rastrero corría;
ya, pues, de rama en rama,
al rústico seguía,
y saltando en la grama,
parece que decía:
"Dame, rústico fiero,
mi dulce compañía";
y a mí que respondía
el rústico: "No quiero".

XXXIV

A sus amigos

Ya de los altos montes
las encumbradas nieves
a valles hondos bajan
desesperadamente.
Ya llegan a ser ríos
las que antes eran fuentes,
corridas de ver mares
los arroyuelos breves.
Ya las campañas secas
empiezan a ser verdes,

his sad moans. Now with sad harmony, trying harder, he would repeat his many complaints; now tired he would be silent, and to renewed grief he would now noisily return; now he would fly in circles, now run about dragging [his wings]; finally from branch to branch he would follow the countryman, and jumping on the grass, seemed to be saying to him: "Give me, cruel countryman, my sweet company"; and it seemed to me the countryman would answer: "I don't want to." *XXXIV, To His Friends:* Now from the high mountains the lofty snows descend to the low valleys desperately. Now they get to be rivers, which formerly were springs, indignant to see little brooks converted into seas. Now the dry countryside begins to be

y porque no beodas,
aguadas enloquecen.
Ya del Liceo monte
se escuchan los rabeles,
al paso de las cabras
que Títiro defiende.
Pues, ea, compañeros,
vivamos dulcemente,
que todas son señales
de que el verano viene.
La cantimplora salga,
la cítara se temple,
y beba el que bailare
y baile el que bebiere.

SÁFICOS

Dulce vecino de la verde selva,
huésped eterno del abril florido,
vital aliento de la madre Venus,
Céfiro blando.

Si de mis ansias el amor supiste,
tú que las quejas de mi voz llevaste,
oye, no temas, y a mi ninfa dile,
dile que muero.

green and, since it is not drunk on wine, it goes mad on water. Now from Mt. Lycaeus are heard the lutes, as the goats go by which Tityrus protects. So come on, companions, let us live sweetly, for everything gives signs that spring is coming. Let the wine jug come out, let the cythera be tuned; and let him drink who dances, and let him dance who drinks.

SAPPHICS: Sweet inhabitant of the green forest, eternal guest of flowery April, breath of life to mother Venus, gentle Zephyr; if you have discovered my anxious love, you who carried my voice's complaints, listen, don't be afraid, and tell my nymph, tell her that I'm dying. Phyllis once knew of my

Filis un tiempo mi dolor sabía,
Filis un tiempo mi dolor lloraba,
quísome un tiempo, mas agora temo,
temo sus iras.

Así los dioses con amor paterno,
así los cielos con amor benigno,
nieguen al tiempo que feliz volares
nieve a la tierra.

Jamás el peso de la nube parda,
cuando amenace la elevada cumbre,
toque tus hombros, ni su mal granizo
hiera tus alas.

suffering, Phyllis once wept for my suffering, she loved me once, but now I'm afraid, I'm afraid of her anger. So may the gods with paternal love, so may the heavens with benignant love, as long as you fly happily, deny snow to the earth; never may the weight of the dark cloud, when it threatens the lofty peak, touch your shoulders, nor its evil hail wound your wings.

Sor Juana Inés de la Cruz

(1651–1695)

ROMANCES

2

Acusa la hidropesía de mucha ciencia,
que teme inútil aun para
saber y nociva para vivir.

Finjamos que soy feliz,
triste Pensamiento, un rato;
quizá podréis persuadirme,
aunque yo sé lo contrario:
que pues sólo en la aprehensión
dicen que estriban los daños,
si os imagináis dichoso
no seréis tan desdichado.
Sírvame el entendimiento
alguna vez de descanso,
y no siempre esté el ingenio
con el provecho encontrado.
Todo el mundo es opiniones
de pareceres tan varios
que lo que el uno que es negro,
el otro prueba que es blanco.
A unos sirve de atractivo

BALLADS, 2, *She brings accusations against the dropsy of great studiousness, which she fears is useless even to knowledge and is harmful to life:* Let's pretend that I am happy, sad thoughts, for a while; perhaps you can convince me, although I know the opposite: for since only in being apprehensive they say the harm consists, if you imagine yourself happy, you won't be so unfortunate. Let my intelligence serve me for once as a comfort, and let not my ingenuity always be opposed to my own betterment. The whole world consists of such various opinions and appearances that what one person ex-

lo que otro concibe enfado;
y lo que éste por alivio,
aquél tiene por trabajo.
El que está triste, censura
al alegre de liviano;
y el que está alegre, se burla
de ver al triste penando.
Los dos Filósofos Griegos
bien esta verdad probaron:
pues lo que en el uno risa,
causaba en el otro llanto.
Célebre su oposición
ha sido por siglos tantos,
sin que cuál acertó, esté
hasta agora averiguado;
antes, en sus dos banderas
el mundo todo alistado;
conforme el humor le dicta,
sigue cada cual el bando.
Uno dice que de risa
sólo es digno el mundo vario;
y otro, que sus infortunios
son sólo para llorados.
Para todo se halla prueba
y razón en que fundarlo;
y no hay razón para nada,
de haber razón para tanto.
Todos son iguales jueces;
y siendo iguales y varios,

periences as black, another does as white. Some people are attracted by what others consider repellant; and what this one thinks is relaxing, that one thinks is work. The sad man criticizes the gay one as superficial; and he who is gay makes fun of seeing the sad one suffer. The two Greek philosophers demonstrated this truth well: for what caused in one of them laughter, in the other caused tears. Their opposition has been famous for many centuries, without its having been ascertained so far which of them was right; to the contrary, the whole world has enlisted under their two banners; as one's temperament dictates, each person chooses his side. One says that the varied world is solely worthy of laughter; another, that its sufferings can only be lamented. For any argument proof is found, and reason on which to base it; and there is no reason for anything if there are reasons for so many different things. Everyone is equally a judge; and being equally qualified

no hay quien pueda decidir
cuál es lo más acertado.
Pues, si no hay quien lo sentencie,
¿por qué pensáis, vos, errado,
que os cometió Dios a vos
la decisión de los casos?
¿O por qué, contra vos mismo
severamente inhumano,
entre lo amargo y lo dulce,
queréis elegir lo amargo?
Si es mío mi entendimiento,
¿por qué siempre he de encontrarlo
tan torpe para el alivio,
tan agudo para el daño?
El discurso es un acero
que sirve por ambos cabos:
de dar muerte, por la punta;
por el pomo, de resguardo.
Si vos, sabiendo el peligro,
queréis por la punta usarlo,
¿qué culpa tiene el acero
del mal uso de la mano?
No es saber, saber hacer
discursos sutiles, vanos;
que el saber consiste sólo
en elegir lo más sano.
Especular las desdichas
y examinar los presagios,
sólo sirve de que el mal

yet varying, no one can decide what opinion is most correct. So, if there is no one to give a verdict, why do you think, in your error, that God granted to you final judgment in such cases? Or why, being severely cruel to yourself, between the bitter and the sweet, should you wish to choose the bitter? If my intellect belongs to me, why should I always find it to be so inept to comfort, so keen to damage? Reason is a sword which is useful at both ends: for killing, with the point, and with the pommel, for security. If you, aware of the danger, want to use its point, how can you blame the sword for the clumsiness of the hand? It isn't knowledge to know how to invent vain, subtle reasonings; for knowledge consists only in choosing what is healthiest. To speculate on misfortunes and to investigate the omens only serves to in-

crezca con anticiparlo.
En los trabajos futuros,
la atención, sutilizando,
más formidable que el riesgo
suele fingir el amago.
¡Qué feliz es la ignorancia
del que, indoctamente sabio,
halla de lo que padece,
en lo que ignora, sagrado!
No siempre suben seguros
vuelos del ingenio osados,
que buscan trono en el fuego
y hallan sepulcro en el llanto.
También es vicio el saber:
que si no se va atajando,
cuando menos se conoce
es más nocivo el estrago;
y si el vuelo no le abaten,
en sutilezas cebado,
por cuidar de lo curioso
olvida lo necesario.
Si culta mano no impide
crecer al árbol copado,
quita la substancia al fruto
la locura de los ramos.
Si andar a nave ligera
no estorba lastre pesado,
sirve el vuelo de que sea
el precipicio más alto.
En amenidad inútil,

crease one's suffering by suffering in advance. Focused upon future trials, one's attention, oversubtle, tends to imagine the threat to be more formidable than the actual danger. How happy the ignorance of him who, unlearnedly wise, finds sanctuary from what he suffers in what he doesn't know! Daring flights of the intellect do not always ascend securely, for they seek a throne in the fire and find a burial in tears. Knowledge is also a vice: for if one doesn't keep it under control, when one least expects it, the destruction is most harmful; and if one doesn't restrain its flight, baited by subtleties, in its concern for sophistication it neglects the necessities. If a wise hand does not impede the growth of the bushy tree, the wildness of the branches takes substance away from the fruit. If heavy ballast does not keep a light ship from sailing, flight serves to make the fall steeper. Uselessly pleasant, what good

¿qué importa al florido campo,
si no halla fruto el Otoño,
que ostente flores el Mayo?
¿De qué le sirve al ingenio
el producir muchos partos,
si a la multitud se sigue
el malogro de abortarlos?
Y a esta desdicha por fuerza
ha de seguirse el fracaso
de quedar el que produce,
si no muerto, lastimado.
El ingenio es como el fuego:
que, con la materia ingrato,
tanto la consume más
cuanto él se ostenta más claro.
Es de su propio señor
tan rebelado vasallo,
que convierte en sus ofensas
las armas de su resguardo.
Este pésimo ejercicio,
este duro afán pesado,
a los hijos de los hombres
dió Dios para ejercitarlos.
¿Qué loca ambición nos lleva
de nosotros olvidados?
Si es para vivir tan poco,
¿de qué sirve saber tanto?
¡Oh, si como hay de saber,
hubiera algún seminario

does it do the flowery field, if Autumn finds no fruit, to be showing off flowers in May? What good does it do the intellect to produce many offspring, if quantity is followed by the frustration of miscarriages? And this misfortune is necessarily followed by the disaster of leaving the producer in bad shape, if not dead. The intellect is like fire: antagonistic toward matter, it destroys it the more rapidly the brighter it seems to be. Against its own lord it is such a rebellious vassal that it attacks him with its defensive arms. This most evil entertainment, this harshly cruel passion was given to the sons of men by God in order to train them. What mad ambition makes us forgetful of ourselves? If we're to live so short a time, why do we need to know so much? Oh, if only, as there are seminaries of knowledge, there were

o escuela donde a ignorar
se enseñaran los trabajos!
   ¡Qué felizmente viviera
el que, flojamente cauto,
burlara las amenazas
del influjo de los astros!
   Aprendamos a ignorar,
Pensamiento, pues hallamos
que cuanto añado al discurso,
tanto le usurpo a los años.

56

En que expresa los efectos del Amor Divino,
y propone morir amante,
a pesar de todo riesgo.

Traigo conmigo un cuidado,
y tan esquivo que creo
que, aunque sé sentirlo tanto,
aun yo misma no lo siento.
   Es amor; pero es amor
que, faltándole lo ciego,
los ojos que tiene, son
para darle más tormento.
   El término no es *a quo*,
que causa el pesar que veo:
que siendo el término el Bien,
todo el dolor es el medio.
   Si es lícito, y aun debido,
este cariño que tengo,
¿por qué me han de dar castigo
porque pago lo que debo?

some school where one were taught to learn ignorance! How happily one would live who, carelessly cautious, could poke fun at the threats of the stars' influence! Let's learn to be ignorant, Thought, for we find that the more I add to my intellect, the more I steal from the years of its life. *56, In which she expresses the effects of Divine Love, and proposes to die loving, despite the dangers:* I bear with me a care which is so elusive that I believe that, although I can feel it so deeply, I myself do not perceive it. It is love; but a love which, not being blind, has eyes to make it more tormenting. It is not the *terminus a quo* which causes the pain I see: for since the *terminus* is the Good, all the suffering is but the means. If this love I feel is permissible, and even a duty, why should I be punished because I pay what is due? Oh

¡Oh cuánta fineza, oh cuántos
cariños he visto tiernos!
Que amor que se tiene en Dios,
es calidad sin opuestos.
De lo lícito no puede
hacer contrarios conceptos,
con que es amor que al olvido
no puede vivir expuesto.
Yo me acuerdo, ¡oh nunca fuera!,
que he querido en otro tiempo
lo que pasó de locura
y lo que excedió de extremo;
mas como era amor bastardo,
y de contrarios compuesto,
fué fácil desvanecerse
de achaque de su sér mesmo.
Mas ahora, ¡ay de mí!, está
tan en su natural centro
que la virtud y razón
son quien aviva su incendio.
Quien tal oyere, dirá
que, si es así, ¿por qué peno?
Mas mi corazón ansioso
dirá que por eso mesmo.
¡Oh humana flaqueza nuestra,
adonde el más puro afecto
aun no sabe desnudarse
del natural sentimiento!
Tan precisa es la apetencia
que a ser amados tenemos

what delicacy, oh what tender love I have seen! For the love of God is a value without contradictions. To what is permissible there can be no opposing concepts, so it is a love which cannot live in exposure to oblivion. I remember (oh that it had never been!) that I once loved what exceeded madness and all extremes; but since it was an illegitimate love and made up of contradictions, it easily destroyed itself because of its own being. But now, alas!, it [my love] is so much in its own element that virtue and reason are what keep its flame glowing. Anyone who hears this will say that, if this is so, why do I suffer? But my anxious heart will reply that that itself is the very reason. Oh weakness of our human race, in which the purest affection is unable to free itself of our native regrets! So urgent is the desire

que, aun sabiendo que no sirve,
nunca dejarla sabemos.
  Que corresponda a mi amor,
nada añade; mas no puedo,
por más que lo solicito,
dejar yo de apetecerlo.
  Si es delito, ya lo digo;
si es culpa, ya la confieso;
mas no puedo arrepentirme,
por más que hacerlo pretendo.
  Bien ha visto, quien penetra
lo interior de mis secretos,
que yo misma estoy formando
los dolores que padezco.
  Bien sabe que soy yo misma
verdugo de mis deseos,
pues muertos entre mis ansias,
tienen sepulcro en mi pecho.
  Muero, ¿quién lo creerá?, a manos
de la cosa que más quiero,
y el motivo de matarme
es el amor que le tengo.
  Así alimentando, triste,
la vida con el veneno,
la misma muerte que vivo
es la vida con que muero.
  Pero valor, corazón:
porque en tan dulce tormento,
en medio de cualquier suerte,
no dejar de amar protesto.

which we have to be loved that even knowing that it's useless, we are unable to get rid of it. His reciprocating my love adds nothing; but I can't, no matter how hard I try, cease desiring it. If it's a crime, I already admit it; if I'm guilty, I confess; but I cannot repent, no matter how hard I try. He has seen, who penetrates my inner secrets, that I myself am causing the pains that I suffer. He knows that I myself am the murderer of my desires, for dying among my anxieties, they are buried in my breast. I am dying (who will believe it?) at the hands of that which I love most, and its motive for killing me is the love I feel for it. Nourishing thus, sadly, my life upon poison, the very death I live is the life of which I die. But courage, my heart: for in such sweet torment, in the midst of any fate, I insist upon not ceasing to love.

REDONDILLAS

92

Arguye de inconsecuentes el gusto y la censura de los hombres que en las mujeres acusan lo que causan.

Hombres necios que acusáis
a la mujer sin razón,
sin ver que sois la ocasión
de lo mismo que culpáis:
si con ansia sin igual
solicitáis su desdén,
¿por qué queréis que obren bien
si las incitáis al mal?
Combatís su resistencia
y luego, con gravedad,
decís que fué liviandad
lo que hizo la diligencia.
Parecer quiere el denuedo
de vuestro parecer loco
al niño que pone el coco
y luego le tiene miedo.
Queréis, con presunción necia,
hallar a la que buscáis,
para pretendida, Thais,
y en la posesión, Lucrecia.
¿Qué humor puede ser más raro
que el que, falto de consejo,

QUATRAINS, *92, She argues to be inconsistent the desires and the criticisms of men, who in women find culpable what they themselves cause:* Stupid men who accuse woman without any grounds, without seeing that you are the cause of the very thing that you blame: if with unequaled eagerness you solicit their scorn, why do you want them to be good when you incite them to be bad? You attack their resistance and then, solemnly, you say it was their lightness when it was achieved by your diligence. The valor of your crazy opinion tends to resemble the child who invents the bogey and then is afraid of it. With stupid presumption you want to find her whom you seek to be, while you're pursuing her, a Thais, and after you possess her, a

él mismo empaña el espejo,
y siente que no esté claro?
Con el favor y el desdén
tenéis condición igual,
quejándoos, si os tratan mal,
burlándoos, si os quieren bien.
Opinión, ninguna gana;
pues la que más se recata,
si no os admite, es ingrata,
y si os admite, es liviana.
Siempre tan necios andáis
que, con desigual nivel,
a una culpáis por crüel
y a otra por fácil culpáis.
¿Pues cómo ha de estar templada
la que vuestro amor pretende,
si la que es ingrata, ofende,
y la que es fácil, enfada?
Mas, entre el enfado y pena
que vuestro gusto refiere,
bien haya la que no os quiere,
y quejaos en hora buena.
Dan vuestras amantes penas

Lucretia. What damp whim can be more odd than that which, lacking in counsel, smudges the mirror itself, and then regrets it isn't clear? To favor and to scorn you give the same reception, complaining if they treat you badly, sneering if they treat you well. In reputation no woman gains; for she who is most careful, if she doesn't accept you, is ungrateful, and if she does accept you, is a tramp. You're always so stupid that, with no consistency, you blame one woman as too cruel and another you blame as too easy. Well, how do you want her to be tempered who seeks your love, if she who is ungrateful offends you and she who is too easy angers you? But, in the midst of the anger and suffering revealed by your whims, it's lucky for her who doesn't love you, and so just go ahead and complain. Your loving tor-

a sus libertades alas,
y después de hacerlas malas
las queréis hallar muy buenas.
¿Cuál mayor culpa ha tenido
en una pasión errada:
la que cae de rogada,
o el que ruega de caído?
¿O cuál es más de culpar,
aunque cualquiera mal haga:
la que peca por la paga,
o el que paga por pecar?
Pues ¿para qué os espantáis
de la culpa que tenéis?
Queredlas cual las hacéis
o hacedlas cual las buscáis.
Dejad de solicitar,
y después, con más razón,
acusaréis la afición
de la que os fuere a rogar.
Bien con muchas armas fundo
que lidia vuestra arrogancia,
pues en promesa e instancia
juntáis diablo, carne y mundo.

ments put wings on their liberties, and after making them bad you want them to be very good. Who is more to blame in a sinful passion: she who falls because she's begged, or he who begs because he's so fallen? Or who is more to blame, whatever the evil done: she who sins for pay, or he who pays for sin? But why are you surprised at your own guilt? Either take them as you make them, or make them as you like them. Stop soliciting, and then you'll have more right to accuse the fondness of her who solicits you. I am right to argue that your arrogance fights with many weapons, for in your promises and insistence you unite the devil, the flesh and the world.

SONETOS

145

Procura desmentir los elogios que a un retrato de la Poetisa inscribió la verdad, que llama pasión.

Este, que ves, engaño colorido,
que del arte ostentando los primores,
con falsos silogismos de colores
es cauteloso engaño del sentido;
éste, en quien la lisonja ha pretendido
excusar de los años los horrores,
y venciendo del tiempo los rigores,
triunfar de la vejez y del olvido,
es un vano artificio del cuidado,
es una flor al viento delicada,
es un resguardo inútil para el hado;
es una necia diligencia errada,
es un afán caduco y, bien mirado,
es cadáver, es polvo, es sombra, es nada.

147

En que da moral censura a una rosa, y en ella a sus semejantes.

Rosa divina que en gentil cultura
eres, con tu fragrante sutileza,
magisterio purpúreo en la belleza,

SONNETS, *145, She tries to refute the praises dedicated to a portrait of the poetess by truth, which she calls prejudice:* This colored deception that you see, which, displaying the charms of art, with its false syllogisms of color is a cunning deception of one's sense [of sight]; this thing, in which flattery has attempted to avoid the ravages of the years, and by overcoming the cruelty of time, to triumph over old age and oblivion, is a vain contrived artifice, is a delicate flower exposed to the wind, is a useless defense against fate; it is a foolish, mistaken effort, is a failing eagerness, and, rightly viewed, is a corpse, is dust, is shadow, is nothing. *147, In which she morally censures a rose, and through the rose things similar to it:* Divine rose who, gently reared, with your subtle fragrance are a purple lesson in beauty, a

enseñanza nevada a la hermosura;
amago de la humana arquitectura,
ejemplo de la vana gentileza,
en cuyo sér unió naturaleza
la cuna alegre y triste sepultura:
¡cuán altiva en tu pompa, presumida,
soberbia, el riesgo de morir desdeñas,
y luego desmayada y encogida
de tu caduco sér das mustias señas,
con que con docta muerte y necia vida,
viviendo engañas y muriendo enseñas!

148

Escoge antes el morir que exponerse a los ultrajes de la vejez.

Miró Celia una rosa que en el prado
ostentaba feliz la pompa vana
y con afeites de carmín y grana
bañaba alegre el rostro delicado;
y dijo:—Goza, sin temor del Hado,
el curso breve de tu edad lozana,
pues no podrá la muerte de mañana
quitarte lo que hubieres hoy gozado;
y aunque llega la muerte presurosa
y tu fragante vida se te aleja,
no sientas el morir tan bella y moza:
mira que la experiencia te aconseja
que es fortuna morirte siendo hermosa

snowy course in loveliness; imitation of human architecture, example of vain gentility, in whose being nature has joined the gay cradle and sad sepulchre: how proudly in your pomp, presumptuously and haughtily you scorn the danger of dying, and then, fainting and shriveling, you give withered evidence of your failing existence, whereby, by your wise death and foolish life, you deceive as you live, and as you die, you teach a lesson! *148, She prefers dying rather than exposing herself to the indignities of old age:* Celia looked at a rose which on the meadow was ostentatiously happy in its vain pomp and with crimson rouge gaily bathed its delicate face; and she said, "Enjoy, without fear of Fate, the brief course of your blooming youth, for tomorrow's death can never take from you what you have enjoyed today; and even though death is approaching fast and your fragrant life is departing from you, don't regret dying so lovely and young: consider that experience advises you that it is good fortune to die while you are beautiful

y no ver el ultraje de ser vieja.

152

Verde embeleso de la vida humana,
loca Esperanza, frenesí dorado,
sueño de los despiertos intrincado,
como de sueños, de tesoros vana;
alma del mundo, senectud lozana,
decrépito verdor imaginado;
el hoy de los dichosos esperado
y de los desdichados el mañana:
sigan tu sombra en busca de tu día
los que, con verdes vidrios por anteojos,
todo lo ven pintado a su deseo;
que yo, más cuerda en la fortuna mía,
tengo en entrambas manos ambos ojos
y solamente lo que toco veo.

164

En que satisface un recelo con la retórica del llanto.

Esta tarde, mi bien, cuando te hablaba,
como en tu rostro y tus acciones vía
que con palabras no te persuadía,
que el corazón me vieses deseaba;
y Amor, que mis intentos ayudaba,
venció lo que imposible parecía:
pues entre el llanto, que el dolor vertía,
el corazón deshecho destilaba.

and not to suffer the indignity of being old." *152:* Youthful captivator of human life, mad Hope, gilded frenzy, complex sleep of those who are awake, as empty of treasures as of dreams; soul of the world, blossoming senility, decrepit imaginary youthfulness; the today hoped for by the lucky, and the tomorrow of the unlucky: let those pursue your shadow in search of your daylight who, wearing wishful spectacles of rosy glass, see everything painted in the color of their desires; for I, saner in my fortune, hold in both hands both my eyes and only see what I can touch. *164, In which she answers a fear with the rhetoric of tears:* This afternoon, my love, while I was talking to you, since I could see by your face and actions that I was not convincing you with my words, I wished that you could see my heart; and Love, who helped my efforts, achieved what seemed to be the impossible: for in my tears, shed in grief, I poured out my heart dissolved. Enough, my

Baste ya de rigores, mi bien, baste;
no te atormenten más celos tiranos,
ni el vil recelo tu quietud contraste
con sombras necias, con indicios vanos,
pues ya en líquido humor viste y tocaste
mi corazón deshecho entre tus manos.

165

Que contiene una fantasía contenta con amor decente.

Detente, sombra de mi bien esquivo,
imagen del hechizo que más quiero,
bella ilusión por quien alegre muero,
dulce ficción por quien penosa vivo.
Si al imán de tus gracias, atractivo,
sirve mi pecho de obediente acero,
¿para qué me enamoras lisonjero
si has de burlarme luego fugitivo?
Mas blasonar no puedes, satisfecho,
de que triunfa de mí tu tiranía:
que aunque dejas burlado el lazo estrecho
que tu forma fantástica ceñía,
poco importa burlar brazos y pecho
si te labra prisión mi fantasía.

166

Resuelve la cuestión de cuál sea pesar más molesto en encontradas correspondencias, amar o aborrecer.

Que no me quiera Fabio, al verse amado,

love, of your harshness; be no longer tortured by tyrannous jealousy, nor let low fears disturb your tranquillity with foolish imaginings, misleading evidence, for in a liquid humor you have seen and touched my heart dissolved between your hands. *165, Which restrains an amorous fantasy, contenting it with decency:* Halt, reflection of my elusive love, image of the charm I most adore, lovely illusion for whom I gaily die, sweet fiction for whom I sadly live. If to the attractive magnet of your graces my heart responds like an obedient needle of steel, why do you woo me with flattery if you are later to deceive me by fleeing? But you cannot brag, self-satisfied, that your tyranny is triumphing over me: for although you escape from the tight noose which bound your fantastic form, it little matters whether you escape my arms and breast if you are imprisoned within my imagination. *166, She settles the question of which suffering is harder to bear, in opposed affections: to love or to hate:* That Fabio doesn't love me while I love him is a

es dolor sin igual en mí sentido;
mas que me quiera Silvio, aborrecido,
es menor mal, mas no menos enfado.
 ¿Qué sufrimiento no estará cansado
si siempre le resuenan al oído,
tras la vana arrogancia de un querido,
el cansado gemir de un desdeñado?
 Si de Silvio me cansa el rendimiento,
a Fabio canso con estar rendida;
si de éste busco el agradecimiento,
 a mí me busca el otro agradecida:
por activa y pasiva es mi tormento,
pues padezco en querer y en ser querida.

167

Continúa el mismo asunto y aun le expresa con más viva elegancia.

Feliciano me adora y le aborrezco;
Lisardo me aborrece y yo le adoro;
por quien no me apetece ingrato, lloro,
y al que me llora tierno, no apetezco.
 A quien más me desdora, el alma ofrezco;
a quien me ofrece víctimas, desdoro;
desprecio al que enriquece mi decoro,
y al que le hace desprecios, enriquezco.
 Si con mi ofensa al uno reconvengo,
me reconviene el otro a mí, ofendido;
y a padecer de todos modos vengo,
 pues ambos atormentan mi sentido:

grief without equal in my experience; but that Silvio loves me while I hate him is a lesser evil, but no less annoying. Whose patience will not be worn out if in his ear is forever sounding, after the arrogant vanity of a loved one, the wearisome moaning of one scorned? If Silvio's devotion wearies me, I weary Fabio by being devoted; if I seek the latter's gratitude, the other man seeks mine: both actively and passively I am tortured, for I suffer in loving and in being loved. *167, She continues the same subject, expressing it with even more vivid elegance:* Feliciano adores me and I hate him; Lisardo hates me and I adore him; for him who ungratefully doesn't desire me, I weep, and him who tenderly weeps for me I don't desire. To him who criticizes me most, I offer my soul; him who offers me sacrifices, I criticize; I despise him who enhances my reputation, and him who detracts from it, I praise. If I complain of one because he offends me, the other complains of me because he's offended; and either way I suffer, for they both torture my feelings: one,

aquéste, con pedir lo que no tengo;
y aquél, con no tener lo que le pido.

168

Prosigue el mismo asunto, y determina que prevalezca la razón contra el gusto.

Al que ingrato me deja, busco amante;
al que amante me sigue, dejo ingrata;
constante adoro a quien mi amor maltrata;
maltrato a quien mi amor busca constante.
Al que trato de amor, hallo diamante,
y soy diamante al que de amor me trata;
triunfante quiero ver al que me mata,
y mato al que me quiere ver triunfante.
Si a éste pago, padece mi deseo;
si ruego a aquél, mi pundonor enojo:
de entrambos modos infeliz me veo.
Pero yo, por mejor partido, escojo
de quien no quiero, ser violento empleo,
que, de quien no me quiere, vil despojo.

PRIMERO SUEÑO
que así intituló y compuso la Madre Juana Inés de la Cruz, imitando a Góngora.

[fragmento introductorio]

Piramidal, funesta, de la tierra

by asking for what I do not have; and the other, by not having what I ask him for. *168, She continues the same subject, deciding that reason should prevail over pleasure:* Him who ungratefully abandons me, I lovingly seek; him who lovingly pursues me, I ungratefully abandon; I steadfastly adore him who abuses my love; I abuse him who seeks my love steadfastly. Him whom I treat lovingly, I find to be hard, and I am hard for him who treats me lovingly; I want to see the triumph of him who kills me, and I kill him who wants to see my triumph. If I reward the latter, my own desires suffer; if I beg the former, my pride suffers: either way I'm unhappy. But I, as the better alternative, choose to serve him, whom I don't love, against my will rather than to be, of him who doesn't love me, the despised victim.

FIRST DREAM, *so entitled and composed by Mother Juana Inés de la Cruz imitating Góngora [introductory fragment]:* A pyramidal, funereal shadow

nacida sombra, al Cielo encaminaba
de vanos obeliscos punta altiva,
escalar pretendiendo las Estrellas;
si bien sus luces bellas
—exentas siempre, siempre rutilantes—
la tenebrosa guerra
que con negros vapores le intimaba
la pavorosa sombra fugitiva
burlaban tan distantes,
que su atezado ceño
al superior convexo aun no llegaba
del orbe de la Diosa
que tres veces hermosa
con tres hermosos rostros ser ostenta,
quedando sólo dueño
del aire que empañaba
con el aliento denso que exhalaba;
y en la quietud contenta
de imperio silencioso,
sumisas sólo voces consentía
de las nocturnas aves,
tan obscuras, tan graves,
que aun el silencio no se interrumpía.

Con tardo vuelo y canto, del oído
mal, y aun peor del ánimo, admitido,
la avergonzada Nictimene acecha
de las sagradas puertas los resquicios,
o de las claraboyas eminentes
los huecos más propicios

born of the earth was aiming toward Heaven its proud point of vain obelisks, attempting to scale the Stars; but their lovely lights—free always, always sparkling—so distantly evaded the dark war which with black vapors was being declared upon Heaven by the fearful, fleeting shadow that its blackened frown did not even reach the upper convex surface of the sphere of the Goddess which shows herself to be thrice beautiful with three beautiful faces [the Moon], and it was left the master only of the air which it smudged with the dense breath which it exhaled; and satisfied with the quietness of its silent empire, it consented only to the submissive cries of nocturnal birds, so dark and heavy that the silence was not even broken. With slow flight and song, scarcely accepted by the ear, and even less by the spirit, shameful Nyctimene [the screech owl] spies at the chinks of the sacred doors or at the lofty skylights' most propitious hollows, opening a

que capaz a su intento le abren brecha,
y sacrílega llega a los lucientes
faroles sacros de perenne llama,
que extingue, si no infama,
en licor claro la materia crasa
consumiendo, que el árbol de Minerva
de su fruto, de prensas agravado,
congojoso sudó y rindió forzado.

Y aquellas que su casa
campo vieron volver, sus telas hierba,
a la deidad de Baco inobedientes,
—ya no historias contando diferentes,
en forma sí afrentosa transformadas—,
segunda forman niebla,
ser vistas aun temiendo en la tiniebla,
aves sin pluma aladas:
aquellas tres oficïosas, digo,
atrevidas Hermanas,
que el tremendo castigo
de desnudas les dió pardas membranas,
alas tan mal dispuestas
que escarnio son aun de las más funestas:
éstas, con el parlero
ministro de Plutón un tiempo, ahora
supersticioso indicio al agorero,
solos la no canora
componían capilla pavorosa,

breach sufficient for her purpose, and sacrilegiously she reaches the gleaming sacred lamps of perennial flame, which she extinguishes, if she does not desecrate them, by consuming the fatty matter in the clear liquid which Minerva's tree [the olive], from its fruit, weighed down by presses, in anguish sweated and yielded under pressure. And those damsels, which saw their house turned into fields, their fabrics into grass, being disobedient to Bacchus' deity—no longer telling different stories, but transformed into disgraceful shapes—form a second mist, still fearing to be seen in the darkness, winged featherless birds: those three laborious, daring sisters, I mean, whose awful punishment gave them dark naked membranes, wings so ungainly that they are the laughingstock of even the most sinister birds [the three daughters of Minyas, changed into bats for slighting Bacchus' festival]: these three, along with Pluto's onetime talkative servant, now a superstitious indication to the fortune-teller [the barn owl, formerly Ascalaphus], by themselves composed the unmusical frightful choir, intoning

máximas, negras, longas entonando,
y pausas más que voces, esperando
a la torpe mensura perezosa
de mayor proporción tal vez, que el viento
con flemático echaba movimiento,
de tan tardo compás, tan detenido,
que en medio se quedó tal vez dormido.

Este, pues, triste són intercadente
de la asombrada turba temerosa,
menos a la atención solicitaba
que al sueño persuadía;
antes sí, lentamente,
su obtusa consonancia espacïosa
al sosiego inducía
y al reposo los miembros convidaba,
—el silencio intimando a los vivientes,
uno y otro sellando labio obscuro
con indicante dedo,
Harpócrates, la noche, silencioso;
a cuyo, aunque no duro,
si bien imperïoso
precepto, todos fueron obedientes—.

El viento sosegado, el can dormido,
éste yace, aquél quedo
los átomos no mueve,
con el susurro hacer temiendo leve,
aunque poco, sacrílego rüido,
violador del silencio sosegado.
El mar, no ya alterado,

"maxims," "blacks," and "longs" [various notes], with pauses more than sounds, sometimes waiting for the slow and clumsy measure of greater dimensions which the wind marked with phlegmatic movement, at so slow a rhythm, so dilated, that sometimes it fell asleep in between. This sad intermittent sound, then, of the frightened, fearful crew excited attention less than it invited sleep; slowly, rather, its obtuse, spacious harmony induced one to calm and invited one's limbs to repose—the night, a silent Harpocrates, hinting silence to the living by sealing both dark lips with index finger; to whose, although not harsh, nevertheless imperious precept, all were obedient—. The calmed wind, the sleeping dog, the latter lies, the former quietly does not move its atoms, fearing with light rustle to make a sacrilegious noise, though slight, violating the calm silence. The sea, no longer

ni aun la instable mecía
cerúlea cuna donde el Sol dormía;
y los dormidos, siempre mudos, peces,
en los lechos lamosos
de sus obscuros senos cavernosos,
mudos eran dos veces;
y entre ellos, la engañosa encantadora
Alcïone, a los que antes
en peces transformó, simples amantes,
transformada también, vengaba ahora.

En los del monte senos escondidos,
cóncavos de peñascos mal formados
—de su aspereza menos defendidos
que de su obscuridad asegurados—,
cuya mansión sombría
ser puede noche en la mitad del día,
incógnita aun al cierto
montaraz pie del cazador experto,
—depuesta la fiereza
de unos, y de otros el temor depuesto—
yacía el vulgo bruto,
a la Naturaleza
el de su potestad pagando impuesto,
universal tributo;
y el Rey, que vigilancias afectaba,
aun con abiertos ojos no velaba.

stirred up, did not even rock the unstable, blue-green cradle in which the Sun was sleeping; and the sleeping fish, always mute, in the slimy beds of their dark cavernous nooks, were twice mute; and among them the deceptive enchantress Halcyon [the kingfisher] now avenged those whom, as simple lovers, she had formerly transformed into fish, by being transformed herself. In the hidden nooks of the mountain, crudely formed of concave crags—less defended by their roughness than by their darkness made safe—whose somber mansion can be night in the middle of the day, unexplored even by the sure forest foot of the expert hunter—set aside the ferocity of some, and the timidity of others set aside also—the animal mob lay, to Nature paying the universal tribute imposed by its power; and the King [the lion], pretending vigilance, even with open eyes was not awake. He who was attacked by his own dogs, formerly a famous monarch, now a timid deer [Actaeon], with vigilant hearing moves back and forth his acute ear at the calm surroundings' least perceptible movement changing the atoms, and

El de sus mismos perros acosado,
monarca en otro tiempo esclarecido,
tímido ya venado,
con vigilante oído,
del sosegado ambiente
al menor perceptible movimiento
que los átomos muda,
la oreja alterna aguda
y el leve rumor siente
que aun le altera dormido.
Y en la quietud del nido,
que de brozas y lodo, instable hamaca,
formó en la más opaca
parte del árbol, duerme recogida
la leve turba, descansando el viento
del que le corta, alado movimiento.

De Júpiter el ave generosa
—como al fin Reina—, por no darse entera
al descanso, que vicio considera
si de preciso pasa, cuidadosa
de no incurrir de omisa en el exceso,
a un solo pie librada fía el peso
y en otro guarda el cálculo pequeño
—despertador reloj del leve sueño—,
porque, si necesario fué admitido,
no pueda dilatarse continuado,
antes interrumpido
del regio sea pastoral cuidado.
¡Oh de la Majestad pensión gravosa,

perceives the light rustle which disturbs him even while asleep. And in the quietness of the nest, an unstable hammock which it has built of brambles and mud in the darkest part of the tree, sleeps withdrawn the lightweight mob [the birds], the wind resting from the winged movement which cuts it. The noble bird of Jupiter—since after all it is the Queen [eagle]—, in order not to yield entirely to rest, which she considers a vice if it exceeds the strictly necessary, concerned not to fall into the excess of neglect, balancing entrusts her weight to a single foot and in the other keeps the little stone—her light slumber's alarm clock—, so that, if necessary sleep has been permitted, it may not be able to extend continuously, but will rather be interrupted by her regal, pastoral duty. Oh heavy burden of Majesty, which does

que aun el menor descuido no perdona!
Causa, quizá, que ha hecho misteriosa,
circular, denotando, la corona,
en círculo dorado,
que el afán es no menos continuado.

El sueño todo, en fin, lo poseía;
todo, en fin, el silencio lo ocupaba:
aun el ladrón dormía;
aun el amante no se desvelaba...

not allow even the slightest carelessness! Perhaps the mysterious reason why the crown is circular, indicating by its golden circle that zeal is no less continuous. Sleep, finally, possessed everything; everything, finally, was occupied by silence: even the thief was sleeping; even the lover was not lying awake . . .

Biobibliographical Notes

HERNANDO DE ACUÑA (*ca.* 1520–1580), a native of Valladolid, led a military career in Africa, Italy, and Germany. He belongs, with Gutierre de Cetina, to the first wave of Renaissance poets and shows the usual Italian and Classical influences, with a special emphasis on the heroic tradition. His sonnet, "Ya se acerca, señor, o ya es llegada," a standard anthology piece, expresses the imperialistic religious spirit of sixteenth-century Spain; it is usually supposed that he addressed it to Charles V, but it would be equally appropriate to Philip II, after the naval victory of Lepanto. His widow published his collected *Varias poesías* (Madrid, 1591), recently edited by Luis F. Díaz Larios (Cátedra, 1982). N. Alonso Cortes is the author of a book-length biographical study (Valladolid, 1913), but there is no good critical study of Acuña's poetry.

BALTASAR DE ALCAZAR (1530–1606) was born in Seville and served various noblemen in a military and administrative capacity. Although he wrote typical Petrarchan and religious sonnets, his own personal note is one of witty, lightly ironic "realism." In addition to amusing epigrams and sonnets, his octosyllabic *canciones* are his most well-known works. The best edition and study of Alcázar are found in a volume by F. Rodríguez Marín (Madrid, 1910).

FRANCISCO DE ALDÀNA (1537–1578) was born and raised in Italy and led a military career, dying with King Sebastian of Portugal at the Battle of Alcazarquivir, in Africa. His poetry ranges from the most sensual and imperialistic to a meditative Neoplatonic epistle of religious and scholarly detachment from the world. His poetry was posthumously published by his brother, Cosme, in two volumes (1589 and 1591), which have been recently reprinted (Madrid: CSIC, 1953). His life and works have been studied by A. Rodríguez-Monino and E.L. Rivers the latter has edited, with an introductory study, an anthology of his poetry in the "Clásicos Castellanos" series. A more recent and complete edition is that of José Lara Garrido (Cátedra, 1985).

LUPERCIO (1559–1613) and BARTOLOMÉ (1562–1631) L. DE ARGENSOLA, brothers, were born in Barbastro (Aragon) and studied in Huesca and Zaragoza. The older brother served the Count of Lemos in Madrid and Naples; the younger, an ordained priest, served Lemos as chaplain in Naples and was later a canon of Zaragoza Cathedral and the official chronicler of Aragon. Their poetry is generally moralistic and of a classical sobriety; Horace and Juvenal are major influences. Their elegies and epistles are worthy of study;

their sonnets are more widely known. Their works were published together, posthumously, in 1634. There is a good critical edition by J. M. Blecua (Zaragoza, 1950–1951); Lupercio's life and works have been studied by O.H. Green (Philadelphia, 1927). A more recent and accessible edition is that of J.M. Blecua, 1972-74 (Clásicos Castellanos, vols. 173, 184, 185).

JUAN DE ARGUIJO (1567–1623) belonged to a wealthy family of Seville and was himself a patron of the arts. Heavily charged with the archaeological erudition typical of his region and period, he was an exquisite formalist, particularly in his elegantly plastic sonnets on Classical themes. His works have been edited by Stanko B. Vranich in 1972 (Clásicos Castalia) and in 1985 (Albatros Hispanófila).

JUAN BOSCÁN (*ca.* 1490–1542), or Joan Boschá Almugáver, belonged to the bilingual (Catalan- and Castilian-speaking) upper middle class of Barcelona. He received a humanistic education and was associated with the cosmopolitan court of Charles V; he served as the youthful Duke of Alva's tutorial companion. In 1526 he began experimenting in Spanish with Italian verse forms and poetic genres, persuading his friend Garcilaso to do likewise. Garcilaso, in turn, persuaded Boscán to translate Castiglione's *Cortegiano* and to publish his translation in 1534; it is the Renaissance model of elegant Spanish prose. Upon Garcilaso's death in 1536, Boscán became his friend's literary executor, arranging in 1542, just before his own death, for the joint publication of their experimental verse (*Las obras de Boscán y algunas de Garcilaso de la Vega,* Barcelona, 1543); this volume, often reprinted during the sixteenth century, established the Renaissance tradition in Spanish verse.

As a whole, Boscán's *canzoniere* (sonnets and odes) is modeled on Petrarch's, but in poetic texture it is more profoundly influenced by the Catalan poetry of Ausias March (*ca.* 1395–*ca.* 1460); its dominant note is one of an almost masochistic desire for a desperation sufficiently constant to withstand the fluctuating sufferings of love. Much more humanistic in tone is his retelling of the story of Hero and Leander and, above all, his Horatian epistle to Diego Hurtado de Mendoza, extolling the simple pleasures of married life on his country estate. There are two modern critical editions of Boscán's poetry, Knapp's (Madrid, 1875) and Riquer's (Barcelona, 1957——), of which only one volume has so far appeared. Boscán's *Cortesano* has been more or less carelessly reprinted many times. The major general critical study is that of M. Menéndez y Pelayo, in the final volume of his *Antología* . . . See also M. de Riquer, *Juan Boscán y su cancionero barcelonés* (Barcelona, 1945); A, Parducci, *Saggio sulla lirica di Juan Boscán* (Bologna, 1952); and A. Armisén, *Estudios sobre la lengua poética de Boscán* (Zaragoza, 1982).

RODRIGO CARO (1573–1647) was an Andalusian antiquarian and archaeologist whose fame as a poet rests upon a single work, the *Canción a las ruinas de Itálica.* In this somewhat insipidly neoclassical poem to the ruins of a Roman town just outside of Seville, Caro, in typically Renaissance fashion, attempts simultaneously to relive Classical antiquity and to lament time's inexorable destruction of all things human; we are reminded of Castiglione's "Superbi colli . . ." and DuBellay's *Antiquités de Rome*. The best edition is that found in P. Blanco Suárez's anthology; S. Montoto's book-length biographical and critical study (Seville, 1915) should be supplemented by E. M. Wilson's article in the *Revista de Filología Española,* Vol. XXIII (1936).

CRISTÓBAL DE CASTILLEJO (*ca.* 1490–*ca.* 1550), born in Ciudad Rodrigo, spent his life in the service of the Hapsburgs. He is known primarily as the leader of a traditionalist reaction against the Italianate metrical innovations of Boscán and Garcilaso. Nevertheless his own poetry often shows traits typical of Renaissance humanism. His works have been edited, with an introductory study, by J. Domínguez Bordona, in four volumes of the "Clásicos Castellanos" series.

GUTIERRE DE CETINA (*ca.* 1510–*ca.* 1554) received a classical education in Seville and led an apparently romantic life, as a soldier, in Italy, northern Europe, and finally Mexico, where he seems to have met with a violent death. He belongs, with Diego Hurtado de Mendoza and Hernando de Acuña, to the first group of Renaissance poets in Spain, influenced primarily by Petrarch and Ausias March. Herrera accuses him of cultivating a too Italian, un-Spanish "softness" of style. His madrigal "Ojos claros, serenos" is his standard anthology piece, but he experimented in other genres and imitated many different Italian models. He may be viewed as the major link between Garcilaso and Herrera, consolidating the Italian innovations and simultaneously continuing medieval traditions of courtly love. His works have been edited in two volumes by J. Hazañas y la Rúa (Seville, 1895); see especially Begoña López Bueno, *Gutierre de Cetina, poeta del renacimiento español* (Seville, 1978) and her edition of *Sonetos y madrigales completos* (Câtedra, 1981).

SAN JUAN DE LA CRUZ, or St. John of the Cross (1542–1591), born Juan de Yepes, was closely associated with Saint Teresa of Avila in her hard-won reform of the Spanish Carmelite Order. He studied at the University of Salamanca and suffered imprisonment at the hands of his unreformed Carmelite brethren. His major works are three poems of mystic rapture, filled with highly erotic imagery, and their three accompanying exegetical commentaries in prose: the *Noche oscura,* the *Cántico espiritual,* and the *Llama de amor viva.* Considerably more refined and theologically sophisticated than Saint Teresa's comparable writings, these works by St. John of the Cross are considered by the Roman Catholic Church (which beatified him in 1675, canonized him in 1726, and finally declared him a Doctor of the Church in 1926) to be as authoritative in the area of mystical knowledge as St. Thomas Aquinas' in the theological area. But for the reader of poetry, St. John's verse itself speaks strongly and directly, expressing a tremulous passion that is not restricted by ecclesiastical sectarianism or traditional religiosity. His other poems, written predominantly in the popular genres of the *villancico* and the *romance,* tend to be less rapturous than the three major poems, written in "*lira*" stanzas, more intellectually paradoxical, and even at times directly theological.

The handiest edition of San Juan's complete works, with bibliographies, is that of the "Biblioteca de Autores Cristianos" (Madrid, 1955); the most important literary study is that of Dámaso Alonso, *La poesía de San Juan de la Cruz (desde esta ladera)* (Madrid, 1958). Among the many books on San Juan, see especially J. Baruzi, *St. Jean de la Croix et le problème de l'expérience mystique* (Paris, 1924), and E. A. Peers, *Spirit of Flame* (New York, 1944).

Sor Juana Inés de la Cruz (1651–1695) was born in a Mexican village as Juana de Asbaje y Ramírez, the perhaps illegitimate daughter of a Mexican woman and a Spaniard. Literarily most precocious, she was taken to the viceroy's court in Mexico City when she was still quite young; there she learned Latin and soon impressed scholars with her erudition. She entered a convent, primarily, it seems, in order to avoid men and to be able to pursue her studies; the position in Hispanic society of an attractive feminine intellectual, always difficult, was particularly precarious in seventeenth-century Mexico. She wrote a great deal of poetry, both for religious festivals and in the tradition of the love lyric; she also wrote secular and religious plays. Her *Primero sueño* is the most ambitious philosophical poem written during the Golden Age of Spanish letters. In 1690 she wrote a theological critique, soundly based on patristic orthodoxy, of a certain Jesuit preacher; a bishop's sympathetic reprimand provoked an eloquent defense of her own intellectual life. But shortly thereafter she abandoned her studies, sold her library for charitable purposes, and died caring for her sisters during an epidemic. Two volumes of her works were published in Spain during her lifetime, and a third posthumously. A modern critical edition, in four volumes, with introductory studies, has been published by A. Mendez Plancarte (Mexico, 1951-1957); important essays on Sor Juana are those by D. Schons, O. Paz, G. Sabat de Rivers.

Pedro Espinosa (1578–1650), born in Antequera (Andalusia), was the industrious collector, in his youth, of the most important anthology of lyric poetry published during the Golden Age of Spanish literature, the *Primera parte de las flores de poetas ilustres de España* (Valladolid, 1605). His own delicately colorful poetry is also of considerable interest, occupying an intermediate position in the central Renaissance-Baroque tradition of Spanish poetry. His Ovidian *Fábula de Genil,* written in *octavas reales,* is generically related to Garcilaso's *Egloga III* and Góngora's *Fábula de Polifemo y Galatea.* His sonnet beginning, "Como el triste piloto que por el mar incierto," is noteworthy for its unusual use of the *alejandrino,* a 14-syllable line with a caesura in the middle; this type of sonnet was not revived until the end of the nineteenth century, by the great *modernista* Rubén Darío. Espinosa's works have been studied (1907) and edited (1909) by F. Rodríguez Marín; see also the handier edition by F. López Estrada (Clásicos Castellanos, 1975).

Andrés Fernández de Andrada, an otherwise virtually unknown poet of Seville, owes his fame to having written, shortly before 1613, the *Epístola moral a Fabio*. This poem marks the culmination of the Horatian epistle in Spanish literature, a tradition that began with Boscán, Garcilaso, Hurtado de Mendoza, and Cetina, and was subsequently cultivated by almost every major Spanish poet. The author, in this case, speaks as a native of Seville to a fellow Andalusian pursuing his worldly ambitions at the royal court in Madrid; with grave simplicity he warns him against such vain pretensions and advocates a melancholy disillusion and withdrawal, an elegiacally Stoic resignation to the transitory nature of all things human. The author expresses in perfect classical form a vast store of moral commonplaces stemming from the Old Testament, Seneca, and many other authors, in addition, of course, to Horace. For a recent discussion of this epistle's authorship and date, see *Dos españoles del siglo de oro* (Madrid, 1960), by Dámaso Alonso, and his critical edition and study of the poem (Madrid, 1978).

Garcilaso de la Vega (1501–1536) was the second son of a noble Toledan family named Laso de la Vega. Like his older friend and fellow poet, Boscán, he received a humanistic education and was associated with the court of Charles V and with the family of the Duke of Alva. As a young soldier he fought for the king against the 1520 revolt of the Comunidades and, with Boscán, took part in the 1522 expedition to defend Rhodes against the Turks. In 1523 he was made a knight of the Order of Santiago and spent the next seven years in the constant service of the king, fighting first in northern Spain against the French. In 1525 Charles V sponsored his marriage to the noble Elena de Zúñiga, by whom he had three sons in the next three years. Simultaneously Garcilaso became emotionally attached to Isabel Freire, a Portuguese lady-in-waiting who later married Antonio de Fonseca and died in childbirth in 1533 or 1534; we see her poetic reflections in the Galatea and the Elisa of Eglogas I and III. We also know that Garcilaso had an illegitimate son and at least one other affair, with a peasant girl in Extremadura. In 1529 he accompanied the Emperor to his coronation in Italy; the following year he was sent on a diplomatic mission to France. In 1531 he witnessed the forbidden betrothal of a nephew and thereby incurred the lasting wrath of Charles V, who exiled him first to an island in the Danube (see Canción III) and then to Naples.

Naples was then governed by a Spanish viceroy, Pedro de Toledo, a member of the Duke of Alva's family; under his patronage (see dedication of Egloga I), Garcilaso completed his Renaissance education among Italian humanists, poets, artists, and musicians; he developed new emotional attachments and wrote his own best poetry, in Latin and in Spanish. In 1533 and 1534 he revisited Spain as an official messenger to Charles V. In 1534 he participated in the Spanish expedition to Tunis, was wounded, and returned to Naples by way of Sicily (see Elegia II). In 1536 he went on his last campaign, in northern Italy and southern France, where he was killed near Fréjus in a skirmish with peasants.

Garcilaso's poetry shows a gradual development away from the introverted anguish, abstractions, and wordplay of Ausias March and the fifteenth-century *cancioneros* toward a syntax of flowing periods, an imagery of refined pastoral sensuousness, and a sweetly melancholy, Neoplatonic idealism; this transition typifies perfectly the establishment of the Renaissance tradition in Spanish poetry. His works, first published posthumously with those of Boscán in 1543, were frequently republished during the sixteenth and seventeenth centuries. The earliest scholarly editions, with emendations, notes, and additional texts, date from 1574 and 1577 (Francisco Sánchez de las Brozas, or El Brocense), 1580 (Fernando de Herrera), 1622 (T. Tamayo de Vargas), and 1765 (José Nicolás de Azara). The best-known modern edition is that of T. Navarro ("Clásicos Castellanos"), based on Herrera's. Hayward Keniston (1925) and E. L. Rivers (1964) have edited critical texts based primarily on the first edition of 1543. The best general study of Garcilaso's life and works is H. Keniston, *Garcilaso de la Vega* (New York, 1922). An important study of his major Renaissance themes is Margot Arce, *Garcilaso de la Vega* (Madrid, 1930, and Puerto Rico, 1961). His poetic evolution is established with great insight by Rafael Lapesa, *La trayectoria poética de Garcilaso* (Madrid, 1948); this book is the best introduction to Garcilaso's poetry. See also A. Blecua, *En el texto de G.* (Madrid, 1970).

Luis de Góngora (1561–1627) is as important for the development of Baroque poetry in seventeenth-century Spain as Garcilaso de la Vega was for establishing the Renaissance tradition in the sixteenth century. Born in Cordova, he studied at Salamanca and thereafter held an ecclesiastical benefice in the Cathedral (a converted mosque) of Cordova, where he became known as a great card-player and attender of bullfights. In 1617 he was ordained to the priesthood so that he could hold a royal chaplaincy in Madrid; he spent most of the last ten years of his life at court, trying to get a more lucrative appointment and feuding literarily and personally with Lope de Vega and Francisco de Quevedo, his greatest rivals as poets. Ingenious virtuosity is Góngora's hallmark as a poet; whatever the genre, whether belonging to the popular tradition or to the most learned, he carried to their ultimate consequences, even to the point of burlesque, that genre's implicit potentialities. Because of his major poems' uncompromising formal rigor, they have been passionately attacked and defended from the seventeenth to the twentieth centuries.

Among Góngora's minor poems we may note a wide range, extending from the authentic folk tradition of Romancillo XLIX ("La más bella niña"), dated 1580, to the wittily ironic *romance* based on Ariosto's episode of Angelica and Medoro (1602) and the burlesque treatment of a classical story in *Píramo y Tisbe* (a *romance* dated 1618); the range of his *letrillas, villancicos,* and sonnets is similarly impressive. His major poems, which are the ones that have given rise to the great polemics, exhibit less stylistic variety. The *Fábula de Polifemo y Galatea* (1613), based on Ovid, is of an elevated *cultista* style with complex metaphors that challenge the sharpest *conceptista* wit. It is a poetry of extreme chiaroscuro, balancing the grotesquely monstrous hideousness of the giant Polyphemus against the delicate beauty of the sea-nymph Galatea. The *Soledades,* which belong to the same period and general style, are more loosely constructed. Instead of the *ottava rima* stanza, they are written in the *silva,* a stanza freely combining, with irregular rhymes, hendecasyllabic and heptasyllabic rhymes. Their "plot" is much vaguer, more episodic, with a wanderer as the central figure. Only the first Soledad, of more than 1,000 lines, was completed; the second is somewhat fragmentary, and the remaining two, if actually planned, were never begun. The substance of this poetry is a highly stylized pastoral landscape, presenting innumerable facets continuously refracted by a complicated play of metaphors that emphasizes the gemlike, colorful details of physical reality, the musicality of rare learned words, and the tension of difficult allusions and displaced syntactic elements, a tension that can, however, always be satisfactorily resolved by the adequately erudite and industrious reader. Like Yeats' Byzantine artificer, Góngora glorifies the material world by taking natural things out of nature and giving them "such a form as Grecian goldsmiths make / Of hammered gold and gold enamelling / To keep a drowsy Emperor awake . . ."

This difficult poetry was defended and annotated by friendly contemporary scholars and was wittily attacked, and surreptitiously imitated, by Góngora's greatest rivals and their friends. After dominating the seventeenth century, Góngora's major poems were virtually lost until "rediscovered" in the 1920's by a new generation of scholar-poets. The best complete editions of Góngora's works are those of R. Foulché-Delbosc (1921) and J. & I Millé y Giménez (1943); a good anthology is that of J. M. Blecua in the "Clásicos Ebro" series. Important book-length studies have been published in French (by L.-P. Thomas), in German (by W. Pabst), and in English (by E. Joiner Gates); there is also the verse translation into English of the *Soledades,* a veritable *tour de force,* by E. M. Wilson. But the bulk of the critical work has been done in Spanish: essays by G. Diego, Salinas, Lorca, Alberti, Guillén; major studies by Alfonso Reyes of Mexico (1923, 1927), Artigas (1925), Cossío (1927), and, above all, Dámaso Alonso. By the latter one should note especially the edition of the *Soledades* (1927), *La lengua poética de Góngora* (1935), *Ensayos y estudios gongorinos* (1955), and *Góngora y el "Polifemo"* (1961); the last-mentioned work contains an anthology. Another excellent introductory anthology is that of A. Carreira (Castalia, 1986).

FERNANDO DE HERRERA (*ca.* 1534–1597) held an ecclesiastical benefice in his native city of Seville; an austerely dignified scholar, his chief ambition was to write a great national epic poem that would match that of the Portuguese Camoens. Although he never fulfilled this ambition, he did write a series of hymns or Pindaric odes that, with their grandiloquent echoes of the Old Testament, define his heroic organ voice. More important to Herrera's career as a poet was the literary *tertulia* of the Count and Countess of Gelves. To the latter he devoted all of his love poetry, in which he exquisitely suffers and delights as he yearns for "Luz." He gave to the current Neoplatonic theories of love their fullest poetic expression in Spain. And, at the same time that he fulfills the Renaissance trends initiated by Boscán and Garcilaso, he anticipates the Baroque achievement of Góngora in the color, the intellectualized density and complexity, and the chiseled forms of his poetic idiom.

Herrera's voluminously annotated edition of Garcilaso's poetry (1580) reveals his full awareness of rhetorical devices and of the literary tradition, both ancient and modern, within which he was writing; it is a major work of humanistic scholarship, embodying a complete poetic. A year after his countess's death, he published a limited edition (1582) of selections from his love poetry; a much fuller edition, with many new readings, was published posthumously, in 1619. He died in 1597, having set for Spain the model of the aristocratically aloof scholar-poet. Though too often pedantic and even mechanical, his verse is a technical achievement in some ways comparable to that of Milton. The French Hispanist, Adolphe Coster, reedited with great care both the 1582 and 1619 editions of his poetry; the former is also available in the "Clásicos Castellanos" series. J. M. Blecua published from manuscripts his *Rimas inéditas* (1948). Major general studies of Herrera are those of Coster (1908) and Oreste Macrí (1959). J.M. Blecua and C. Cuevas have edited the complete poetry.

FRAY LUIS DE LEÓN (1527–1591) was born in Belmonte (Cuenca), the descendant of Jewish converts to Christianity. He studied at the University of Salamanca, where he took vows as an Augustinian friar and held various chairs. As professor of Scripture, he aroused the opposition of Dominican scholastics by insisting upon the primacy of the Hebrew text of the Old Testament; his belligerence won him personal enmities among his fellow professors, and he was denounced to the Inquisition. He spent four years in prison before winning an acquittal and returning to his university. He was chosen to edit the works of Saint Teresa of Avila, the reformer of the Carmelite Order, and was elected provincial of his own order just before his death. He did his strictly professional writing in Latin, but he was eager to make the Bible and theology more accessible to the people; he published in 1583 a popular handbook on the ideal wife *(La perfecta casada)* and a Platonic dialogue on Christology *(De los nombres de*

Cristo), both of them based on Scriptural and patristic authorities, particularly St. Augustine. He also translated into Spanish, with penetrating commentaries, the Song of Solomon and the Book of Job. Other translations from the Bible, in verse, are selected Psalms and Proverbs.

Fray Luis was also a classical Latin scholar and translated into Spanish verse the *Eclogues* and part of the *Georgics* of Virgil, and selected *Odes* by Horace. His own poems, typically odes written in "*lira*" stanzas, show some pastoral Virgilian elements, but more significantly an Horatian linear development of anecdote and argument. Urbane Horatian satire, praising the simple country life and condemning political and commercial greed, merges with a more transcendental philosophy and emotional soaring, based upon Pythagorean, Ptolomaic, Neoplatonic, and Christian ideas of universal harmony. Though limited in range and quantity, Fray Luis's original poems are often of the highest quality and seem to typify the Hispanic Christianization of the Italian Renaissance. He collected, but did not publish, his verse, considering it no doubt inappropriate for a Biblical scholar and an Augustinian; it circulated in manuscript until published by Quevedo in 1631. Very useful for the modern reader is the one-volume edition of his *Obras completas castellanas,* in the "Biblioteca de Autores Cristianos" series (Madrid, 1951). The latest attempt at a critical edition of the original poems is that of A. C. Vega (Madrid, 1955), but the sound bilingual editions of O. Macrí (Florence, 1950 & 1964) are in many ways superior. There are several book-length studies of Fray Luis de León; see especially those of A. Bell, A. Coster, A. Guy, and K. Vossler.

LOPE DE VEGA, or Lope Félix de Vega Carpio (1562–1635), born of humble parents in Madrid, was a precocious student in that city and at the University of Alcalá. He led an unruly life, combining and recombining simultaneously his roles as lover, soldier, husband, private secretary, and priest. He was also a phenomenally productive writer in almost every genre of prose fiction, narrative poetry, dramatic poetry, and lyric poetry, frequently interpolating lyrics into the other genres. His stylistic trademark is one of facile emotionalism, sweetly tender, intense, variable. But his creative experiments range widely, inspired by everything from the most authentic folk poetry to the most classical erudition. He wrote novels pastoral *(La Arcadia),* religious *(Los pastores de Belén),* and adventurous *(El peregrino en su patria).* His greatest literary achievement was the establishment of Spain's popular theatrical tradition; he dominated the Madrid stage, producing literally hundreds of fast-moving comedies, in varying combinations of octosyllabic and hendecasyllabic verse, based on many different literary and historical themes and erotic situations. He also wrote (to be read, not staged) an ambitious humanistic tragicomedy in prose, *La Dorotea.* Among the narrative poems that he published we should here mention *El Isidro* (the story of Madrid's patron saint), *La Jerusalén conquistada* (*cf.* Tasso), and *La corona trágica* (the story of Mary, queen of Scots).

As for his lyric poetry itself, we can give here only a cursory survey of the works that he himself published. His folk songs, authentically traditional, are found chiefly inserted in his plays. His *romances,* or ballads, are not traditional, but rather are accounts of his own love affairs, disguised in pastoral or Moorish garb; many of these were published in the *Romancero general* of 1600, and others, of a maturer tone, appear in *La Dorotea* (1632). The *Rimas humanas,* consisting of 200 sonnets, came out in 1602, along with his *Angélica (cf.* Ariosto) and *Dragontea* (an epic poem on Sir Francis Drake). Many of these sonnets belong to the Petrarchan tradition of the sixteenth century; others analyze women less adoringly or depict mythological and pastoral scenes. In his love poetry, autobiographical elements are often close to the surface. His *Rimas sacras* (1614) contain 100 devotional and hagiographic sonnets, in which the expression of his love for Christ is sometimes remarkably similar in tone to that of his secular loves; this volume also contains *octavas, glosas, romances, canciones, tercetos, edilios,* and *villanescas.* All of it tends to be highly personal poetry, expressing a very special Spanish religiosity. Along with his mythological *Circe* (1624) he published six poetic epistles, an eclogue, 44 sonnets, and several verse psalms. His *Triunfos divinos* (1625) contain more sonnets, octosyllabic *canciones,* etc. Finally, under a transparently ironic pseudonym, he published the semiburlesque *Rimas humanas y divinas del licenciado Tomé de Burguillos* (1634), containing many new sonnets, as well as *espinelas,* eclogues, and the *Gatomaquia,* a mock-heroic cat fight.

In the latter part of the eighteenth century these works were re-edited rather carefully in a multivolume collection of Lope's *Obras sueltas.* Some of them have been more recently reprinted in facsimile. The best anthology and study of Lope's lyrics is that of J. F. Montesinos, in the "Clásicos Castellanos" series; see also the anthologies of L. Guarner (Bergua) and J. M. Blecua ("Clásicos Ebro"). Further studies by J. F. Montesinos are found in his *Estudios sobre Lope* (Mexico, 1951). The standard biography of Lope is that of H. A. Rennert (1904), especially in the revised Spanish translation of A. Castro (1919). General studies of his life and works are those of J. Entrambasaguas (Labor) and A. Zamora Vicente (Gredos).

ESTÉBAN MANUEL DE VILLEGAS (*ca.* 1589–1669), a native of the Rioja region of northern Spain, was educated in Madrid and Salamanca. In 1618 he proudly published his youthful poetry, after careful revision, under the general title of *Las eróticas o amatorias.* Many of these poems reveal him to be, for this period in Spain, an unusually meticulous imitator of the Classics, particularly of Horace, Anacreon, and the elegiac poets; the *heptasílabo* predominates, and he even attempts to imitate in Spanish the quantitative metrics of Greek and Latin. In the simplicity of his classicism he often seems to hark back to the humanistic innovators of the Renaissance and simultaneously to anticipate the neoclassicism of the eighteenth century, when his poetry was to be more influential in Spain than that of any other seventeenth century poet. He devoted much time in later life to classical scholarship and to translating Boethius. A generous selection from his *Eróticas* has been published, with a biographical and critical introduction, by N. Alonso Cortés in the "Clásicos Castellanos" series.

FRANCISCO DE MEDRANO (1570–1607), a native of Seville, was for 15 years associated with the Jesuit order and with various colleges in Castile, particularly at the University of Salamanca. In 1602 he left the order and returned to Seville to spend his last five years as a literary gentleman of property. He occupies, chronologically, a position between Herrera and Góngora. We can see the influence of Fray Luis de León in his translations, adaptations, and free imitations of Horace's odes. His sonnets reveal a similar classicism of form and, at times, a spiritualized sensuality that strikes us as peculiarly modern. His works were first published at Palermo in 1617. To Dámaso Alonso and Stephen Reckert we owe an excellent modern edition (1958); Alonso is also responsible for the only full study of his life and works (1948).

FRANCISCO DE QUEVEDO (1580–1645), born of aristocratic parents in Madrid, studied with the Jesuits of that city before attending the universities of Alcalá and of Valladolid; in the latter city he made his début at court and also as a poet, in Espinosa's *Flores de poetas ilustres* of 1605, initiating simultaneously his feud with Góngora. Following the court back to Madrid, he began his major works of prose fiction, the violently picaresque *Buscón* (published 1626) and the fantastically satirical *Sueños* (published 1627), as well as a nationalistic apology for Spain *(España defendida)*. He also continued to write, and translate, poetry. In 1613 he joined the Duke of Osuna in Sicily as his private secretary and became deeply involved in Spanish court politics. Later, with the death of Philip III and the fall of Lerma and Osuna, he was exiled from court. To this period in his life, around 1620, belong his epistle in verse (more satirical than poetic) to Olivares and the gestation of his treatise *La política de Dios* (published 1626). We may also assume that his erotic adventures reached their Platonic climax, in his sonnets to Lisi, during this period; in 1624 he was definitely having a less Platonic affair with a certain Señora Ledesma, and had reestablished himself with the royal court, under Philip IV and Olivares. With the publication in 1626 and 1627 of the prose works mentioned above, Quevedo's fame as a satirist spread rapidly; this, in addition to his other polemical activities, led once more to his exile from court in 1628.

To Olivares he dedicated in 1631 his editions of the sixteenth-century poetry of Francisco de la Torre and of Fray Luis de León, which were part of his campaign against the Gongoristic baroque style; his own style, however, is very far from their relatively simple classicism, and his favor at court continued to vacillate as he added to the number of his personal enemies the many victims of his ferociously satirical pen. At the age of fifty-four he was talked into reluctant matrimony with a well-born widow; he lived with her only very briefly. He spent the next years in retirement at his country estate, writing attacks upon his enemies, who in turn denounced him and his works repeatedly to the Inquisition. In 1639 he was imprisoned, on what charges we do not know; he was not released until after Olivares' fall, in 1643. He spent his last years, a sick man, in complete retirement, but still reading, writing, and thinking violently about the social and political problems of Spain. Although Quevedo was the first great Spanish author to be acutely aware of his country's decline, this concern is not often reflected directly in his poetry, the major theme of which is the more general one of time and death, the destruction of love and beauty. This theme, a commonplace of the Renaissance tradition, takes on an intensely personal pathos, an almost metaphysical anguish, in Quevedo. His command of the Spanish language ranges from the heights of a desperately Platonic devotion and Stoic solemnity to the depths of foul gutter speech and cynical burlesque; dark shadows obscure any glimmers of color in his poetry.

Quevedo died having published only a small volume of his poetic translations, but he had been famous as an original poet since 1605, largely on the basis of his *romances* published in anthologies and circulating, with satires and sonnets, in manuscript. Three years after his death, one part of his poetic remains was published in Madrid under the title of *El Parnaso español* (1648); a second part was published in 1670. The problems of authenticity and variant versions are complex and indeed, at times, insoluble. By far the best modern edition of Quevedo's poetry is that of J. M. Blecua (Barcelona, 1963); his introduction is also the best brief biographical, bibliographical, and critical study. A good anthology, chosen by R. E. Scarpa of Chile, is available in the "Colección Austral." There are many articles on Quevedo's works; among others, the studies of E. Carilla, *Quevedo (entre dos centenarios)* (Tucumán, Argentina, 1949), O. H. Green, *Courtly Love in Quevedo* (Colorado, 1952), and A. Mas, *La Caricature de la femme, du mariage et de l'amour dans l'oeuvre de Quevedo* (Paris, 1957), deserve mention here. The best introduction is J.O. Crosby's *Poesía varia* (Cátedra, 1981).

Francisco de Rioja *(ca.* 1583–1659), a scholarly theologian born and educated in Seville, occupied important positions both in that city and in Madrid, particularly during the primacy of Olivares. His poetry reveals a special interest in painting and colors; he is known for his delicately sensuous description of flowers. The usual epicurean or moralizing overtones are in his case muted. *(The Canción a las ruinas de Itálica* and the *Epístola moral a Fabio* were for a long time attributed to him.) The best edition of his poetry is that of B. López Bueno (Cátedra).

Francisco de la Torre is an otherwise unknown sixteenth-century poet whose works, like those of Fray Luis de León, were first published by Quevedo in 1631, as part of the latter's characteristically reactionary campaign to revive in the seventeenth century, as an antidote to baroque complications of style, the relatively simple Renaissance style associated with Salamanca. (The so-called Salamanca school, led by Fray Luis de León, is generally considered to include F. de Figueroa and F. de Aldana, as well as F. de la Torre.) Francisco de la Torre's style is one of gentle Neoplatonic melancholy, with a keen sense of nature and a pre-Romantic appreciation of the night. His works have been carefully edited, in the "Clásicos Castellanos" series, with an introductory study, by A. Zamora Vicente. See also *Poesía completa* edited by María Luisa Cerrón Puga (Cátedra, 1984).

General Bibliography

I. STUDIES

Alonso, A. *Materia y forma en poesía.* Madrid: Gredos, 1955.
Alonso, D. *Poesía española: ensayo de métodos y límites estilísticos (Garcilaso, Fray Luis de León, San Juan de la Cruz, Góngora. Lope de Vega, Quevedo).* Madrid: Gredos, 1957.
Blecua, J. M. *Sobre poesía de la edad de oro.* Madrid: Gredos, 1970.
Bleiberg, G., and J. Marías, editors. *Diccionario de literatura española.* Madrid: Revista de Occidente, 1964.
Brenan, G. *The Literature of the Spanish People.* Cambridge University Press, 1951.
Cossío, J. M. de. *Fábulas mitológicas en España.* Madrid: Espasa-Calpe, 1952.
Díaz-Plaja, G. *Historia de la poesía lírica española.* Barcelona: Labor, 1948.
________, editor. *Historia general de las literaturas hispánicas.* 3 vols. Barcelona: Barna, 1949–53.
Escandón, B. *Los temas de "Carpe diem" y la brevedad de la rosa en la poesía española.* Universidad de Barcelona, 1938.
Fucilla, J. G. *Estudios sobre el petrarquismo en España.* Madrid: González de CSIC, 1960.
Green, O. H. *Spain and the Western Tradition.* Vol. I. Madison: University of Wisconsin, 1963.
Guillén, J. *Language and Poetry: Some Poets of Spain.* Cambridge: Harvard University Press, 1961.
Henríquez Ureña, P. *Estudios de versificación española.* Buenos Aires: Universidad de Argentina, 1961.
Hurtado, J. and A. González-Palencia. *Historia de la literatura española.* Madrid: SAETA, 1949.
Jones, R. O. *A Literary History of Spain. The Golden Age: Prose and Poetry.* New York: Barnes & Noble, 1971.
Menéndez y Pelayo, M. *Antología de poetas líricos castellanos.* 10 vols. Santander: CSIC, 1944–45.
Navarro, T. *Arte del verso.* Mexico: C. G. E., 1959
________. *Métrica española: reseña histórica y descriptiva.* Syracuse University Press, 1956.
Nelson, L. *Baroque Lyric Poetry.* New Haven: Yale University Press, 1961.
Pierce, F. *La poesía épica del siglo de oro.* Madrid: Gredos, 1961.
Río, A. del. *Historia de la literatura española.* New York: Dryden, 1948 (2nd edition, New York: Holt, Rinehart, 1963).
Salinas, P. *Reality and the Poet in Spanish Poetry.* Baltimore: Johns Hopkins University Press, 1940.
Valbuena Prat, A. *Historia de la literatura española.* 2 vols. Barcelona: Gili, 1950.
Vossler, K. *La poesía de la soledad en España.* Buenos Aires: Losada, 1946.
Wardropper, B. W. *Historia de la poesía lírica a lo divino.* Madrid: Revista de Occidente, 1958.

II. ANTHOLOGIES

Blanco Suárez, E. *Poetas de los siglos XVI y XVII.* Madrid: Instituto Escuela, 1933.

Blecua, J. M. *Floresta lírica española.* 2 vols. Madrid: Gredos, 1963.

Buchanan, M.A. *Spanish Poetry of the Golden Age.* University of Toronto, 1947.

Castro, A. de. *Poetas líricos de los siglos XVI y XVII* (Vols. 32 and 42 of the "Biblioteca de Autores Españoles"). Madrid: Atlas, 1950–51.

Cohen, J. M. *The Penguin Book of Spanish Verse.* Baltimore: Penguin Books, 1960.

Fitzmaurice-Kelly, J. *The Oxford Book of Spanish Verse.* Oxford University Press, 1945.

Lapesa, R. *Poetas del siglo XVI.* Barcelona: Rauter, 1947.

Marín, D. *Poesía española.* Mexico: Andrea, 1958.

Menéndez y Pelayo, M. *Las cien mejores poesías (líricas) de la lengua castellana.* Buenos Aires: Sopena, 1945.

Moreno Báez, P. *Antología de la poesía lírica española.* Madrid: Revista de Occidente, 1952.

Pierce, F. *The Heroic Poem of the Spanish Golden Age: Selections.* Oxford University Press, 1947.

Sánchez, A. *Poesía sevillana en la edad de oro.* Madrid: Castilla, 1948.

Turnbull, E. L. *Ten Centuries of Spanish Poetry.* New York: Grove Press, 1955.

Wardropper, B. W. *Spanish Poetry of the Golden Age.* New York: Appleton-Century-Crofts, 1971.

Important series of texts edited for students and currently kept in print, containing either complete works or anthologies of individual authors, are the "Clásicos Castellanos" and the "Colección Austral," published by Espasa-Calpe of Madrid, the "Clásicos Ebro" of Zaragoza, "Clásicos Castalia" and "Letras Hispánicas" (Cátedra) of Madrid. See also A. Terry, *An Anthology of Spanish Poetry 1500-1700*, 2 vols. (Oxford: Pergamon, 1965-68); A. Prieto, *La poesía española del siglo xvi*, 2 vols. (Cátedra, 1984-87); María Pilar Manero Sorolla, *Introduccíon al estudio del petrarquismo en España* (Barcelona: PPU, 1987).